Marriage Markets

Marriage Markets

How Inequality Is Remaking the American Family

JUNE CARBONE

and

NAOMI CAHN

OXFORD
UNIVERSITY PRESS

OXFORD
UNIVERSITY PRESS

Oxford University Press is a department of the University of Oxford.
It furthers the University's objective of excellence in research, scholarship,
and education by publishing worldwide.

Oxford New York
Auckland Cape Town Dar es Salaam Hong Kong Karachi
Kuala Lumpur Madrid Melbourne Mexico City Nairobi
New Delhi Shanghai Taipei Toronto

With offices in
Argentina Austria Brazil Chile Czech Republic France Greece
Guatemala Hungary Italy Japan Poland Portugal Singapore
South Korea Switzerland Thailand Turkey Ukraine Vietnam

Oxford is a registered trade mark of Oxford University Press
in the UK and certain other countries.

Published in the United States of America by
Oxford University Press
198 Madison Avenue, New York, NY 10016

Library of Congress Cataloging-in-Publication Data
Carbone, June.
Marriage markets : how inequality is remaking the American family / June Carbone and Naomi Cahn.
   p.   cm.
Summary: "June Carbone and Naomi Cahn examine how macroeconomic forces are transforming marriage,
and how working class and lower income families have paid the highest price"—Provided by publisher.
   ISBN 978–0–19–991658–0 (hardback); 978–0–19–026331–7 (paperback)
  1. Families—Economic aspects—United States. 2. Marriage—Economic aspects—United States.
3. Domestic relations—United States. 4. Equality—United States. 5. Working class—Economic aspects—
United States. 6. Social classes—United States. I. Cahn, Naomi R. II. Title.
   HQ536.C348 2014
      306.850973—dc23
                                              2013045704

1   3   5   7   9   8   6   4   2

Printed in the United States of America on acid-free paper

CONTENTS

ACKNOWLEDGMENTS

In writing a book about marriage markets, we have incurred many debts—of gratitude—to so many people for their support of our work on this project. We've benefited from discussion and editing from numerous colleagues, friends, and family members. For their review of our work and engagement with our ideas, we thank Bill Black, Don Braman, Tonya Brito, Maxine Eichner, Martha Fineman, Tony Gambino, Marsha Garrison, Jill Hasdsay, Pat Hernandez, Nancy Levit, Linda McClain, Hanna Rosin, and Buffie Scott. Thank you to our OUP editor, Dave McBride, for believing in what we are "selling." We are particularly grateful to Michael Guttentag for sharing some of his experiences as a teenager talking to his mother, Marcia Guttentag, about the development of her book on sex ratios. We've benefited from presenting early pieces of this book at numerous conferences and faculty fora, including Bowdoin College, Boston University, Hofstra University, New England School of Law, St. Louis University, the University of Florida, the University of Miami, Michigan, Michigan State, Missouri, and Wisconsin, and we have appreciated the work of numerous law review editors at Hofstra, New England, Michigan State and the University of Nevada-Las Vegas as they have worked on articles related to the book. We would also like to thank the many colleagues who have listened to us—for many years—as we have explored the ideas in this book, including Jewel Allers, Barbara Glesner-Fines, Michele Goodwin, Viviana Grieco, Mary Kay Kisthardt, Mary Kay O'Malley, and those who have helped us with research, including Mary Kate Hunter, Jodi LeBolt, and Jessica Qian. We have benefited from the generous research support of the Universities of Missouri-Kansas City and Minnesota and George Washington University.

For their belief in equality, and for their understanding of the seemingly infinite amount of time consumed by our writing this book, we thank our own families—Bill, Galen, Genina, and Kenny, Tony, Louisa, and Abigail.

Introduction

The American family is changing—and the changes guarantee that inequality will be greater in the next generation. For the first time, America's children will almost certainly not be as well educated, healthy, or wealthy as their parents, and the result stems from the growing disconnect between the resources available to adults and those invested in children. The time to address the *real* explanation for the changing American family is now.

The changes themselves, of course, have been the subject of endless commentary, both positive and negative. The age of marriage is going up, the rate of marriage is falling, and almost half of all marriages fail. An increasing number of states allow women to marry women, and men to marry men. The number of children born outside of marriage is drawing equal with the number of children born within marriage. And, the percentage of children growing up in single-parent households is the highest in the developed world. These changes, however, do not affect everyone equally. Describing how the "average" family has changed hides what is really going on: economic inequality is remaking the American family along class lines, and families are not going through the same changes together. To understand what is happening to the American family—and how family law locks in the growing class divisions—requires examining the links between family change along the continuum from the top to the bottom of the American economy.

In the process, many of the existing explanations for why the American family today is so radically different from the American family of fifty years ago will prove hollow. The right blames declining moral values, the pill, welfare as we knew it, the rise of "soulmate" marriage, and a host of other social ills without providing a convincing explanation of why these changes affect one group more than another. The left celebrates individual choice, sexual liberation, and women's equality without acknowledging that not all sources of change are benign and that the consequences of some of the changes they support contribute to the growing inequality they oppose. Neither group provides a complete explanation of these changes, and without a better explanation of why the top and bottom of American families are moving in opposite directions, efforts at family reform will remain futile.

A complete explanation of family change requires taking seriously the role of class in scripting our lives as well as the effect of greater economic inequality in remaking the terms of marriage, divorce, and childrearing. Such an explanation needs to address not just why marriage has disappeared from the poorest communities, but also why, in a reversal of historical trends, elite women have become the *most* likely to marry. It requires the ability to explain why divorce rates, which for decades moved in the same direction for the country as a whole, are now diverging, falling back to the levels that existed before no-fault divorce for the most educated while continuing to rise for everyone else. A comprehensive analysis must also be able to make sense of the decisions of working-class women, who often describe themselves as religious or conservative, to have children on their own even when the fathers of their children are willing to propose.

In short, a full explanation cannot look at the family in isolation from economic forces. Any attempt to respond to family change must include reconstruction of the script for the college educated, prompting investment in careers and marriages that can withstand the stresses of career changes, children's illness, and geographic mobility. It also must address the destruction of the pathways that helped the working class aspire to the same combination of financial and family security.

The story accordingly starts with the greater inequality that characterizes the American economy. Rising inequality has affected men more than women, increasing both the number of men at the top who are eager to pair with high-status women and the number of men at the bottom who no longer play productive roles. These changes fundamentally alter the "gender bargain," that is, the terms on which men and women find it worthwhile to forge lasting relationships, and they do so in ways that push the top and the bottom of the socioeconomic system in different directions. At the top, increasing disparities among men and among women have made both pickier about potential mates and wary of early commitments that might limit future opportunities. Women used to "shop around" for successful men. Male executives used to marry their secretaries, who would take care of them at home the way they did in the office. Now both look for mates who reflect (and enhance) their own expectations about the ability to enjoy the good life. Two substantial incomes rather than one make the difference between the home overlooking the golf course and the modest tract house in the less tony school district, and even if money is not at issue, the stay-at-home spouse with the Ph.D. possesses much more social status than does a high school graduate playing the same domestic role.

College graduates still largely forge lasting relationships and they typically will do so with one another, but they hedge their bets by delaying marriage and childbearing until they have a better idea of where they (and the partners to whom they commit) are likely to end up—concentrating elite advantage in the process as overwhelming numbers of them raise their children in financially secure, two-parent families.

For those whose incomes place them in the bottom third of the population, increasing disparities between men and women have made both more likely to give up on each other. International and interstate comparisons demonstrate that higher rates of inequality tend to be associated with chronic unemployment, high rates of imprisonment, and substance abuse—factors that disproportionately affect men.[1] Women in these communities view commitment to a man who runs up the credit card bill, cycles in and out of jobs, or deals drugs on the side as more of a threat than an asset to the ability to care for children. Men view women who take their money when they have it but do not stand by them when they flounder with distrust. These patterns encourage women to invest in their own resources rather than in the men in their lives and men to move on to new relationships when their current ones hit rough patches. Family stability is an inevitable casualty.

The hardest patterns to analyze are those of the middle—the group clustered around the fiftieth percentile of family income in the United States. This group, which used to be called the "white working class," is now more racially diverse than both its comparable cohort of fifty years ago and the college-educated upper third of today. This group was once associated with well-paying blue-collar manufacturing jobs, but manufacturing jobs are no longer numerous or distinct enough to define the group. Education is perhaps the best proxy. Members of this group are high school graduates but lack a B.A. Many start at a university but do not finish, or they earn a community college or vocational degree. The women from these families in the middle have done well. Unlike those in the top group, where sons are more likely than daughters to graduate from college and where the gender gap in income has widened, the women in this middle group have outpaced the men. They earn higher grades, stay in school longer, and are more likely to return to complete an unfinished degree later in life. When they have the same level of education and work the same number of hours as the men, the income gender gap narrows. With these changing fortunes, this larger group of successful women in the center seeks to pair with a shrinking group of comparable men. Female high school graduates used to be able to marry men with a college education; today they are much less likely to get married at all. And sociologists find that women in this center group, particularly among whites, cohabit more than American women in any other group; they live with a partner, marry, divorce, and cohabit with

someone else to a greater degree than in any other group.[2] We are providing a
portrait of the changes that remade the country in the years 1990–2007. But
the jury is still out as to whether the family patterns of the center, which used
to look more like the family patterns at the top, will eventually resemble those
of the poor.

These economic changes, which have increased the dominance of high-
income men at the top, marginalized a large number of men at the bottom,
and reduced the number of men in the middle, have unsettled the foundations
of family life. To be sure, the family does not change with the stock market
ticker or the seasonal adjustments in the unemployment rate. Instead, shifts in
the economy change the way men and women match up, and, over time, they
alter young people's expectations about each other and about their prospects
in newly reconstituted marriage markets. These expectations go to the core
of what many see as a shift in values. The ambitious college students, who are
said to have mastered the "hook-up," know that attending to their studies pays
off in terms of both marriage and career prospects and that too early a commitment to a partner or to childbearing may derail both. Yet, they still largely
believe that when they are ready, a suitable partner—male, female, or the product of a sperm bank—will be there for them. Women who do not graduate
from college are more likely to see childbearing as the event that will most give
meaning to their lives, and they are more likely to respond to experiences with
unreliable and unfaithful partners by giving up on men and investing in themselves and their children. These differing expectations, treated as the subject of
moral failings, women's liberation, and cultural clashes, are a predictable consequence of the remaking of marriage markets. At the top, there are more successful men seeking to pair with a smaller pool of similarly successful women.
In the middle and the bottom, there are more competent and stable women
seeking to pair with a shrinking pool of reliable men. What we are watching
as the shift in marriage markets rewrites family scripts and increases gender
distrust is the re-creation of class—of harder edged boundaries that separate
the winners and losers in the new American economy.

These developments and their connections to growing economic inequality do more to explain changing marriage patterns than does any discussion
of shifting social mores taken in isolation. The class dimension means that all
of the previous explanations for family change—women's independence, welfare, changing moral values, the embrace of soulmate marriage—ring hollow.

If we want to understand why our lives have changed, why our children's
marriages are shaky, and why our grandchildren cannot count on the resources
their parents enjoyed, we must be willing to confront the consequences of
greater inequality. This book attempts to tell the story of what has happened to
the American family, and though the tale is at times complex, the conclusion

is short and simple: it's the economy, stupid. And any analysis or proposed solution that does not take growing inequality into account is based on a lie. Inequality matters to overall social health, and it matters to the well-being of future generations.[3]

* * *

In attempting to link family change to inequality and class, we start with two conundrums: Just what does *class* mean in American society, and isn't a marriage market an oxymoron? Americans often reject the very idea of class—of social constructions that separate families on one part of the economic spectrum from others—as an "un-American" concept. They are more likely to see divisions in racial or ethnic terms, and they are more likely to identify with religious, cultural, or ideological categories. Yet, whether we acknowledge it or not, class is critical to the understanding of contemporary families. It is critical because it shapes the attitudes and expectations that underlie culture as well as the practical consequences that channel resources to the next generation. In this book, therefore, we use class as a functional category that explains the structure of marriage markets, educational expectations, and the possibilities for movement up and down the socioeconomic ladder.

Marx, of course, defined class in terms of antagonism between the interests of the "capitalists," who owned the means of production, and the workers, who depended on wages for their labor but had little ability to shape the terms of employment. Yet, Marxian notions do not apply directly to a post-industrial economy, and Marx himself did not anticipate the development of a "middle class" independent of the capitalists. Since Marx's time, much of the discussion of class has largely been relegated to those who chart the course of financial progress in Asia, Latin American, and the rest of the developing world. While this literature treats the size and health of the middle class as a primary subject of attention, it pays little attention to the re-emergence of class divisions in countries such as the United States. Accordingly, we recognize that our efforts to describe class do not piggyback on existing definitions and that we may sometimes seem to use terms in ways that may not always be precise or entirely consistent because the meaning of the terms we are using have not jelled into coherent definitions. To try to limit some of that confusion, we set forth the following concepts, which inform our discussion throughout the book.

For our purposes, class is a social construct that is often—but not always—correlated with income. It is a term designed to make more visible the way that society creates expectations about behavior and/or channels societal resources, such as wealth and income, parental time and attention, and human capital acquisition. We use the idea of class most critically in this book to describe who is likely to marry whom, who is willing to live with whom, and how prospective parents view the appropriate family structures for raising children. The most voluminous, consistent, and reliable data on these issues are from the census and distinguish among three groups. First, college graduates are a group constituting roughly one-third of today's young adults though a smaller percentage of the overall population.[4] Every recent study of marriage indicates that college graduates have become more likely to marry fellow graduates.

The second group, which is harder to define precisely, is the "middle" of the American population, including those who graduated from high school, but not college, and those who, while perhaps struggling economically, are not poor. The group can be defined demographically: a household at the fiftieth percentile of the American population in 2011 earned a little over $42,000,[5] and the average American adult graduated from high school and attended college but did not complete a four-year degree.[6] This group has lost ground over the past twenty years, with shrinking income distinctions between those with some skills and those without, and while this group continues to differ from the bottom group, distinctions between them, in terms of both income and marriage, have become less pronounced than they were in the middle of the twentieth century.

The third group is the poor or the marginalized. This group includes high school dropouts, but it is certainly broader than the 7.4 percent of those between the ages of sixteen and twenty-four who lack a high school degree.[7] It includes most of the 15 percent of Americans below the poverty line.[8] In terms of family characteristics, it is a group for whom marriage is rapidly disappearing.

Our three family groups overlap with, but are not identical to, the use of class terms for economic or political analysis.[9] The top group, college graduates, roughly constitutes what in the nineteenth century would have been called the middle class. That is, they are a group whose political and economic standing depends on investment, most commonly, investment in the education or skills of their children.[10] Within this group is a small, but distinct, elite. This is Marx's capitalist class or the 1 percent in today's political discourse. Members of this elite group differ from college graduates more generally in that they have the resources to ensure the success of their offspring; they also have relationship patterns that are somewhat different from those who need two incomes to be able to afford to buy a house in D.C. or San Francisco. While it wields disproportionate political and economic power, this elite group is too small to influence family patterns more generally.

Throughout this book we use the terms *college graduates, college-educated middle class, upper middle class,* and *upper* or *elite third* to refer to roughly the same group. Yet the terms are not identical, and the group of college graduates, even if we exclude the 1 percent, is not uniform. We recognize that the meaning of a college degree is not the same for all races or parts of the country.

For example, about half of those over the age of twenty-five who live in Washington, D.C., are college graduates, and a quarter have advanced degrees, as compared to such middle-American cities as Memphis, Tennessee, or San Antonio, Texas, where the number of college graduates is roughly one-quarter of the population.[11] Accordingly, class and social distinctions become more important in the D.C. area than in parts of the country where people have fewer years of formal education, between those with advanced degrees and those with only bachelor degrees, or between high-income professionals and other college graduates. Racial differences among college graduates also may carry different meanings in different places, especially if interracial marriage or parenting is less common in a particular area or if the ratio of men to women differs markedly from national averages. We try to call attention to racial and geographic differences where the data are available and the differences matter, but overall we treat the college-educated third as a whole.

In the quarter century between 1975 and 2000, the line between college graduates and the second, middle group became sharply defined, while the line between the second and third group was blurred. The group we describe as the middle group is what has historically been described as the "working class," particularly the white working class. That is, it is a group of less skilled workers whose well-being depends on the stability of their employment and on-the-job training rather than formal education. The group at the bottom differs from the middle, in part, because it includes the marginalized (e.g., minorities who suffer from isolation, discrimination, and/or exclusion from the advantages of American society or the rural poor who may lack access to better opportunities and resources) and the dysfunctional of all races, such as those who cannot hold a job because of physical or mental limitations. It also includes those in prison or on probation or parole, a group that has grown markedly because of policies of mass incarceration. In times of high unemployment or financial instability, job loss and downward mobility erode many of the economic and social distinctions between the stable working class and the poor. A generation or two ago, the family patterns of the middle looked much more like those of the top third of American society; today, they increasingly resemble the patterns of the bottom third.[12]

We use these class-based groups to construct "marriage markets" or, more accurately, to explain how mate choice occurs in the twenty-first century. In so doing, we are very aware that many from all political and philosophical persuasions object to the very idea of treating intimate relationships as something that should ever be the product of exchange. We believe, however, that to explain why the family has become a marker of class requires looking at the mechanisms that connect a changing society to what takes place in the family. We believe that the way men and women, gays and lesbians, and intimate partners of all kinds match up in a given community has a lot to do with the resulting understanding of family values. To understand how the shift in the organization of the economy has affected the assumptions that underlie family behavior for the rich, the poor, and the middle, it *is* important to see marriage and other intimate relationships as the product of markets. That is, relationships do occur as a result of an exchange, just like the purchase of the latest iPhone. Intimate markets, however, are special ones. They depend on trust, they incorporate assumptions about gender, and they reflect community reinforcement (or obstruction in the case of same-sex couples) of institutions like marriage. These exchanges, like other kinds of human interactions, also reflect supply and demand.

In all societies, marriage declines if there is an imbalance in the number of willing partners. Yet the impact of market changes is not simply a shift in marginal price, a few more men who have to work harder to find the right woman and a few more women who will end up alone. Instead, changes in supply and demand affect the factors that underlie trust—can a partner, for example, be expected to be faithful and dependable? And trust in turn affects a host of other decisions: Is it important to stay in school to land the right type of partner? Is staying in school a realistic possibility? Is one better able to provide for children by investing in oneself or one's mate? Are intimate relationships likely to be temporary or long-term? These considerations are part of what we think of as "values," and they in fact reflect mundane changes in supply that reverberate through communities in predictable ways.

We have a rich literature that looks at the way men and women match up across different countries, time periods, and neighborhoods. That literature finds that when the marriageable men outnumber marriageable women, community norms look a lot like those of college graduates. The women can be picky about their choice of intimate partners, and the men find that they have to shape up, work hard, and be respectful to win over the women they desire. Where the women outnumber the men, however, family understandings look more like the behavior of those losing out on the American dream. The most desirable men (the ones with jobs) find that they can play the field rather than commit. They disappoint enough women that the women invest in themselves rather than their partners. Over time, family stability increases in one community and declines in the other; investment in children increases in one community and declines in the other.

The stakes, like the facts themselves, are now impossible to deny. Increasing inequality has remade the pathways into the middle class, secured class advantages for those who are winning the "rugrat race," and pulled up the ladders that once allowed the diligent working class to find ways to a better life.

In the first section of this book, we explore the forces that led us to where we are today: the remaking of the relationship between home and market increased women's autonomy while the subsequent growth of economic inequality changed the way men and women match up. In the second section, we show how these forces skew marriage markets, altering the terms on which men and women come together and creating different class-based norms. The third section turns to the law, analyzing how family law contributes to the dismantling of the system of gender subordination and institutionalizes the new marital model of, and for, the elite. This new model, which replaces dependence with interdependence, restricts post-divorce obligations among spouses, and insists on the continuing involvement of both parents following a breakup, protects the interests of successful men and makes marriage a bad deal for women paired with unreliable men. For the middle, it also makes family law the focus of an on-going fight over gender power.

In the fourth section we argue that restoring family stability depends on the prospects for more equal and secure participation in the country's economy. Technological change and globalization set the stage for women's greater economic independence and greater inequality among men. The more steeply banked hierarchies and winner-take-all compensation systems that resulted, however, also increased the emphasis on short-term earnings at the expense of longer term institutional concerns and created incentives for executives to shortchange worker and community interests. Economic reconstruction requires renewed attention to the relationship between employment security and flexibility, and a rethinking of the connections that link executive rewards, job creation, worker training, and social insurance.

The other half of societal reconstruction requires reconsideration of the channeling of resources to the next generation. The increase in family-based and economic inequality skews not only the financial but the parental resources available to the next generation. In 1970, high school and college graduate parents spent about the same amount of time interacting with their children. Today, higher income mothers spend an hour a day more with their children in the first year of life. These differences correspond to gaps in cognitive performance that emerge before the age of two and produce a widening gulf in teen success and adult capabilities. Without renewed investment in all of our children and in the infrastructure that allows parents to raise their children, the result will be cultural understandings that diverge by class and that interact with the changing economy to solidify class boundaries, making social mobility more difficult and reducing overall human capital investment in the next generation.

SECTION I

THE PUZZLES OF TODAY'S FAMILIES

Tyler did everything right.[1] He graduated from a college in the Midwest and worked in the same city, where he met his first real girlfriend. They broke up when he realized she thought marriage meant that she would find a man who would support her while she took care of the house and the children. He wanted no part of that, and the relationship did not last long. He moved to another city and decided that law school would provide him with the financial security he needed. His parents, both well-paid professionals, supported his decision—and were able to pay most of his law school tuition.

In his second year of law school, Tyler met Amy, a fellow law student. Amy was ambitious, smart, and also knew how to party. They fell very much in love and planned to marry soon after graduation. When we asked Tyler how he knew she was the one, he told us that she was the first woman he had ever dated who was as disciplined and confident as he was.

We checked in with Tyler again just as he was about to graduate from law school. He and his fiancée were to be married a week later. We asked them about their plans. While students at the top of their law school classes were going off to work for prestigious judges or for high-powered law firms, they had graduated closer to the middle. She had landed a six-month job, with the possibility that it might turn into a permanent position if the office's finances improved. He accepted a temporary, unpaid internship with a judge that promised to get him valuable experience. He told us he could count on his parents to lend him enough money to get by, but then he sheepishly told us that his fiancée had offered to take a second job if they needed the money.

We asked if they hoped to have children. He said they wanted at least two, but he figured it would be years before they could afford to have them. Tyler is in his early thirties; his fiancée is twenty-eight. Amy put herself through school, and the two will finish law school with tens of thousands of dollars in student loan debt between them. There's a good chance that, with the probability of two incomes, they will never need public welfare, but they nonetheless feel very insecure about their financial future.

*   *   *

Lily was in tears in June's kitchen in Kansas City. She was from a rural area in the state more than an hour from the city. She was unmarried and four months pregnant; her boyfriend, Carl, didn't have a job, and still lived with his mother, but that's not what concerned her. The car that she needed to get to the two jobs in the city that kept her afloat had broken down. Her parents had lent her the money to pay for it, but they were both ill and their finances were stretched thin. She told us that she had bought the car because the dealer told her "he was a Christian," and she trusted him. Now, she had discovered that the car, which she had purchased a couple of weeks before, was a lemon and needed thousands of dollars' worth of work to run at all. She had found a lawyer, who thought he could get her money back and wanted to know what we thought. We had no idea what the odds were, but she clearly thought the lawyer was her only hope. We wondered more about the baby, but she told us that she had a group of friends who would help her get through the birth.

We later ran into a mutual friend. She told us that Lily and her family were good Christians and that Lily would never have considered an abortion. But she also never thought seriously about marrying Carl. Here's how Lily sees it, the friend informed us: She is sure she can support herself; she always has. She knows it will be hard, but she is confident she can support herself and the baby. She just can't support herself, the kid, *and* him.

*   *   *

Tyler and Lily grew up not too far from each other. They share a German heritage and are descendants of families who originally came from Europe to settle the American plains. In another era they both likely would have remained close to home. Even if one attended college and the other did not, their family lives would not have differed all that much. In the fifties, they might have even lived on the same street, attended the same church, and had the same expectations for their children. They almost certainly would have led lives that were even better than their parents'. Today, they will lead very different lives—differences that reflect different pathways into jobs, relationships, and childbearing.

1

Class, Marriage Markets, and the New Foundations for Family Life

In 1960 we could talk about such a thing as "the American family." We could imagine that a typical family and its form would not differ whether they were high school dropouts or college grads, whether they lived in a city like Boston or a farm community in Iowa. If intimate partners lived together, they were likely to be married, and, indeed, almost everyone married eventually. The children of the immigrant families that had flooded the United States at the turn of the twentieth century were catching up with the native-born in education. And everyone, it seemed, was having children, with only small differences in their views of the ideal age to marry or the number of children.

What held middle-American families together in that era were jobs, good jobs that paid a family wage even to the unskilled. The silver screen emblem of the era was Marlon Brando. In *A Streetcar Named Desire*, Brando played the virile Stanley Kowalski, whose strength and passion contrasted with the fading (and penniless) graces of the old southern family into which he married. Male high school graduates of that era, who made up the center of the American economy, were not only married (88 percent); almost all men (96 percent of high school graduates) were employed. More than 80 percent of wives with young children, in contrast, stayed home with the children.[2] Married mothers in the workforce were limited to a small number of the most educated women and a larger number of the poor.

Perhaps most strikingly, the men, whether white collar managers or blue collar workers, put in about the same number of hours. More jobs were there for the asking, and few worked the sixty-hour weeks required to make partner or enter into the top executive ranks. And yet both fathers and mothers spent *less* time interacting with their children than they do today. There really was a village—or an urban neighborhood block or a new suburban development—in the background that made their lives easier.

Of course, even in that era of relative equality and prosperity exceptions existed. Overall poverty rates were higher, and isolated populations on Native-American reservations, in Appalachia and other rural areas; and, most notably, African Americans did not share in the general prosperity, and their families were changing. In the first half of the century, African Americans had been *more* likely to marry than whites, and at earlier ages. By 1960, African-American families had begun to change. Gender relationships had long been rocky, and informal desertion rates appear to have been higher. After World War II, however, the birth rates of unmarried parents rose steadily, and by 1960 they had become a source of concern. Although no one realized it at the time, African-American men were already losing access to the high-paying blue-collar jobs that had fueled American postwar prosperity, and the loss was beginning to remake the family. Flash forward. Today only one group in the entire country has seen its marriage rates increase since 1970—the women with the top 5 percent of incomes.[3] A half-century ago, female college graduates were less likely than their peers with less education to be married; today they are the top catches in the marriage market. Everyone else is more likely to be single. Fifty years ago, during the *Mad Men* era, an executive might marry his secretary; today he is much more likely to marry another executive or a doctor or an accountant. Among high school graduates, the odds that the man is married have fallen to 54 percent; he is less likely to be employed, less likely to be the sole source of support for his family (73 percent of wives of high school graduate men are employed), and much less likely to be working in manufacturing.

By 2013, we had lost any sense of family as an enterprise built on a common foundation. College graduates have become more culturally conservative than they were thirty years ago and more likely to raise children in two-parent households than they were a quarter century ago. The young professionals who are often portrayed as part of a "hook-up culture" on college campuses are no more likely than their parents to give birth outside of marriage. The bottom third in the meantime has all but given up on marriage as a way of life, even if they still idealize the white picket fence. For African Americans, 70 percent of all births—and 96 percent of those to high school dropouts—are non-marital. The most surprising changes are to those in the middle of all races. Good Christian families like the Palins support their daughters when they choose not to have an abortion. They also often express relief when their daughters do not marry the Levi Johnstons (the ex-fiancé of Bristol Palin) of the world.

The problem is explaining how far we have grown apart as a society. In our last book, *Red Families v. Blue Families*, we tried to make sense of why the changes in the American family had mapped onto the political system and how family law, which in the postwar era had not differed all that much from Massachusetts to Alabama, had become a site of political polarization. In the process, we showed the regional differences in the family: a new "blue" family system had taken hold in the states most likely to have supported the Democratic presidential candidates in 2004 and 2008—those states have higher average ages of marriages and lower divorce rates, lower overall fertility and fewer teen births, and higher abortion rates and more support for contraception. In contrast, the states that had backed the Republican candidates and in 2004 had more voters listing "family values" as a concern, also had families with more children, younger ages of marriage and first birth, and less stable marriages. These differences corresponded to an ideological gulf among elites: red states have more religious and conservative elites and a working class that attends church less than they do while blue states have more secular elites and a working class that is more religious than those with higher incomes. Yet we also knew we were seeing something else: blue states are richer, and a big part of the explanation for the demographic differences between red and blue involves wealth.

If there was any chart that inspired our last book, it was one showing that divorce and teen birth rates mapped onto red/blue differences. And if there is any chart underlying this book, it is the one showing that divorce and nonmarital births have become markers of class. In the nineties, we heard good news—the divorce rate had leveled off. We, like the sociologists who studied these matters, assumed that these trends, like the ones before them, affected the country as a whole. We were wrong.

As we were pulling together the material for our last book, we saw a chart that captures the growing class division in the American family and that inspired us to write this book (see figure 1.1).

What this chart shows is that the divorce rate did not really plateau in the nineties. It was simultaneously declining steadily (the lower line on the graph) *and* rising precipitously (the higher line on the graph)—just for different groups. Thus the averages were misleading. Divorce rates were not plateauing for *anyone*. Instead, the averages cloaked two different trends. For college graduates, divorce rates were steadily declining; for everyone else, divorce rates, after a brief hiatus, resumed their upward climb. Families have always differed somewhat by class: the middle class and the elite have long been more likely than the poor to marry before giving birth, less likely to divorce, and less likely to end up at the altar solely because of a pregnancy. Yet, trend lines were historically the same. As the chart shows, for those who married in the seventies, divorce rates increased both for college graduates and everyone else. To be sure, college graduates had lower divorce rates, *hence* the difference in the two lines. Both curves move upward at about the same rate.[4]

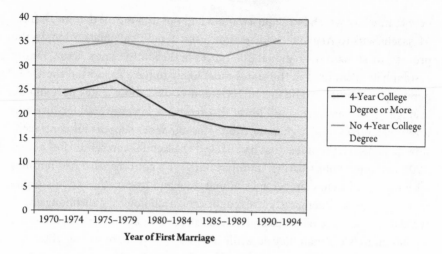

FIGURE 1.1: First Marriages Ending in Divorce within 10 Years as a Percentage of All First Marriages by Female Educational Attainment
Naomi Cahn and June Carbone, *Red Families v. Blue Families: Legal Polarization and the Creation of Culture* 40 (2010)

Starting with couples who married in 1980, however, the slopes of the curves begin to change, with divorce rates dropping sharply for the well educated while declining modestly for the rest of the population. For those who married at the end of the eighties (examined ten years later, at the end of the nineties), the divorce rates of those without college degrees *change direction* and rise significantly but continue to decline for the well educated. The net result: by 2004, the divorce rates of college graduates were back down to what they were in 1965—before no-fault divorce, the widespread availability of the pill and abortion, or the sex revolution.[5] In the meantime, the divorce rates of the less well educated reached all-time highs. These increasing divorce rates occurred well after the legal changes in the role of fault. The change in the incidence of divorce thus involved two very different time periods. During the seventies, what we now think of as the period of the sex revolution and the seismic shift in gender roles, divorce rates rose for the country as a whole. During the nineties, a class divide appeared in family behavior. College graduates, who marry much later than those who do not attend college and who have become much more likely to marry one another, began to create much more stable families. Class differences were remaking the family.

The Elite Commitment to Marriage and Children

Complementing the puzzle of diverging divorce rates has been the increase in non-marital births. This has been the part of the changing family that has attracted the most study and concern. The changes are striking. When the age of marriage began to rise for the college educated in the seventies, so too did the age of first birth. The result postponed family formation and lowered overall fertility. For high school graduates, the big delay in the average age of marriage came later—and it came with an increase in non-marital births.[6] Young women who used to get pregnant and then marry the father still get pregnant, though a little bit later than they did in the fifties or seventies. It's just that they no longer marry the father. While the age of first birth has continued to rise for college graduates, the increases leveled off after 1990 for other women.[7] The result—a steady increase in non-marital births but not for everyone. The chart in figure 1.2 shows that, in 1982, the non-marital birth rate for women with moderate education more closely resembled that of higher educated women than of women with the least education. Today, the opposite is true. College graduates continue to hold the line on non-marital births, even as that line erodes for everyone else.

The results are even more dramatic when race is taken into account. The non-marital birth rate for white college graduates has remained at 2 percent, with no change in the twenty-five-year period that started in the mid-eighties. During that period, twenty-somethings became more likely to live on their own. Journalists began to discuss the "hook-up" culture on college campuses, with casual sex becoming the norm.[8] Cohabitation increased, and overall marriage rates dropped. The stigma against non-marital births rapidly eroded. Yet, white college graduates held the line. The delay in starting families produced a delay in births but not a lack of emphasis on marriage. Indeed, a fourteen-year-old daughter of college graduates was *more likely* to be raised in a two-parent home in 2006–2008 than in the early eighties; the same held true for

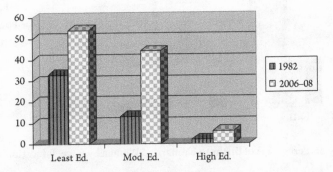

FIGURE 1.2: Percentage of Births to Never Married Mothers, Ages 15–44

Nat'l Marriage Project, The State of Our Unions 2010, *When Marriage Disappears: The New Middle America* 23 fig. 5 (W. Bradford Wilcox & Elizabeth Marquardt eds., 2010), *available at* http://www.virginia.edu/marriageproject/pdfs/Union_11_12_10.pdf.

African Americans as well as whites.[9] One of the things that separates couples like Tyler and Amy from Lily and Carl is that Tyler and Amy still believe that they can make marriage work and that they should wait until they have found the right partner before having a child.

For those without college degrees, in contrast, a delay in marriage has meant an increase in non-marital births—and in the number of those likely never to marry. For the most disadvantaged women, non-marital birth rates were already high in 1982, and they continued to rise. Today, for example, the non-marital birth rate for African Americans without a high school degree is 96 percent. Marriage has all but disappeared in the poorest communities. As figure 1.3 shows, the group that experienced the largest increase in the period from the mid-eighties until 2008, however, was white high school graduates— a group once among the most likely to marry. The non-marital birth rate for this group was 4 percent in 1982, just barely higher than the rate for college grads. By 2008, the rate had increased to 34 percent, close to the 42 percent rate for white high school dropouts. African-American high school graduates also became much more likely to give birth outside of marriage during the same period, with the percentage of non-marital births rising from 48 to 74 percent. Moreover, the huge recent expansion in the non-marital birth rate, which has had a dramatic impact on the middle of the American public, has largely been to women in their twenties; teen births have fallen across the board.

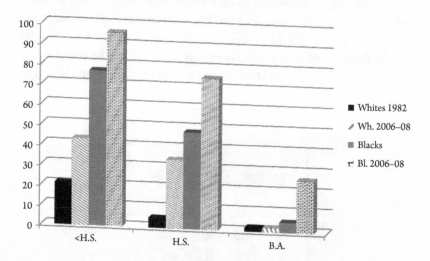

FIGURE 1.3: Percentage of Births to Unmarried Women by Race, Education, and Year, Ages 15–44

W. Bradford Wilcox, *When Marriage Disappears: The Retreat From Marriage in Middle Amercia,"* The State of Our Unions: Marriage in America 2010 (Charlottesville, Va., National Marriage Project at the University of Virginia and the Institute for American Values, 2010), 56 Figure S2, http://stateof ourunions.org/2010/SOOU2010.pdf.

These figures also correlate with class-based shifts in attitudes toward divorce, sexuality, non-marital births—and marital satisfaction. Between 1990 and 2010, the percentage of white college graduates who described themselves as in "very happy marriages" increased from 58 to 63 percent. During that same period, the percentage of the white working class who could say the same plummeted from 38 to 23 percent.[10] The rates for African Americans are even lower. The 2010 "State of Our Unions" report describes the combination that emerges from the divorce and non-marital birth trends as the "disappearance of marriage" from Middle America. The report's authors asked a group ranging in age from twenty-four to forty-four whether "marriage has not worked out for most of the people they know." Of those with the least education, over half (53 percent) said yes, marriage has not worked out for most people they know. Those with moderate amounts of education follow close behind, with 43 percent expressing skepticism about marriage. Among the most highly educated, only 17 percent agree; that is, 83 percent indicate that marriage has worked for most of the people they know.[11] Tyler and Amy are in the group that still believes in marriage, even though Tyler's parents are divorced. Lily grew up in a rural community with two married parents, but we suspect that she is much less likely than Tyler and Amy to see marriage succeeding for those around her.

While high-profile conflicts like those over same-sex marriage get the most attention, they are not the most far-reaching changes. The story of the American family is not a story of the privileged left undermining the family values of the conservative middle. Nor is it a story of the liberated seeking more creative ways to make family work. Indeed, the elite do not lead the way out of marriage; they are too busy buying back into it. The well-educated and prosperous upper third of the country has reembraced marriage. The highly educated are more likely than their parents to believe that divorce should be more difficult to obtain (48 to 36 percent) or that premarital sex is always wrong (21 to 15 percent).[12] In their parents' generation, the more education a woman had, the less likely she was to marry. Today, the opposite is true—more highly educated women are substantially more likely than other women to be married and to raise their children within a two-parent family.

In the meantime, those with less education have become less "traditional" in their beliefs and practices. They place less faith in marriage than their parents did and have become less likely to favor restraining divorce or treating non-marital sex as wrong. They are more likely to have children before marriage.

Marriage, once universal, once the subject of rebellion, has emerged as a marker of the new class lines remaking American society. Stable unions have become a hallmark of privilege. The flight away from marriage is not a flight of elites. Instead, stable marriage has become increasingly hard to obtain for much of the country. For the majority of Americans who haven't graduated from college, marriage rates are low, divorce rates are high, and a first child is more likely to be born to parents who are single than to parents who are married.[13] Yet, for those who make marriage work, it continues to pay off handsomely for the lives of the next generation.

2

Blinded by the Light

The pieces of the puzzle—why have young couples such as Tyler and Amy become *more* likely to raise their children in a two-parent home while couples like Lily and Carl have given up on marriage altogether?—have been there all along had we been willing to see them. Instead, the study of the family has been shouted down, stuck in extended detours down blind alleys and mired in ideological division. A consistent (and well-funded) drumbeat repeats from decade to decade that economic change cannot explain a change in values, that Lily's decision not to marry the father of her child cannot be attributed to anyone's job prospects. Instead, the parents' behavior, their feelings of shame (or pride) about the birth, and their sense of obligation (or entitlement) operate on their own tracks, and society must address the mores and the behavior rather than talk about employment.

The problem with these theories is that the stories of Tyler and Amy, Lily and Carl, and the data that document the emerging class divisions that underlie the family defy the predictions elicited by these theories. Explaining how these two couples have moved so far apart requires *combining* mores with economics and explaining how men and women find each other in the marriage markets of the new century. We repeat our question: what happened? Answering that question requires working through the detours and distractions of the highly contentious family debate in order to recognize that the answers have always been there, right before our eyes.

This long detour has been driven by the psychological need to separate the change in mores from the changing economy. Numerous explanations for diverging family structures insist that the change in sentiment is somehow independent of economics.[1] That insistence—and the difficulty in explaining the relationship between sexual bargains and material ones—lies at the heart of the refusal to accept the explanation we are about to offer. So we start with the detours, which provide their own clues to the full explanation of the family and class system that emerged in full force in the 1990s.

The Late and Great Moynihan

We've known about the connection between the economy and the family at least since the Moynihan report in 1965. His claim—that the loss of jobs causes changes in family structure—remains as controversial today as when it was made. A half-century after his infamous Report, no government officials who wish to keep their jobs are likely to attempt an explanation for the racial differences in marriage.[2] Indeed, in 2012, an in-depth U.S. government report on marriage rates blandly noted that there have been two sets of explanations for diverging marriage rates, cultural and structural, and called for more research. But, of course, "culture" and "structure" are not two different explanations, but rather are deeply intertwined. The causal links that connect them remain obscure and politically explosive.

What Did Moynihan Discover?

> The gap between the Negro and most other groups in American society is widening. The fundamental problem, in which this is most clearly the case, is that of family structure. The evidence—not final, but powerfully persuasive—is that the Negro family in the urban ghettos is crumbling. A middle-class group has managed to save itself, but for vast numbers of the unskilled, poorly educated city working class the fabric of conventional social relationships has all but disintegrated. . . . So long as this situation persists, the cycle of poverty and disadvantage will continue to repeat itself.
>
> The Moynihan Report, 1965[3]

> LBJ's 1965 War on Poverty was triggered in part by the famous "Moynihan Report" finding that the black out-of-wedlock birthrate had hit 26 percent; today, the white rate exceeds that, the overall rate is 41 percent, and over 70 percent of African-American babies are born to single parents—a prime sociological indicator for poverty, pathology and prison regardless of race or ethnicity.[4]
>
> "The Marriage Vow," 2011

Daniel Patrick Moynihan's 1965 report, *The Negro Family: The Case for National Action* (now known as the Moynihan Report after its primary author), set the standard for explanations that attempt to combine cultural and structural change. It also provides a cautionary tale for what it is possible to discuss in the political arena. Moynihan tried to explain how a change in the economy (the disappearance of well-paying blue-collar jobs in the inner cities of the rustbelt north) produced a change in family culture (female-headed households) that he argued locked successive generations into a cycle of poverty. The relationship he documented between employment and family culture is a fundamental insight into explaining today's class divergence; yet, the causal explanations he proffered remain contested—and, many would say, rightly so.

Fifty years after its publication, the Moynihan Report's attempt to identify the causal links between increases in male unemployment and higher rates of divorce and non-marital births still inflames. It does so because Moynihan took on the intersection of race and gender in the production of culture. Moynihan sought to explain why an increase in unemployment might affect family structure more readily among blacks than whites. In doing so, he addressed the assault on black manhood that he treated as a legacy of slavery, characterized the African-American family as a "tangle of pathologies," and attributed many of its problems to the "matriarchy" that resulted when African-American women stepped into the breach left by the lack of reliable male breadwinners. As two researchers concluded in 2009:

> The Moynihan report asserted that a determining factor in the increasingly "desperate" situation of so-called "lower-class" Negroes was family instability as displayed by the growing prevalence of out-of-wedlock childbearing, female-headed families, and the decreasing reliance on men's earnings for family support. The stated and unstated implications of these trends were clear. Although black women were not responsible for the joblessness and underemployment of black men, their apparent assumption of economic and social responsibilities for their households served to emasculate their men and undermine men's efforts to be proper husbands and fathers.[5]

The liberals of Moynihan's era insisted that the African-American family must be accorded greater respect as an adaptive response to the problems of racism, just as many today maintain that family creation should be viewed entirely as a matter of individual choice. And conservatives, then and since, have treated the Report as a critique of African-American moral failings while conveniently overlooking its emphasis on the disappearance of jobs as the cause of the problem. Moynihan's insistence that economic change could transform family structure, and that the resulting change, however understandable or even adaptive, could exacerbate class and racial barriers, remains a combustible mix.

Moynihan's Meaning Today

Determining Moynihan's legacy is accordingly a tricky matter. His effort to link changing employment patterns to cultural norms, such as the acceptability of female-headed households and non-marital births, adds an important piece to the puzzle of understanding today's American families, but his causal agents—race and gender—are at best incomplete and, though they reflect the best sociological thinking of his era, arguably wrong. Moreover, whatever the merits of his substantive claims, the language, he used, which was intended to galvanize a response to what he saw as a pressing social issue, remains jarring. In the Report, Moynihan declared, without qualification, that "At the heart of the deterioration of the fabric of Negro society is the deterioration of the Negro family.... [U]nless this damage [to the family] is repaired, all the effort to end discrimination and poverty and injustice will come to little."[6]

At the time Moynihan wrote those lines, he was a brash, young assistant secretary of labor who wanted to catch the president's attention.[7] Lyndon Johnson had declared "war on poverty" in his first State of the Union message in January 1964. Johnson came to office committed to addressing the issue of poverty, and his presidency came at a time when "sustained economic growth, [and] steadily increasing affluence seemed now an enduring and irreversible reality of American life." At a time of general prosperity and Cold War détente, the country felt willing and able to address the needs of the less fortunate.[8] The challenge was to figure out how to reach those who had been left behind, and the war on poverty devoted particular attention to the rural poor and concentrated poverty in the inner cities.

Moynihan, despite his intellectual pedigree, had grown up poor in the worst neighborhoods of New York. His father had deserted the family. His mother moved from tenement to tenement in some of New York's roughest neighborhoods.[9] After graduating first in his high school class in Harlem and working as a longshoreman, Moynihan attended City College when tuition was free and completed his education on the GI bill. Like Johnson, he cared personally about the issue of poverty, urban poverty in particular. He sought to do two things with the Report. He sought to define a problem—the role of family structure in perpetuating racial inequality, an issue on which no one was focused at the time—and to encourage the federal government to help solve it.[10] His most innovative suggestion was to increase postal delivery to twice a day; he understood that jobs for the least employable men were critical to any solution.

Instead, the reaction to the Report effectively derailed discussion of family form for at least a generation. In fact, criticism of the Report preceded its publication and—in an era before the Internet—before many of the reviewers had even seen the document.[11] The most intense ideological response came from the left, and one of the most influential critics, William Ryan, coined a term to dismiss Moynihan's ideas. He called it "blaming the victim." As he observed:

> The explanations almost always focused on the supposed defects of
> the Negro victim as if those—and not the racist structure of Ameri-
> can Society—were the cause of all woes that Negroes suffer. The

Moynihan Report single[s] out "the unstable Negro family" as the cause of Negro inequality. But the statistics reflect current effects of contemporary discrimination. They are results not causes.[12]

Twenty-five years later, Adolph Reed Jr. and Julian Bond would still refer to "Moynihan's racist, scurrilously sexist 1965 Report."[13]

Today, scholars are more inclined to say that Moynihan was right, though they do not necessarily agree on what he was right about. In particular, few, even among those who cite Moynihan with admiration, combine his emphasis on structure *and* culture. Instead, they cherry pick the parts of the analysis that fit their own worldviews. Many African Americans, for example, still bristle at the suggestion that Moynihan described a particular weakness of the African-American family.[14] Instead, the easiest way to get broader agreement is to say that he was remarkably prescient in describing structural change, a change that plays out along lines of class and affects whites as well as blacks. Stated in these terms, a retrospective on Moynihan in 2009 concluded that "Moynihan's core argument was really rather simple: whenever males in any population subgroup lack widespread access to reliable jobs, decent earnings, and key forms of socially rewarded status, single parenthood will increase, with negative side effects on women and children."[15]

This description, however, downplays Moynihan's emphasis that the structural forces (widespread lack of access to reliable jobs) do not change the family directly (any man who loses his job is at risk of divorce) but indirectly by altering the sexual and gender norms of the group (women generally begin to rely more on their own earnings and become less dependent). Moynihan emphasized that the consequences affected the African-American community as a whole, concluding that "the Negro community has been forced into a matriarchal structure which, because it is [so] out of line with the rest of the American society, seriously retards the progress of the group."

Those on the right, on the other hand, often cite Moynihan's description of the effect on culture, conveniently omitting his recital of the loss of jobs as a necessary causal agent. When a conservative Christian group cited Moynihan in promoting a "Marriage Vow" during the 2012 Republican primaries, for example, it treated the changing family as an independent cause of poverty and identified the War on Poverty as an effort to address family change, reversing the time line of the events.[16] We similarly found in 2011, when we submitted a blog on the connection between employment and family values, that even among readers of a liberal publication like the *Huffington Post*, few make the connections.

What Moynihan almost certainly discovered were the initial effects of the disappearance of stable manufacturing jobs from the urban north. He was one of the first to recognize that at the height of the Civil Rights movement the circumstances in heavily African-American inner-city communities were getting *worse, not better*.[17] His description, with light of hindsight, reads as a roadmap for what would later happen to the country as a whole as the widespread loss of reliable jobs transformed gender expectations. Moynihan explained that while divorce rates did not differ by race in 1940, by 1964 the non-white rate exceeded the white rate by 40 percent. Non-marital births during the same period grew from 16.8 percent to 23.6 percent for blacks (compared to an increase among whites of 2 to 3.07 percent). In addition, while well-educated African Americans had fewer children than well-educated whites, African Americans with less education had more children at younger ages than their white counterparts. The net effect of the changes created a picture of two groups moving in opposite directions. Between 1940 and the mid-1960s, the percentage of female-headed households fell for whites and increased for blacks.[18] Moreover, within the African-American community, the overall statistics cloaked increasing class divisions as the stable African-American middle class placed "a higher premium on family stability and the conserving of family resources than does the white middle-class family."[19]

Moynihan was thus most prescient when he emphasized that male unemployment was the single most critical cause of the change in African-American family structure.[20] Indeed, he observed that the impact of that unemployment was "the least understood of all the developments that have contributed to the present crisis. There is little analysis because there has been almost no inquiry."[21]

Drawing on the few studies that did exist, Moynihan reported that male African-American employment had peaked during World War II and the Korean War, while white men were off at war and the demand for black labor increased. African-American male unemployment, however, rose steadily after 1951, particularly in the urban areas of the north. Moynihan explained:

> The conclusion from these and similar data is difficult to avoid: During times when jobs were reasonably plentiful . . . the Negro family became stronger and more stable. As jobs became more and more difficult to find, the stability of the family became more and more difficult to maintain.[22]

Moynihan insisted that what jobs—particularly for men—do is to restore the family's proper hierarchy of men over women, in accordance with society's dominant (if not inevitable) order.[23]

In establishing the connection between unemployment and family instability, Moynihan's causal connection was the pernicious effects of "matriarchy" imposed on a black community already weakened by the legacy of slavery.

And, indeed, even today some cite that insight with approval, insisting that "a society that fails to give respect and responsibilities to males, is grossly inferior to one that does, in terms of outcomes."[24] At the same time, others reject Moynihan altogether for the suggestion that African-American women, by emasculating the men, were responsible for the condition of the African-American family. The notion of gender hierarchy remains critical to Moynihan's analysis and to his legacy.

So just what was Moynihan right about? He was clearly right that the family was changing. He was right that it was doing so along class lines. He was right that race was a factor, though there is no agreement then or later on why race mattered. He was almost certainly right that the changes worsened the circumstances of African-American children. He was right that employment was a significant cause and that, indeed, African-Americans were the canaries in the mine, experiencing the early impact of the loss of industrial era manufacturing jobs. The most difficult issue he raised, however, is on the elusive question of causation—how does a loss of employment change cultural norms and how does gender affect the result—which will occupy us for the rest of the book.

How the Culture Wars Derailed the Inquiry

The leading theorists of the family all tell a version of the same story:

> Boy meets girl. Boy falls for girl. Girl keeps him at bay until he comes up with the right signs of devotion: a ring, sober behavior, fidelity, employment and ideally all of the above. By the time they have 2.3 or even 1.98 children, the romance has faded but they stay together because marriage and community tell them what roles to play, and social pressure, financial dependence, moral obligation, and a gendered system of power keep them together. Alter the script and the family—and society—falls apart.

These tales have very little to say about why the family has diverged along class lines. Indeed, this scenario predicts that the independent women enjoying college hook-ups should have the bleakest marital prospects when in fact they have become the most likely to manage stable relationships and carefully planned and pampered children. But these morality tales have one advantage that the Moynihan Report did not: they provide a justification for bankrolling the careers of those who from the pulpits of ever more prosperous megachurches or the comfortable sinecures of well-funded think tanks are prepared to wage culture war. If the left shouted down Moynihan for his suggestion that African-American culture could be a causal factor in explaining the persistence of poverty, the right has long insisted that *only* the combination of cultural failings and individual weakness can explain an increase in non-marital births. The furor over the Moynihan Report shut down public discussion of the family for a generation. When discussion resumed, it would be hijacked by the "moral majority" and the nascent conservative movement.

3

Blaming the Victim: The Morality Tale

Americans, to a greater degree than Europeans, see the individual as responsible for his or her fate. The opportunities are there; it is simply a matter of seizing them. And conservatives, in this and every other century, view the existing order as one that rewards virtue; as a result, if you haven't succeeded, it is your fault. No one has captured this ethic better than Charles Murray. His most famous book, *The Bell Curve*, written with Harvard psychologist Richard Herrnstein and published in 1994, argued that societal success—and failure—increasingly reflect intelligence and are therefore difficult for the government to change. In his two books on the family—*Losing Ground* in the eighties and *Coming Apart* in 2012—he maintains that what matters is hard work, marriage, and religion. He wrote in the eighties to argue that government intervention was misguided and counterproductive, uniting the libertarian elite that disdained government assistance for the poor with the growing social conservative base that wished to bring back traditional values.

We take up Murray's work with some reluctance. Moynihan, though a public intellectual who wished to influence policy, drew on the best academic work of his day. He caused a furor because he took that work to its logical conclusions, explaining that loss of jobs combined with racism to create cultural obstacles to community renewal. Murray, in contrast, writes as a movement conservative. He positions his critique outside the framework of mainstream research, ignoring the issues that would complicate his conclusions. His scholarship is not as rigorous as Moynihan's nor the better sociological work before and since. Yet, unlike Moynihan, he succeeded in redirecting social policy and really does blame the victim. To understand the failure to see the forces remaking the American family therefore requires understanding why more than half of the American public still believes Murray's claim that welfare caused the changes in U.S. families and why Murray has managed to insist over the course of three decades with ample evidence to the contrary that economic change had nothing to do with the changes in the family.

Murray's work in the eighties, which focused on the African-American underclass, stepped into the vacuum left after the reaction to the Moynihan Report. His more provocative title, however, came with an op-ed in the *Wall Street Journal* in the early nineties calling attention to "The Coming White Underclass."[1] In 2012, he completed the analysis with a new book, *Coming Apart: The State of White Ameri*ca. By then, the characteristics that had alarmed Moynihan in the mid-sixties about African Americans better described whites. The non-marital birth rate in 2010 approached 30 percent of all white births; divorce rates, which leveled off for college graduates after 1980, continued steeply upward for the working class; and the incidence of children raised in single-parent families was heavily concentrated in poorer communities.[2] In 1963, the likelihood that a child lived with both biological parents exceeded 90 percent for the entire population with few class differences among whites; in 2005, the differences had grown so large (90 percent of children still lived with two biological parents in the top 20 percent of white households compared to 35 percent for the white bottom third) that Murray argued that they constituted "different family cultures."[3] Even marital happiness corresponded increasingly to class.[4] The result, Murray warned, was the creation of a white underclass[5] characterized by an increase in crime, deterioration of neighborhood schools, rising unemployment, and the weakening of communities.[6]

Murray can be called a "once and future culture warrior." He has consistently blamed family instability on lack of character and misguided government intervention. We do not quarrel with his description, both in the eighties and more recently, of the class-based nature of family change. Instead, what is startling is his explanation for the creation of a yawning class gap: the deterioration of the moral character of those at the losing end of economic changes. He indicts the culture of the working class as a problem standing on its own. And to the extent he concedes that any of the threats to American families do not result from individual responsibility alone, he blames misguided government intervention. His banner for the newly energized right of the eighties could be summarized as moral failings that "welfare let me get away with." *Mother Jones* characterized Murray's take on the cause of social decay: "It's an age-old problem: the government gives you food stamps, and the next thing you know, your marriage has collapsed, you've quit your job, you've turned your back to God, and you're facing 5 to 10 for holding up a Piggly Wiggly."[7] The one explanation Murray aggressively took off the table was the one Moynihan emphasized—the argument that the decline in "good jobs" for working class men destabilized their communities.

Murray's 2012 book continues the saga with a stunning and depressingly accurate description of the effects of the growing class divide in the United States, while denying that greater economic inequality had anything to do with the results.[8] Instead, Murray attributes the decline to the erosion of work, religiosity,[9] and marriage—and the private discipline that once made such traits more universal. His earlier work provides almost a caricature of conservative thinking by insisting that discipline can only come from stigma and punishment. As Murray explained in 1993,

> To restore the rewards and penalties of marriage does not require social engineering. Rather, it requires that the state stop interfering with the natural forces that have done the job quite effectively for millennia.
>
> ... Throughout human history, a single woman with a small child has not been a viable economic unit. Not being a viable economic unit, neither have the single woman and child been a legitimate social unit. In small numbers, they must be a net drain on the community's resources. In large numbers, they must destroy the community's capacity to sustain itself. *Mirabile dictu,* communities everywhere have augmented the economic penalties of single parenthood with severe social stigma.[10]

What reforms mores is shaming the individual; anything that might help the desperate plight of that individual therefore dooms community well-being.

In 2012, Murray shifted his focus from condemnation of women's sexual and reproductive autonomy to men's employment failings, but the framework of moral blame remained the same. He relentlessly documented the loss of work. The percentage of elite families with at least one family member working forty hours a week or more did not change between 1960 and 2010—it has remained close to 90 percent in the affluent community he calls "Belmont." For the bottom group of whites in working class "Fishtown," however, the number fell from 80 to 60 percent,[11] and the number of males not in the workforce at all doubled.[12] Murray acknowledges the loss of high-paying union jobs and the wage stagnation for the unskilled. Yet, he concludes that there is "no evidence" that men were out of work because of a lack of jobs—plenty of low-paying jobs exist that employers have trouble filling, despite the fact that many economists call the so-called shortage a myth.[13] Instead, he finds that the "simpler explanation" is that white males of the 2000s were less industrious than they had been and that somehow this loss of industry only affected the working class. They just lack the ability "to get up every morning and go to work."[14] What could explain the class division? Murray concludes that if men *need to work to survive*—an important proviso—falling hourly income does not discourage work."[15] Today, men do not need to work to survive because they mooch off either the government or the women in their lives.[16] He endorses George Gilder's analysis that men arrive at adulthood as "barbarians" who are civilized by women through marriage. Take away marriage—and their families' dependence on male income—and the men remain barbarians.[17] Women, given the choice, are quite happy to do without them. Murray argues that the solution must therefore be to reinstill the right values. The feckless men "must once again be openly regarded by their fellow citizens as lazy, irresponsible and unmanly."[18]

Murray, in his insistence that "economics cannot explain our cultural divide,"[19] refuses to recognize that the cultural aspirations might still be shared (yes, Charles, poor people still value marriage) but that forces beyond the control of the individual tear up the pathways that make realization of those aspirations possible. Thomas Keneally writes of the destructive impact of famine, whether in Ireland or India, "The victim becomes a new person. The fastidious become slovenly; the kindly become aggressive; the moral are caught up in the great amorality of famine. Fraternity and love wither."[20] By contrast, Murray, like the neoliberals of their time who advocated in London editorials that the Irish and the Indians deserved their fate,[21] would point to these changes and say, see, these people are starving *because* they have become slovenly, aggressive, and amoral. Let them stay hungry and they will reform themselves.

After thirty years of declining working-class incomes, the Murray-inspired abolition of welfare as we know it, greater inequality (and greater returns for the most successful), and the stalled mobility of the bottom half of the American population, Murray offers no explanation of why hard times have not worked their prescribed magic. He seems to suggest only that we have not made those losing ground sufficiently desperate or chided them enough for their failings.

In the meantime, what neither Moynihan could foresee nor Murray acknowledge is that women's employment, rather than weakening the families in Murray's well-off Belmont, seems to have strengthened it. Murray writes as though families like those of law students Tyler and Amy are identical to the fifties' families with stay-at-home moms in every respect except their willingness to sneer at Lily and Carl. Murray, neither in the eighties nor today, can explain how women's employment somehow manages to strengthen marriage in the well-off communities in Belmont while discouraging marriage in working-class Fishtown. All he can manage to propose is that the well-off come out of their gated communities and "preach what they practice," which ideally seems to involve marriage between two lawyers, pharmacists, or investment bankers in their early thirties. These unions may in fact be fairly stable, and we do have high hopes for Tyler and Amy, but Murray is one of the few writers we have encountered who would uphold the avatars of Wall Street as moral exemplars, culpable only for their failure to chastise the economy's losers. The story he refuses to acknowledge, though it is at the heart of everything he writes, is the re-creation of class and women's roles in remaking the pathways to success.

Misunderstanding Marriage

The two most celebrated theories of the family, which do look at women's roles, come from economics and sociology. But rather than provide a more complex account of family change, they provide an academic explanation of why the changing roles of women must inevitably lead to family decline. Chicago economist Gary Becker won a Nobel Prize in economics in part for his extension of the imperial discipline of economics into the realm of the family. His 1981 *Treatise on the Family* sought to bring the hallmark of rational choice theory, that is, simplifying assumptions that people act rationally to maximize their well-being, reductionist models, and equations that validate the models, to explain such non-material behavior as marriage and the sexual division of labor within it. Central to Becker's *Treatise* was his claim that a major advantage of marriage comes from specialization between men and women, with the man's focus on the market and the woman's on the home maximizing the benefits derived from their union. In accordance with this model, Becker predicted that those with high wage rates will tend to marry those with lower wage rates ("negative assortative mating") and that with women's greater workforce participation, lesser specialization would reduce the gains from marriage, leading to less marriage and more divorce. Based on these predictions, one would expect an ambitious law student like Amy to invest less in marriage than a woman like Lily, who has fewer prospects for a high-paying job. And, indeed, we suspect that Lily would welcome a bargain that allowed her to use her housekeeping skills (she cleans houses on the side) to land a man with a higher income than she could earn on her own. Becker would further expect Tyler, who is investing heavily in his own earning capacity, to look for a woman like Lily who would happily take on the cleaning, shopping, errand running, and child care that Tyler has no interest in doing himself. Today, even economists who continue to genuflect to Becker guffaw at the notion that such thoughts motivate modern partner selection. Tyler is marrying Amy because, not in spite, of the fact she is likely to earn as much as he does. Yet, even economists who point out how badly Becker's predictions turned out continue to begin almost every paper on the family with reference to his theories.[22]

Sociologists place less faith in equations and considerably more in the institutions that make up society. It is perhaps unsurprising, therefore, that they view the changing family with concern and term the changes "deinstitutionalization." Perhaps the most influential article describing the trends was by sociologist Andrew Cherlin in 2004. By then, the increases in divorce, cohabitation, and non-marital births were unmistakable; so too was the class-based nature of the changes in marriage rates. Cherlin defined "de-institutionalization" as the move away from the social norms that once guided young people into marriage (primarily we are to assume by stigmatizing non-marital sex and childbearing) and kept them there through the assumption of gendered roles that marked their entry into adulthood. In contrast, he terms today's later marriages as "status symbols" attainable only by those who have achieved maturity and financial stability and modern relationships as part of a quest for individual expression and fulfillment rather than societally mandated institutional obligations. Cherlin describes these changes within the context of a centuries-long move toward greater individualism and as part of a stalled revolution that dismantled sharply differentiated marital roles assigned by gender without replacing them with either egalitarian or other shared understandings about family organization. He thus acknowledges the class-based nature of the changes in the family while maintaining that the future offers a choice between permanently more fragile unions or an unlikely reduction in women's labor force participation and a return to more gender-typed family roles.[23] Cherlin discusses Becker's influence, even as he notes the failure of his predictions, and fellow sociologists routinely refer to Cherlin's deinstitutionalization hypothesis whether or not they agree with the prescriptions the analysis suggests.

Becker and Cherlin, though certainly not identical to each other, create academic frameworks that dovetail with many popular—and less nuanced—accounts. Family instability starts with the change in woman's autonomy. Societal stability depends on the foundational role of marriage, and marriage is an institution designed to provide for childrearing through the assumption of complementary roles.[24] Dismantle the idea of gender, leave family arrangements to individual negotiation, and the institution dissolves. Same-sex marriage often appears in these narratives as a symbol of everything that is wrong with the modern family. To be sure, the elite, the motivated, the disciplined, the lucky, the old-fashioned traditionalists may still find a way to stay together, but marriage becomes associated with class because of the erosion of the societal pathways that once shepherded everyone else into marriage and kept them there.

These accounts from economists, sociologists, moralists, and pundits bemoan that we have rewritten the ancient script. In the popular press, the pundits argue that the new script has become

> Boy meets girl. They have the hots for each other and jump in the sack. If she is disciplined and ambitious, she's been on the pill since puberty. If not, she gets pregnant. She decides she can deal with the baby. He thinks she can, too. They both adore the child, but not necessary each other. They stay together only so long as the sex stays hot, their tempers stay cool, and a better opportunity does not present itself. Then they part and society goes to hell.

If the story were really that simple, we could add contraception to the water and the problem would be solved; to tell something more than a stick figure vignette requires understanding why the solutions that work so well for the elite third do not work for everyone else and why the upper third, who first embraced the move away from gendered marital roles, today lead the way back into the remade institution.

Getting Closer: The Rediscovery of Marriage Markets

An ethnographic study of working class whites in San Francisco in the early sixties observed that working class courtship was typically sexual and brief; it quotes a young man about his marriage, "If a girl gets pregnant you married her. There wasn't no choice. So I married her."[1]

Calvin, the father of her child, was not going to drive up in a Chevy and take his rightful place at the head of the table one day soon because Bethenny was already occupying it, not to mention making the monthly payments on the mortgage, the kitchen renovation, and her own used car. Bethenny was doing too much, but she was making it work and she had her freedom. Why would she want to give all that up?[2]

Moynihan argued that the "very essence of the male animal, from the bantam rooster to the four-star general, is to strut." He concluded that when the lack of employment and matriarchal women deprive men of that opportunity, the family falls apart. Murray maintained that a hard worker can always strut, and when a man loses his $25 an hour factory job, his family will still have him if he works at Home Depot for $10 an hour and supplements that with a second shift and then a third.

So what happens if Moynihan was right that women won't marry unemployed men? And what happens when women become financially independent?[3] We're finding out. In fact, as journalist Hanna Rosin shows, women are too busy taking charge of their lives to worry whether the men will stick it out at Home Depot. The women may not accept even if the men are willing to propose.

Conservative critics assert that when a generation of college women, supposedly deluded by feminists like Gloria Steinem, led the charge to dismantle the connections between sex, marriage, and childbearing, it left the working class with no one to prod them to do the right thing.[4] These critics blame the problems of Lily and Carl on what Amy and Tyler do in the bedroom. And both liberals and conservatives agree that class divergence starts with the fact that when Lily has sex, she still gets pregnant while when Amy has sex, she does not. It's just that they utterly disagree on what this has to do with marriage.

So it is time to come back to the issue of sex. While volumes focus on the question of why Lily and Carl no longer marry, we think the far more interesting question is why Amy and Tyler still do. Both liberals and conservatives agree that part of what has changed is the death of the shotgun wedding as the response to pregnancy. What both groups have a more difficult time explaining is why anyone bothers to get married without it. The answer to that question lays the foundation for the creation of a new middle-class strategy for love and the war to climb the corporate ladder.

Economics Revisited: Akerlof, Yellen, and Katz and the End of the Shotgun Marriage

In 1996, economists George Akerlof, Janet Yellen, and Michael Katz set the stage for many of the conservative critiques. They argued that the pill and the legalization of abortion led to the end of the shotgun marriage and, with it, the rise in non-marital births.[5] Perhaps ironically, these relatively liberal economists made Murray's case linking the sexual revolution to the increase in male fecklessness. They provide an explanation for how a widespread cultural change—the increase in women's reproductive autonomy—could simultaneously make well-educated women better off and decrease the power of less-educated women to snooker men into marriage. Like Moynihan and Murray, they focus on what happens to those at the bottom of the socioeconomic order. Yet their analysis also combines those observations with insight into the re-creation of marriage markets at the top—and the impact on everyone else.

Akerlof is a Nobel laureate, who was then at Berkeley. His wife, Janet Yellen, became head of the Federal Reserve Board in 2014 and is a former chair of President Obama's Council of Economic Advisors. Together with their associate Michael Katz, they tried to model the change in women's decision-making about reproduction. Because of women's vulnerability to pregnancy in the era before the widespread availability of contraception and abortion, they argued that unmarried women would engage in sex only with at least an implicit promise that the man would marry them if they became pregnant. Adoption served as the primary fallback. They calculate that about 60 percent of premaritally conceived first births for whites and 35 percent of those for blacks resulted in marriage before the birth of the child. In contrast, less than 30 percent of the women who did not marry kept the child, showing the importance of the fallback option.[6] Given the stigma associated with what were then called "illegitimate" births, the increase in non-marital sex during the fifties drove down the age of marriage (with a much higher percent following pregnancy) *and* increased the adoption rate, reversing the trends of the preceding century and a half. In 1960, 30 percent of brides gave birth within eight and a half months of the nuptials, a figure last seen in 1800. The age of marriage also fell, and with it women's educational parity with men. The seventies would reverse these trends and re-create class gaps in the process.

The economists argue that the birth control pill and the legalization of abortion changed the terms of the bargains that united sex and marriage. In the fifties, college women and high school dropouts alike shared the consequences of sex in the backseat of a Chevy. With the advent of the pill and the legalization of abortion, women who wanted sex could engage in it on the same terms as men—without commitment. If the woman became pregnant, she could make the decision to have an abortion on her own. The man in her life did not necessarily have a say in the decision whether or not to bear the child.[7] He might feel obligated to contribute to the cost of an abortion, but if she chose to have the child, he did not feel the same obligation to marry her. Akerlof, Yellen, and Katz maintain that the result had the greatest effect on women who wanted children and those who either because of lack of discipline or religious scruples failed to use contraception or seek an abortion. They became less able to secure a desired betrothal and more likely to have a child on their own.

The article is clever, original, and continues to be widely cited. The principal challenge to its reasoning has come from the right. James Q. Wilson, for example, responded that, in explaining the rise in non-marital births, what needed attention was the moral shift, not the economic calculus.[8] Wilson repeats the conservative mantra that what matters is character, individual responsibility, and values and that these are somehow independent of such structural factors as the availability of employment or the legalization of abortion. In fact, Akerlof, Yellen, and Katz did address the change in moral sensibilities. The intensity of the stigma against non-marital births had long depended on the association between the prohibited sex and the embarrassing pregnancy. The economists argued that once the availability of the pill changed the acceptability of the sex, the stigma associated with non-marital births changed quickly and, with it, much of the pressure that produced the shotgun marriage disappeared.[9] Within five years of the legalization of abortion, the birth rate fell dramatically and the adoption rate fell in half. Women became more likely both to prevent the unintended birth and to keep the children they bore. Adoption, like back-alley abortions, had overwhelmingly been a response to intense social disapproval of the circumstances of the conception.[10]

While the economists thus provide an explanation for the disappearance of the stigma that had once prompted the shotgun wedding, they do not attempt to explain why marriage was becoming a class-based practice. In their account, the women using contraception wanted sex on the same terms as the men—with no commitment. The women losing out were the ones who wanted a betrothal.[11] Yet those college women most associated with the embrace of sex and contraception were becoming the ones most likely to marry at the same time that single women having unplanned children were the ones rejecting marriage, uninterested in securing a gold band for the fourth finger of their left hand. When journalist Hanna Rosin recounted the twenty-first-century relationship between Bethenny and Calvin we cited at the beginning of this chapter, it was Bethenny, not Calvin, who determined whether or not the relationship would continue.[12]

So how did the women engaging in the college hook-up later persuade a man to marry them without getting pregnant? And why did the women having children at younger ages become more critical of the men who might, with a little effort, be willing to make a trip to the altar? As the relationship between sex and marriage became more attenuated, the reasons to marry—or not—changed as well, in large part because of the pill.

Economics Revisited: The Pill and the Segmentation of Marriage Markets

In their 2002 blockbuster article "The Power of the Pill," Harvard economists Claudia Goldin and Lawrence Katz emphasize that the availability of the pill fundamentally altered the lives of the women who made it through college in the seventies.[13] Their story completes the Akerlof analysis by offering a picture of what happened to the more privileged women, who were not seeking a marriage proposal, express or implied, when they engaged in sex with their fellow students. Goldin and Katz observed that half of women who were born in 1950 and attended college were married by the age of twenty-three. College women, like all other women, feared pregnancy and married early. For those women born a short seven years later who attended college, however, only 30 percent were married by age twenty-three. These women, the ones storming the barricades of the sex revolution, won access to the pill as the age of majority changed from twenty-one to eighteen, eliminating the need for parental approval of their birth control prescriptions, and the Supreme Court guaranteed a right of access to abortion and to birth control. Goldin and Katz find that while both

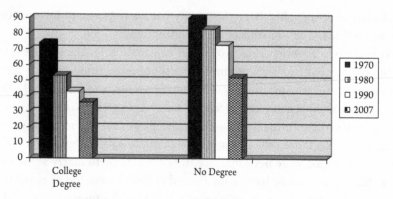

FIGURE 4.1: Percentage of Women Married by Age 25

Adam Isen and Betsey Stevenson, 2010. "Women's Education and Family Behavior: Trends in Marriage, Divorce and Fertility," NBER Chapters, in *Demography and the Economy*, 107–140 National Bureau of Economic Research, Inc., at p. 7 in the NBER version at http://www.nber.org/papers/w15725.pdf.

contraception and abortion influenced the age of marriage, the change in legal access to contraception provided the larger effect.

Indeed, shortly after the pill became available, women with college degrees began to delay marriage, and they did so earlier and to a greater degree than less-educated women. The chart depicted in figure 4.1 demonstrates that the big drop in early marriage came for college graduates in the seventies; a similar drop would not occur for other women until twenty years later.[14]

When Goldin and Katz discuss the consequences of the pill, however, marriage—and the disappearance of the shotgun wedding—is not their primary focus. Instead, they talk about grad school. In the old story, women who could become pregnant needed to be shepherded into marriage. By contrast, those free to time childbearing in accordance with their career plans could take advantage of the opportunities opening up for women in the seventies. The changes were dramatic. The number of women in law school rose from 4 percent in the sixties to 36 percent in 1980; in medical schools, from 1 to 30 percent; in dental schools, from 1 to 19 percent; and in business schools, from 3 to 28 percent.[15] The seventies became the "child-bust" years, with dramatic drops in overall fertility. The one thing that did not change for college graduates, however, was the strong connection between marriage and childbearing. In 1982, non-marital births constituted only 2 percent of all births to those with a bachelor's degree. For whites, those numbers remained unchanged in 2006.[16] And the "baby bust" gave way to a "baby boomlet" in the eighties.

The result transformed the career *and* marital prospects of college graduates. In the nineteenth century, almost half of women college graduates never married.[17] In 1960, 29 percent of college-educated women in their sixties had not done so.[18] Well into the eighties, high school graduates remained more likely than college graduates to marry and be married.[19] Today, however, the percentages have flipped; college graduate women are now "poised to become the most likely to ever marry."[20]

The secret is that as college-educated women delayed marriage, so too did the men. When we headed off to college (June in 1971, Naomi in 1975), we heard hints that we should be on the lookout for the right man while we were there. In fact, when we (and our classmates) didn't get pregnant and didn't press for commitment, the men in our lives didn't marry either. Goldin and Katz comment that the pill, by encouraging the delay of marriage, created a "thicker" marriage market for career women. The difference in the age of marriage between men and women stayed small as the age of marriage increased.[21] Instead, the big effect was to segment marriage markets by class. In the fifties and sixties, the college men who married in their early twenties often married either their high school sweethearts back home or fellow co-eds who dropped out of school after the wedding. The men in our generation who graduated from college married later and became much more likely to marry fellow graduates. The women who postponed marriage found that the most successful of the men were there waiting for them.

By the nineties, the remade marital terms set the stage for the divergence in the incomes of college graduates and everyone else.[22] Between 1960 and 1980, the family incomes of the highly educated and the less educated rose and fell together. After 1980, the two diverged, with household incomes of the

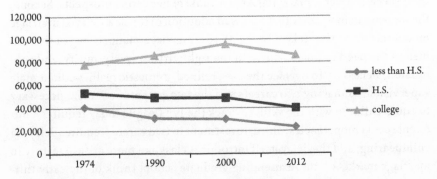

FIGURE 4.2: Median Household Income by Education, 2012 dollars
Source: U.S. Census Bureau, Historical income Tables, Household Tables H-13, H-14, http://www.census.gov/hhes/www/income/data/historical/household/ (last visited Nov. 6, 2013). Tables H-13 and H-14 are based on slightly different educational attainment questions; for example, the college category includes "Bachelor's Degree or More" (Table H-13) in 2000 and 2012, and "College, 4 Years or More" (Table H-14) for 1974 and 1990 and Table H-13 includes a category of "High School, 1-3 years," while Table H-14 includes a category "9th to 12th grade (no diploma)."

highly educated rising as the incomes of other households stagnated or fell (see figure 4.2).[23] A large part of the reason?—the top male and female earners found each other. The leaders of the sexual revolution reaped its benefits and found their way back into traditional family life.

Selection Effects and the Search for the Modern Mr. Darcy

What Akerlof et al. described—college women's embrace of the pill and abortion—did not just change women's career prospects; it also redefined what Gary Becker called "marriage markets." While Becker had predicted that busy executives would prefer spouses who could handle child care and entertaining, that's not true today. Greater investment in women's earning capacity changed the nature of marriage markets. This was the great insight of UCLA sociologist Valerie Oppenheimer, who wrote almost immediately after Becker. Like Becker, Oppenheimer saw dating and mating as the product of exchange.[24] But, unlike Becker, she recognized that changing the organization of the family changed the qualities that spouses sought in each other. When women played the generalist role of wife and mother, ambitious men chose for virtue, housekeeping skills, attractiveness, and the good sense to defer to the head of the household. As women began to play more varied roles, selection of the right mate became more complex. First, when norms change it becomes more critical to find someone on the same page you're on. The women who started investing in careers wanted men who appreciated their success. Tyler is marrying Amy *because of* her career prospects. Second, the increase in inequality that followed adoption of the new delayed marriage model increased the stakes. In the 1840s, marriage manuals began to warn men of the need to find a wife with the right virtues (piety, purity, and submission) necessary to oversee the new, refined, domestic realm without male supervision. Managing two careers *and* the two-parent investment necessary to equip children with the skills to crack the Ivy League today requires a different set of competencies. Third, investment in two careers requires delaying childbearing, and the delay itself introduces class as a more critical feature in marriage markets—those attending graduate school think of the early thirties as the ideal time to settle down while those who go work at Walmart at nineteen see no reason to wait.

In the marriage system of the fifties, men and women married each other with the expectation that they would be socialized into adult roles and appropriate marital behavior after the nuptials. The young men who married because of their bride's pregnancy soon found themselves in workplaces with other fathers and husbands. Middle-class women, likely to have a second child soon after the first, were home in the suburbs with their sisters, friends, and family, surrounded by other women who instructed them in their wifely and motherly obligations. In this world, most men could be expected to be effectively socialized into a breadwinner role—the jobs were there—and most women socialized into homemaking whatever their inclinations as teens. And if the lessons didn't take, the parents were there in the background to reinforce the message that there was nowhere to go. A young wife with two children in tow and a third on the way would be destitute if she left her husband, and the young man would be ostracized from the bowling league, the lunchroom, and sometimes even the local bar if he deserted his family.

The entry of women into the workforce and greater male inequality changed all that. Women, of course, still overwhelmingly took care of young children or hired the babysitters who helped out. But their adult roles were no longer likely to be defined primarily by motherhood or the generalist tasks (cooking, cleaning, child care) that most women could reasonably be expected to master. Instead, women took on new roles: as physicians, journalists, waitresses, or therapists. And, as they did, they looked for men who valued the careers they had chosen and had lives that fit in with theirs. A globe-trotting journalist, male or female, is not likely to marry a restaurant owner rooted to one place. This search builds in more uncertainty—the college student who plans to make a killing on Wall Street may enjoy better marital prospects at thirty-two than at twenty-two but only if he succeeds. The most ambitious of the women who may find him attractive will also wait to see how both of their lives turn out. Mating and dating have become a higher stakes game.

Among Oppenheimer's critical insights is that not only do marriage markets exist (Gary Becker said that), but women's changing roles and greater inequality among men divide the marriage search into submarkets that do not overlap. The woman likely to make partner at a major law firm no longer thinks seriously about marrying her high school sweetheart—unless they run into each other at the right cocktail party for young lawyers years later. And the woman from the working-class background who makes it into Emory often must choose: give up the boyfriend from back home or see him undermine her prospects for later success.[25] The construction of marriage markets reinforces class boundaries in a manner more reminiscent of *Pride and Prejudice* than *A Streetcar Named Desire*. For ambitious college students, male and female, the embrace of the pill and abortion are part of a strategy that takes them into new, more highly segmented and elite marriage markets, allowing them to have some fun along the way.

* * *

With these changes, the new sexual script has become:

> Boy meets girl. Boy likes girl. Girl runs through her checklist: is he a one-night stand? (If so, say yes.) Is he someone she will still want to be with in a month? (If yes, then say no tonight but arrange another date.) Is he someone who can help pay the mortgage on the condo she wants to buy but can't afford? (Flirt some more.) Is she likely to end up picking up his dirty socks *and* his student debt? (No way, unless he's *really* cute.)

By the time our girl has made her decision, we should be at the end of this book, and she will be asking whether he is her last chance to have children or would be better as a sperm donor than as a long-term partner. But in the meantime, it is time to turn to the explanations of what really happened to the American family. Now that we've figured out why the college women of the seventies rallied behind Gloria Steinem (it brought them higher incomes *and* more stable marriages than anyone else), the final piece of the puzzle is why everyone else did not *eventually* follow them. In the following chapter we take up the exacerbation of class-based differences over the past thirty years.

SECTION II

THE NEW TERMS

Amy and Tyler want marriage. They're old enough to feel confident that they know what they're doing, but their parents and friends have been encouraging them to take their time. They are marrying now because they feel incredibly lucky to have found each other. If they stay married, it will be because they respect one another and are committed to making it work. Amy loves the fact that Tyler treats her as an equal; Tyler is pleased that when he picks an argument, Amy argues back. They both believe that marrying someone with similar ambitions and income prospects is a good foundation for family stability. Marriage is a choice, not a social obligation, not a product of pregnancy, and certainly not a result of parental pressure. It is separate from the decision to have children: as excited as they are about their impending nuptials, Tyler and Amy know they are not nearly ready to be parents—financially or emotionally.

With Carl and Lily, the disappearance of social coercion ends things. Yes, they had sex, and, yes, Lily is pregnant, but they don't even know each other all that well, and marriage is not a good deal for either of them. If they married, Lily knows she would have to take care of Carl, but she doubts she would get much in return, however much she enjoyed their brief time together. Carl wishes that Lily were more interested in him, but he is not willing to defer to her, to turn over his limited paycheck, to do more of the chores, or to say no to the friends who want him to hang out. He doubts that he can live up to Lily's expectations, and he's not sure he wants to try.

Amy and Tyler's delight in each other and the wariness that Lily and Carl feel for each other are markers of class division. To understand why they are requires combining economics with cultural change and recognizing how the changes of the past half-century have segmented marriage markets so that young people no longer share the same expectations about the nature of their relationships. The growing class chasm in family life takes place in the context of two broad changes remaking American life.

The first is the transformation in women's roles, a transformation that is also critical to the creation of new pathways into the middle class. As the economy has changed from heavy reliance on manufacturing to a greater emphasis on technology and information, the demand for women's labor has increased and remade the relationship between home and family. The result both increased the advantages to women's workforce participation—the women with the highest incomes are now the most likely to marry *and* best able to contribute to their family's economic well-being—and enhanced women's autonomy within the family. Consequently, all women have become choosier about whom they are willing to marry, if they marry or stay married at all. These changing gender dynamics give women greater ability to choose whether or not to enter into relationships but not necessarily the ability to call the shots after they commit.

The second strand, however, is greater economic inequality. While the change in women's roles took hold in the seventies, the increase in inequality began in the eighties and accelerated in the nineties. For both men and women, the economy has created more "good" and "bad" jobs while shrinking those in the center. In the period of economic prosperity immediately following World War II the families of high school graduates enjoyed the rising wages that accompanied union jobs, while better educated families benefited from the expansion of the corporate middle-management ranks. Both job tracks—blue collar and white collar—provided secure positions, decent benefits, and a family wage. By the late eighties, however, companies began to send blue-collar jobs abroad, to expand the contingent or temporary workforce in lieu of salaried workers, and to trim their management ranks. The prosperity of the late nineties increased the return to investment in education—and CEOs and financial analysts enjoyed outsized increases in income—but blue-collar wages never recovered.

Since then, things have only gotten worse. Through the housing boom, the financial crisis, and the limited recovery, white-collar wages plateaued. Both before the crisis and during the recovery the overwhelmingly male top executive and financial ranks received an even larger share of all economic gains. The increasingly insecure positions in the middle and at the bottom provide few benefits and do little to accommodate parents with young children.[1]

Put the two strands together—the transformation of the economy to reward investment in human capital and the movement toward women's greater autonomy—and you have the elements of a new family strategy increasingly beyond the reach of the working class. For those who do it right—invest in women's as well as men's earning capacity, avoid early marriage and childbirth, achieve a measure of economic independence, and find the right life partner—marriage still works and remains the most reliable way to channel resources to the next generation. For those who fail to follow the new prescription, family stability is increasingly difficult to obtain. In this section, we reach "the heart of the matter," that is, the links that explain why, in an era when women have greater ability to say "no," growing economic inequality produces diverging patterns of family formation.

5

The Heart of the Matter

We see greater inequality in society as the huge, jagged missing piece in the puzzle of the new American family. Greater inequality explains changing family structures and gender dynamics. The revolution in women's roles altered the patterns of mating and dating, but greater inequality changed the stakes. It has remade the role of marriage in ways that exacerbate societal inequality, and it has done so simultaneously for rich and poor.

These forces have been in play since the early nineties, the period in which male income inequality began to accelerate. Yet two factors have stood in the way of putting together the pieces that make up this story or doing anything meaningful about it.

The first is ideological polarization. The ideological right does not want to trifle with any account that attributes the change in the family to something other than the failure to instill the right values. It certainly does not want to hear a Moynihan-type analysis that suggests the solution requires greater financial equality or security. The ideological left, while supportive of economic equality, objects to any effort to pass judgment—it wishes to embrace all families as equally valuable.[2] It certainly does not want to hear that class-based differences in marriage per se should be a concern. Ideology thus blinds both sides to variation in the marriage markets and its connection to cultural change.

The second problem, however, is that the existing accounts rarely integrate the changing family strategies of the elite together with the changing behavior of others. The Moynihan-like accounts that attempt to integrate structural development into an account of shifting values and tie them to the effects of greater inequality, sounded more recently by sociologists like Princeton University's Sara McLanahan, focus on what is happening to the bottom third. Our analysis builds on their insights but adds the critical next step: we argue that inequality remakes the terms of family formation for *everyone*. The increase in marital stability at the top is related to the disappearance of marriage at the bottom, and the fact that these groups are moving in different directions stands in the way of a more complete response to both. Our focus is on how inequality and gender power dynamics tie together what is happening to American family structures.

Ideological and class blinders have stood in the way of the closer examination that we undertake of how family understandings could grow so far apart. Consequently, many explanations of the changes in the family have become an either/or analysis: promote marriage or promote acceptance of all families. Fix values, and we'll fix the family—or fix the economy, and values will take care of themselves. Like most dichotomies, this one is false. We believe that both values and economics are important. What has been missing is identification of the causal mechanism through which economic change affects "sentiment" and the informal expectations that influence behavior. We argue in this chapter that the missing mechanism is inequality, and we explain how inequality has skewed marriage markets. Greater inequality has changed the ways men and women match up, thereby affecting the terms of mating and dating. This in turn affects the question of whether couples can manage a relationship on terms that make marriage—or stable cohabitation—worth it. Most of our focus is on marriage because marriage is the culturally iconic symbol of commitment for heterosexual and same-sex couples, but the same factors affect the duration, stability, and quality of other forms of cohabitation. Class-based changes in marriage, in a society that relies on marriage to secure legal recognition, represent the most visible and easily measured aspect of a wholesale cultural change.

The critical steps in explaining the interrelationship of economics and differing class-based family strategies that show how men and women[3] match up along with their expectations of each other are: (1) demonstrating how economic change affects gender ratios in a given market and (2) analyzing the impact of the ratios on changes in family-formation strategies. Taken together, these steps show how gender ratios influence norms.

The Theory: Gender Ratios and Marriage Markets

"Men are running rampant because of the numbers, treating women however they want with no consequences," said Rhea Nanos, twenty-six, who works at a Manhattan tech start-up. "They can hit on 1,000 girls if they want."

Some men admitted it was true.

"It's just like waiting for a bus or train. Every few minutes another woman will come by—you're stunned and your jaw drops—and on the next block you see another one just as beautiful," said Christian Brown, twenty-four, a teacher and aspiring actor.[4]

Women have outnumbered men in New York City since at least the invention of the typewriter, and the *New York Post* reported in 2011 that they did so by 10 percent for those between twenty-five and twenty-nine. The *Post* had no trouble finding young people who had noticed. Researchers agree that the casual observations reported in the *Post* may be true. As one site reported in an article touting places where women outnumber men, "New York boasts 50,000 young women desperate for a date."[5]

Observations about sex ratios—and their meanings—have a long pedigree. Charles Darwin remarked that almost all species seem to have relatively equal numbers of males and females, even in species where one male fathers large numbers of children with multiple females.[6] Human populations are the same, though they certainly vary from time to time. During war, for example, the number of men may plummet. At other times, immigration may separate male adventurers from prospective brides left at home; Chinese male immigrants to the United States, for example, initially outnumbered the women twenty to one. And some groups vary in the sex ratio at birth: in the nineteenth century, Orthodox Jews in Eastern Europe had an unusually high ratio of boys to girls, while today African Americans tend to bear a higher percentage of girls than the population as a whole, though the absolute differences are small. Sociologists Marcia Guttentag and Paul Secord provided the first sustained examination of the effects of such ratios in 1983.[7]

The two sociologists hypothesized that changes in gender ratios would operate much like changes in supply in any other market. If marriage-age women outnumbered marriage-age men, one would expect a higher percentage of the men to be married at any given time, and empirical evidence tends to support that hypothesis.[8] Guttentag and Secord's more provocative prediction, however, is that a change in gender ratios will affect not just the marriage rate but also the cultural norms of the group. In particular, they suggest that where available men are scarce, they will act exactly like Christian Brown, the young man quoted in the *New York Post*; that is, they will be a bit like a child in a candy store, eager to sample but reluctant to commit.

Guttentag and Secord add a caveat. They argue that what happens next depends on how much power men and women have in a society, distinguishing between what they termed "structural" or societal power and "dyadic" power, the power to choose what happens in relationships.[9] Ordinarily, the ratio of men to women determines dyadic power. If men outnumber women in a community, for example, then women gain greater ability to determine the terms of relationships.[10] But this is where structural power, the comparative privileges associated with each gender, comes in. Guttentag and Secord imagine a society, which they call LIBERTINA, a place where women are few and highly valued.[11] The authors note that such a society actually existed—the Bakweri in Cameroon, Africa, studied by anthropologists during the 1950s.[12] To marry, the men had to pay a substantial bride price. After marriage, the wives often raised money on the side through casual sex with paying customers. The wives controlled the proceeds, and their husbands often resented the wives' sexual activities and economic independence. Yet the most frequent complaint at divorce was not one of infidelity, but the wives' complaint that their husbands did not support them. What made the women's comparative "liberation" possible was the combination of male migration skewing the gender ratio to 236 men for every 100 women, colonial rule that limited the Bakweri men's ability to assert more power in the society, and the women's willingness to use the gender mismatch to generate more income than the men, income that the women used to gain greater power in the society.

Groups like the Bakweri, however, are rare, at least outside of the context of one group of men (the British) marginalizing another group of men (the Bakhari). In most societies, men hold all the cards. The result when men outnumber women in a male-dominated society is that rights of sexual access to women become more "valuable," and women are also more likely to be treated as property.[13] Other men (fathers, pimps) closely supervise valuable women; the men rather than the women reap the benefits of scarcity. For a dramatic example, the authors turn to early Chinese immigrants to the United States, with their 20-to-1 gender ratio at a time when American law forbade interracial marriages.[14] The Chinese Tongs responded by organizing brothels, and given the high cost of recruiting Asian women, they were unforgiving when some of their patrons ran off and married the prostitutes.[15] The women were virtual prisoners who enjoyed little benefit from the high value the men placed on them.

More commonly, however, when men outnumber women, the ability to marry and, indeed, to marry a high-status woman (whatever determines status in the community) becomes more important. Powerful men want women they can monopolize, and men who face intense competition for available women need to be more successful to be able to marry. If women (or their fathers or protectors) have the ability to end the marriage, men who marry also realize that greater fidelity may be the price of staying married. In traditional societies, parents protect their daughters' virtue, aware that it will lead to a better marriage or, in some societies, a higher bride price. They also invest more in their sons' (but not necessarily their daughters') earning capacity. The authors cite the dramatic example of Orthodox Jews in Eastern Europe. The Orthodox refrain from sex during menstruation and encourage it during the period when ovulation is most likely to occur. Perhaps because of these practices, which traditionally were believed to increase male births, boys significantly outnumbered girls in the shtetls of Eastern Europe.[16]

Guttentag and Secord argue that the high sex ratios produced a "virtuous cycle" (pun intended). When women are scarce, men commit. With stable marriages, the parents invest more in their children, and, indeed, Orthodox communities in Europe and the United States had lower infant mortality rates than other communities even when they were desperately poor. The high level of parental investment helped to maintain strict religious practices, which in turn reinforced family stability. The women, though highly valued, did not enjoy much autonomy.

So what happens when women outnumber men? Guttentag and Secord argue that the result depends on who holds power in the society generally. They speculate that if a real-life Amazonia existed, in which society was ruled by women, the most powerful women would safeguard their interests in the available men. They paint a picture of boy toys for the elite, though we also could imagine a more bonobo-like group in which the available men were shared. The women might control income and children (that's what would define a female-dominated society after all), but sexual relationships would become a matter of recreation. Some of our colleagues have suggested that certain parts of Northern Europe may be moving toward such developments, but we leave conclusions about that to the sociologists.[17] Guttentag and Secord, however, could find no example of a society in the eighties or earlier where women both held power (a rare factor in any event) and were more numerous than the available men.

Instead, Guttentag and Secord's real-world examples of groups in which women outnumber men all involved male-dominant societies that produce patterns like the ones the *New York Post* described of the young man on the make.[18] The sociologists maintain that low sex-ratio societies spur the creation of "vicious cycles" in which

- men become less likely commit to any one woman and more likely to cheat if they do promise to commit;
- women feel exploited and become more distrustful of men generally;
- women respond to feelings of exploitation by looking elsewhere; they become more financially independent, less likely to marry, and more likely to divorce or have children on their own.[19]

If the young man who sees great women on every corner plays the field, the women will soon decide that they can't depend on him. And the net result tends to be greater family instability and more women raising children on their own.

Testing the Theory: Gender Ratios and Relationship Stability

Subsequent scholars have tested Guttentag and Secord's theories through a variety of cross-cultural studies. Some analyze different countries. Others look at ethnic groups within the same country. The most intriguing look at college campuses. In the United States today, we are in the midst of something of a natural experiment: women increasingly outnumber men on college campuses, so we can study how dating norms vary from campus to campus.

The first studies, however, ran cross-country statistical analyses testing the Guttentag/Secord hypothesis. The results helped give credence to the theory, though the sociologists did find that the results were more robust in developed rather than undeveloped countries.[20] In one study, researchers predicted that in low gender ratio societies (that is, those with more women than men):

> the surplus of women will encourage promiscuity among men and discourage their commitment to monogamy. Fewer men and women will marry, and those that do will marry later in life. Women's traditional roles will not be highly valued since men enjoy a surfeit of alternatives to their current partners. Marital fertility will be low, but illegitimacy rates will be high. Divorce will also be frequent. Because many women will not be able to rely on their current partners to maintain existing relationships, more will turn to extrafamilial ambitions and pursue educational and career goals.[21]

They also predicted that female depression and suicide rates would be higher. Examining published data, the study found sex ratios that ranged from a low of 80 (80 men for every 100 women) in Swaziland to a high of 119 (119 men for every 100 women) in Brunei.[22] Mortality rates are much higher in the developing world, and together with migration they can skew gender ratios. Mortality rates tend to be much lower in the developed world, and the study looked separately at the effects in highly developed and less developed countries. The researchers found relatively weak correlations in the less developed world, except that low gender ratios (more women than men) led more women to participate in the labor market. In the developed world, however, a relative undersupply of women was associated with higher rates of marriage and fertility, a younger female age at marriage, and lower rates of female literacy.[23] Surprisingly, gender ratios had no significant effect on labor market participation in the more developed countries. And in neither group did the ratios have a significant impact on female suicide rates.[24]

Another study compared ten different European immigrant groups in the United States in the early part of the twentieth century. The sex ratio for each group varied considerably, with Irish women outnumbering Irish men and Italian men outnumbering Italian women by more than two to one. The study found that the more men outnumbered women, the more marriage rates went up for both the women and the men, presumably because the men became more likely to commit. And despite the fact that women were less likely to be in the labor market in groups with more men, the couples in those groups had more income. Economist Josh Angrist concluded that "the results for men are consistent with the view that higher sex ratios cause men to ... try to become more attractive to potential mates."[25] Either the men worked harder when they had to in order to impress a prospective wife or, given a choice, women chose the men with more income for a husband.

Evolutionary psychologists have compared different countries in an effort to determine how mate preferences change with different gender ratios. They began the study with two competing theories. The first theory predicted that as the number of either sex becomes more common, the members of that sex become less picky about mates. For example, if the women outnumbered the men, then women would become more willing to take any available man while the men would become pickier about their choice of women. The second theory predicted that as women outnumber men, men become more willing to sleep with anyone, that is, their standards decline, but they also become less willing to marry, and women give up on them rather than settle for a less satisfactory husband. This study looked at data from thirty-five different countries with sex ratios that ranged from 98.19 in Columbia and 98.51 in Zambia, where the women outnumbered the men, to 105.23 in Norway, 108.26 in India, 108.30 in China, and 108.62 in Taiwan, which have much higher sex ratios. The United States was in the middle, at 100.60. The survey data found that when the number of women increased, men did become somewhat pickier about what they looked for in a woman, though the statistical significance of the correlations was weak. In these societies, however, the women became less likely to marry and their standards for an acceptable husband *increased*.[26] They found, in other words, that when women outnumber men, men become cads. They can play the field, and they do. If women will still have them with their faults, they marry. Otherwise, they don't, enjoying their continued access to new mates. Women become jaded by the men's behavior, and they, too, become more reluctant to commit to a long-term relationship. The result tends to be a cultural shift toward greater promiscuity, more gender distrust, and fewer stable long-term relationships.

The studies have their limitations. The various cultures, whether the Italians and the Irish in the United States or Zambians and Norwegians may differ in a variety of ways that the studies did not anticipate. Studies that examine changes within a single culture, however, show many, though not all, of the same effects. For example, a group of economists examined marriage patterns in France following World War I. World War I male mortality rates differed by region, and the researchers examined the relationship between the resulting sex ratios and marriage patterns. They found that in regions with higher mortality rates (and thus fewer men), men were more likely and women were less likely to marry than in the regions with more men—no surprise there. The men in high-mortality regions were less likely to marry women of lower social classes—they became pickier. In addition, out-of-wedlock births increased, divorce rates decreased, and the age gap between husbands and wives decreased.[27] The fact that men became pickier about social class and that women became less likely to marry and more likely to give birth without being married is consistent with the other studies. The fact that the men were more likely to marry is unsurprising in a traditional society in which marriage is the norm. The fact that the men became less likely to divorce *is* surprising, however, given the men's greater opportunities to find new wives. The authors speculate that perhaps the men were able to arrange better matches in the first place or perhaps something about the experience of war made them less likely to seek a divorce.[28] Cultural differences, however, almost certainly affect these results.

One of the more intriguing studies of the effect of sex ratios in the United States comes from sociologists Mark Regnerus and Jeremy Uecker. They examine sex on college campuses and consider what effect the sex ratio has on the undergraduate dating experience. The students they study are all young Americans, and they control for individual factors, such as race and grades, and institutional factors, such as region of the country and the presence of the Greek life. They find that the percentage of men on campus very much affects campus social life, and the more women outnumber men, the more women report

- negative appraisals of men on campus,
- negative views of their own relationships,
- fewer dates,
- a lower likelihood of having a boyfriend,
- lesser ability to gain commitment in a relationship.[29]

On campuses with more men, women seem to be more likely to find "gentlemen" and to be able to manage stable relationships. All men may not be cads after all! Somehow we do not remember Princeton in the early days of co-education in such terms, but it may have been better than Vassar.

Regnerus and Uecker present some impressive data to back up their observations. Consider the likelihood that a female college student who has a boyfriend has had sex in the last month (see figure 5.1). Looking just at juniors at large public universities with a Greek system outside the northeast, the answer depends on the percentage of men on campus. If women constitute 30 percent of the student body, the likelihood is about fifty-fifty that the woman will have had sex. If the percentage of women is 50 percent, the likelihood that she will have had sex rises to 66 percent. If the percentage of women is 70 percent, then

79 percent of the women with boyfriends will have had sex recently.[30] On the other hand, virginity is more common when women constitute a smaller share of the student body even though, with the more favorable gender ratio, these women should have an easier time finding a compatible mate. And the women have an easier time keeping a boyfriend without having sex. As figure 5.2 shows, 56 percent of the women who have boyfriends are still virgins on a campus where women constitute only 30 percent of the student body. That number falls to 12 percent of the women with boyfriends on a campus where 70 percent of the student body is made up of women. Simply put, the price of a boyfriend rises when men are in short supply, and that price involves sex. Regnerus and Uecker conclude that "[w]hat scholars describe as the 'hook-up culture' may actually be a simple and passive result of this demographic trend—the growing gender imbalance on campus—rather than any active change in Western sexual culture."[31] Perhaps as critically, Regnerus and Uecker's analysis suggests that sexual practices on college campuses may not

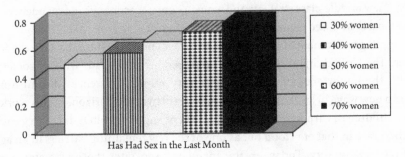

FIGURE 5.1: Likelihood that a Woman with a Boyfriend Had Sex in the Past Month by Percentage of Women on Campus

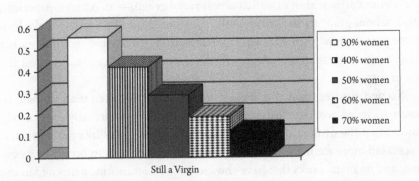

FIGURE 5.2: Likelihood that a Woman Who Has a Boyfriend Is Still a Virgin by Percentage of Women on Campus

necessarily affect post-graduate prospects for stable long-term unions—if the gender ratios that follow graduation differ from those on campus.

Of course, we do wonder exactly how students find themselves on male versus female majority campuses, and part of the answer is that the principal remaining examples of male-majority campuses are tech-oriented universities, such as Cal Tech, military academies like The Citadel, and a small number of bible colleges or rural state schools. It's possible that the students in these schools are a little too much like the characters in the *Big Bang Theory* for meaningful comparisons, but we leave the inquiries into sex on campus to the sociologists.

Adding Inequality: How the Theory Plays Out in Twenty-First-Century America

The gender ratio theory explains how structural forces—greater societal inequality, a new middle-class strategy, and women's greater economic independence—lead to a class-based change in norms and behavior.

First, greater inequality segments marriage markets. Think back to the fifties. The United States was a more homogenous (yes, read "white") society, with the importance of nineteenth-century ethnic differences diminishing and a new wave of large-scale immigration still over the horizon. In this world, the children of carpenters and the children of engineers often did marry each other; race in that era stood out as one of the few remaining barriers in an age of relative equality. Today, greater inequality separates those who stay near home from those willing to relocate for education or employment. It divides the well-educated who postpone marriage and childbearing from those ready to start a family in their early twenties. And it re-creates these regional and class boundaries within as well as across racial groups—an African-American high school graduate in Philadelphia, for example, still primarily seeks intimate partnerships with African Americans from similar backgrounds rather than white high school graduates in the suburbs or college students on the Penn campus.

Second, greater inequality has a different impact on men than women. In most societies, women cluster closer to the mean, and virtually every study shows that the distance from the top to the bottom of the income ladder has increased more for men than for women, with more men in both the executive and financial ranks that have shown the greatest income gains *and* in the blue-collar positions that have shown greater losses. In personal terms, the impact on men has also been greater. Intriguing cross-cultural studies show that greater inequality tends to increase rates of long-term unemployment, violence, and imprisonment and to do so disproportionately for men on the losing end of economic change.[32] In short, greater inequality both historically and today tends to increase the number of men (as opposed to women) at the top and to write off a significant percentage of low-income men, making them effectively unmarriageable. Women, in the meantime, remain more concentrated in the middle, with a shrinking group of mid-range men. Consequently, within the increasingly segregated marriage markets, women at the top have more "desirable" choices, women in the middle have fewer, and women at the bottom have almost none.

Third, gender ratios affect the terms of dating, sex, and marriage within each distinct market. As the number of men at the top increases, and as they seek to marry from within the smaller group of high-status women, Guttentag and Secord predict that the behavior of this group will become more marriage-oriented and relationships will become more stable. As the number of marriageable men declines in comparison with the available women, by contrast, the sociologists predict that the men as a group, employed and unemployed, are more likely to become unreliable cads and the women become more likely to give up on the men and invest in themselves. A hot date with a good-looking guy at his expense is one thing; sharing a credit card or title to a house is another. Harvard sociologist Bill Wilson, writing shortly after Guttentag and Secord published their book, argued that this was the missing piece in Moynihan's research. The African-American family suffered not from "matriarchy," but from the predictable consequences of a shortage of marriageable men.

Does this thesis explain the class divergence in family behavior, along with the hook-up culture and what some journalists misleadingly call the "richer sex" or the "end of men"? We think it may explain what is occurring within relationships (though it does not explain changes in structural power between men and women). So, we turn next to an examination of the evidence for the segmentation of marriage markets (who gets married these days, and whom do they marry?) and the skewing of gender ratios within each segment. Manhattan—New York and Kansas—and the neighboring Belmonts and Fishtowns in some metropolitan areas really may be separate worlds when it comes to the way men and women match up.

Where the Men Are

[T]he biggest reason we probably won't see a lot more college-educated women walking down the aisle with their plumber is one we don't like to say out loud: they want to have smart kids. Educated men and women are drawn to spouses they think will help them produce the children likely to thrive in the contemporary knowledge-based economy. That means high IQ, ambitious, and organized kids who will do their homework and take a lot of AP courses. The preference for alpha kids is the reason there is a luxury market for Ivy League egg and sperm donors. It also explains why, though we don't have solid research distinguishing between elite and State U mating choices, Ms. Harvard will probably not accept a proposal from Mr. Florida State. The economist Greg Mankiw has quipped that "Harvard is probably the world's most elite dating agency." A glance at the *New York Times* nuptial pages suggests he's right.

Kay Hymowitz[1]

Cecelia says it didn't bother her that her husband earned a lot less than she did. But the more I talked with her, the more it seemed in some basic way she did think less of him for it. It was as though he hadn't earned the right to make financial decisions.

Rick Banks[2]

In 1966, Bobby Darin sang a hit song, "If I Were A Carpenter," that asked whether the "lady" in his life would still have him if he was a carpenter, a tinker or a miller. The song suggested that the willingness of the lady to marry the carpenter was the true test of her love, and that the answer the singer looked for was not only that yes, she would, but that she would put him "above" her. And therein lies the rub that suggests that today's "ladies" might respond, "no way."

At its core, the gender ratio thesis is a matter of supply and demand. See how many single men and women live in Brooklyn or show up on occasion from farther away, subtract those who do not want a committed relationship and the drug addicts, convicted felons, and dysfunctional people who cannot manage one, and you have a marriage market. Even, then, however, you need to decide what lines couples in the hunt are unlikely to cross: race? education? physical attractiveness? While demography can create a good sense of how many single men and women of a given race live in an era, determining how they will match up involves more guesswork. Most of the pieces of this account have been tested by others, but no one has entirely solved the relationship riddle.

When we try to construct marriage markets—who is likely to tie the knot with whom—we can start with some obvious divisions. Eighty-year-olds rarely marry twenty-year-olds; indeed, the average age gap between spouses in the United States has fallen to approximately two years. So the most relevant period for gender disparities is around the age of marriage. In the United States, the male/female ratio at birth is 104.8 (that is, 104.8 males for every 100 females). Women outlive men, however, and by age eighty-five the gender ratio falls to 40.7 (40.7 males for every 100 females).[3] The prospects for eighty-five-year-old women who wish to marry do look grim.

Marriage markets also depend on region and race. If you want to know where the boys are, look west. The highest male/female ratios are in Alaska at (107.0), followed by Nevada (103.9), Colorado (101.4), Wyoming (101.2), Hawaii (101.0), Idaho (101.0), and Utah (100.4). The lowest male/female ratios are in Rhode Island (92.5), Massachusetts (93.0), and the District of Columbia (89.0). And the counties with the lowest ratios tend to be in the South.[4]

Some of these differences reflect race. African-American gender ratios are lower than white ratios from birth onward, though the differences at birth are small, and increase more significantly afterwards. The one area where the impact of gender ratios has been noted and studied extensively is among inner-city blacks. Even then, the overall figures may be meaningless without consideration of the effect of intermarriage,[5] mass incarceration,[6] lack of education, and unemployment, to which we will return shortly.

The more difficult issue to study—and the issue we take up in this chapter—is how class affects marriage markets. Education can be used as a proxy for class, but education combines with income and job status to determine social standing. Does anyone really care whether Bill Gates graduated from Harvard? (He dropped out but did not get married until he was thirty-eight—and successful.) And does an ambitious woman change her opinion of the marriageability of the doorman in her apartment building when she finds out he did? Class interacts with age, race, and region in defining acceptable partners, and a big change in recent years has been the effect of income inequality in determining who will marry whom.

When we ask why inequality matters, we already know that part of the answer has to do with the delay in marriage and childbearing. In 1960, the average age of marriage was twenty for women, twenty-two for men. At twenty-two we may have a pretty good idea whether someone will graduate from college, but we don't necessarily know much more than that. Consider what actress Anne Heche told reporters about her parents' marriage. They were high school sweethearts. When they married, her mother, Nancy, thought her father, Don, was "a handsome golden boy, good at everything." At twenty-two, the average age of marriage for men in that era, he would have been a college graduate, studying to be a doctor. But then everything changed. He "dropped out of medical school, he never found a profession that lasted, becoming a part-time church organist and choir director, hatching doomed schemes to make money and stowing his family in rural Ohio in a religious compound." Her father was also a closeted gay man who tormented his son and sexually abused his daughters.[7] He died of AIDS in 1983.

Today, the average age of marriage is older. A man set on medical school is unlikely to marry before his late twenties. By then, he is more likely to be certain of his sexuality. If he succeeds in becoming a doctor, he is likely to want a similarly successful partner. If he quits and fails to find an alternative profession, he also would become less likely to marry at all. For better or worse, delay increases the information available, and more information about oneself and one's prospects makes it more likely that people with similar backgrounds will end up together.

Marriage Markets and the New Marriage-Oriented Elite

The new blue strategy—invest in women as well as men and wait to have children—both increases the available information and changes the time when the well educated and less educated think about forming families. Sociological studies confirm this. According to researchers from UCLA, the likelihood that similarly educated adults will marry each other, a phenomenon sociologists refer to as "assortative mating," increases with later marriage.[8] Between 1940 and 1960, the average age of marriage fell and the likelihood that a husband and wife had the same level of education fell significantly, from 59 to 45 percent. As Tennessee Williams showed in A Streetcar Named Desire, the lady did become more likely to marry the carpenter—or the union guy with the factory job. Since then, the tendency of married couples to share the same educational level has gone back up, exceeding 55 percent in 2003.[9] Over the past several decades, the likelihood that a college graduate will marry someone with only "some college" has fallen and was at a lower level in 2000 than in any decade since 1940.[10] The numbers have increased further since 2000.[11]

This means that, for women, higher education not only produces greater income, but it also increases women's opportunities to marry higher status men; professional men, for example, have become more likely not just to marry fellow college graduates, but to marry fellow professionals.[12] That in turn increases the effects of class in defining marriage markets and in increasing inequality between families. To have access to the highest status men, a woman must complete her own education, hold a job, and avoid having a child until she meets the right man. Tugging a two-year-old along on a date dampens male interest in most social classes;[13] it's particularly rare among women who land the more successful men. All of the evidence indicates that both the ability to earn a college degree and the likelihood of avoiding an early unplanned birth have become more differentiated by class over the past fifteen years. College education has become less affordable, and the likelihood of completion correlates more closely with parental income.[14] Unplanned pregnancies have gone down substantially for college graduates while increasing for the poorest women. Unsurprisingly, therefore, the age at first birth has gone up steadily for women with college degrees while remaining largely unchanged for less educated women.[15] Avoiding early pregnancy and childbirth has become a defining element of middle-class life. It also means that intimate partners who combine their separate six-figure incomes are that much further ahead of less successful couples.[16]

A significant issue for the college-educated, however, is whether the men will be there when the high-achieving, high-earning women reach thirty and hear their biological clocks ticking. The answer—at least for the most successful women—is yes. The great irony of an economy that has dramatically increased economic inequality and enhanced the fortunes of elite men more than the fortunes of elite women is that it has increased the number of *really* good matches. For a distinct part of the American public, intimate relationships have become more stable. Understanding why requires linking the economic changes to increasingly segmented marriage markets.

Marriage Markets and the Market

Family, political, and economic equality in the United States reached their height in the postwar era—the baby boom, during which assortative marriage declined, the age of marriage fell, and women's educational parity with men decreased. Baby boomer economists, who sometimes look back fondly on that time as the period of their youth, call it "The Great Compression."[17] In contrast, they label the period that began in 1980 "The Great Divergence." Since then, levels of societal inequality have risen back to highs last achieved at the height of the Gilded Age and the Great Depression.[18] From 1966–2011, the income of the bottom 90 percent of Americans grew by less than $60, in inflation-adjusted dollars, while the average income for those in the top 10 percent grew by more than $116,000.[19]

The "Great Recession" that followed the financial crisis of 2008 has only made things worse. The *New York Times* reported in October 2012 that income inequality has soared and that the top 1 percent of earners reaped a stunning amount of the income gains in the first full year of the recovery from the 2008 crisis.[20] In 2010, the top 1 percent earned close to 24 percent of the nation's income.[21] In the meantime, the wages of the bottom 90 percent fell between 2009 and 2011.[22]

These disparities, which have set the stage for the family's divergence by class, change the way men and women match up. As economic inequality has increased, it has created a larger number of high-income men because the biggest increases in income have occurred at the top, in positions dominated by men.[23] From 1978 to 2011, CEO compensation increased more than 72 percent, a rise substantially greater than stock market growth and the painfully slow 5.7 percent growth in worker compensation over the same period, with the greatest growth coming in the period between 1993 and 2007.[24] Women remain underrepresented in upper management more generally, including the ranks of younger executives more likely to be still single. In 2012, women held just over 14 percent of the executive officer positions at *Fortune* 500 companies, and more than 25 percent of these companies had no female executive officers.[25] While women do hold some of these top positions, the dramatic increase in income in such a male-dominated sector of the economy means that, overall, women have lost ground.

The second biggest source of the growth in income inequality has been the financial sector. From the forties to the mid-eighties, increases in compensation in that sector had moved in lockstep with other industries. Between 1982 and 2007, however, average annual compensation doubled, exceeding $100,000 per year before the housing bubble burst.[26] In contrast, compensation in the rest of the economy plodded along, increasing from roughly $50,000 to $58,666 in the same period.[27] Yet, the six job categories with the largest gender gap in pay and at least 10,000 men and 10,000 women were in the Wall Street–heavy financial sector: insurance agents, managers, clerks, securities sales agents, personal advisers, and other specialists.[28] Moreover, while the percentage of women in business schools has increased to almost 50 percent, the number of women on Wall Street has dropped off since 2000, and "in 2008 and 2009 the number of sexual harassment charges per woman in the financial industry grew higher" than in previous years.[29]

In other types of positions where women are better represented, compensation has changed to more steeply banked hierarchies rewarding those at the top, who just happen to be overwhelmingly male. Consider the professions. Women have dramatically increased their number among doctors and lawyers, and the most highly paid professionals have increased their incomes substantially. Yet the gender gap has widened even for doctors' starting salaries, rising from a difference of $3,600 in 1999 to $16,819 in 2008.[30] Researchers conclude that the gap cannot be explained by specialty choice, practice setting, work hours, or other characteristics. In law, the differences are smaller, but the percentage of women in law school peaked in 2001 and has been declining since. Because of the decline in graduates, the pipeline into law firms has slowed modestly over the past ten years. Women continue to hold about 15 percent of equity partnerships, the most lucrative positions in the legal profession, and that figure has been largely unchanged for twenty years.[31] In addition, firms have moved toward different compensation tiers, and women do not do as well in the new systems as they did in firms with a single partnership level.

When we put these figures together for the country as a whole, we see a startling change in the gendered wage gap. The ratio between male and female wages had stayed the same for decades. In the seventies and eighties, the gap between men and women in the wages paid to full-time workers narrowed and did so overwhelmingly because of increases in income to highly skilled women.[32] Even through the recession in the early nineties, women college graduates gained on the men.[33] Those trends reversed course with the big growth in income inequality at the end of the nineties. They accelerated during the boom years of the financial bubble, and they continued to grow with the recovery from the financial crisis.[34] During this period, the overall gendered wage gap continued to narrow because of the declining wages for blue collar men, but for the best educated women, the wage gap increased.

What figure 6.1 shows is that in 1990 the wage gap did not vary greatly by education and to the extent that it did, highly educated women earned a higher percentage of male income than less educated women. By 2008, the relationship between education and the wage gap changed. The least educated women are now earning a much higher percentage of male income than the most educated, with the greatest gaps occurring among the highest paid. In 2012, for example, the median weekly earnings for women employed in full-time management, professional, and related occupations was less than 72 percent of what men earned ($951 vs. $1,328).[35] These aggregate figures do not necessarily involve discrimination. Some of the differences in compensation reflect different courses of study, hours worked, or time out of the labor market.[36] Nonetheless, more sophisticated studies confirm the trends. At the ninetieth percentile, the gap between men and women cannot be explained by controlling for education, job experience, or the type of employment. Indeed, looking just at white college graduates with fifteen years of experience, the gap at the ninetieth percentile becomes even more extreme, with women "losing substantial ground."[37]

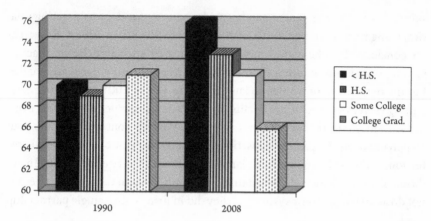

FIGURE 6.1: Female Median Income as a Percentage of Male Median Income by Education

Median Annual Income, by Level of Education, 1990–2009, INFOPLEASE, http://www.infoplease. com/ipa/A0883617.html#ixzz1JFxpOxL9.

The happier news for women, however, is that these economic changes suggest that high-income women enjoy a larger number of high-income men to choose from. The most relevant figures, of course, involve single men and women, and the gender gap is smallest among the young and unattached. Nonetheless, looking at young college graduates during the prime marriage years continues to show a concentration of men in the upper ranks.

Even though women are more likely to graduate from college than men, as the chart in figure 6.2 shows, the average male graduate earns more than the average female graduate, with the greatest disparities occurring at the extreme tail of the distribution, that is, among the top earners. Women looking for re- lationships, of course, want to know about numbers of men rather than the percentages in the chart. Looking at numbers further emphasizes the way men dominate the high end of the employment market—at least among whites. Among white college grads between the ages of twenty-five and thirty-four who work full-time and earn more than $100,000 per year, the men outnum- ber the women by at least 2 to 1. Between $60,000 and $99,000 per year, white men outnumber white women by a little bit less than 2 to 1. At the lower income levels, women outnumber men. Nonetheless, for all white college graduates working full-time at any income level, white men continue to outnumber the women in the twenty-five to thirty-four-year-old age range.[38]

These numbers are further skewed by the question of who the lower earn- ing women college graduates are. Those who herald the "end of men" empha- size the increasing numbers of women college graduates as women outnumber men on college campuses.[39] Looking at broad trends on college attendance, however, the story becomes one of the intersection of gender and class. If we

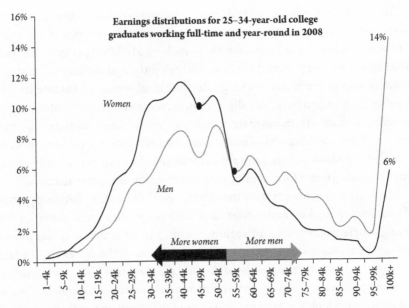

FIGURE 6.2: Earnings Distributions for 25- to 30-Year-Old College Graduates Working Full-Time and Year-Round in 2008

Philip N. Cohen, *Young, educated, and gender-gapped*, FAM. INEQUALITY BLOG (July 23, 2010, 6:00 AM), http://familyinequality.wordpress.com/2010/07/23/young-educated-and-gapped.

look at the dependent [40] sons and daughters of the highest income families heading off to college shortly after high school graduation, there is no gender gap. For the top quarter of households by income, males make up 51 percent of the children entering college from these families. For the same income group among African Americans, the numbers fluctuate more, rising from only 41 percent male in the mid-nineties to 54 percent male in 2003–2004 and then back down to 48 percent in 2007–2008. Among whites, the biggest drop in male attendance has come from households in the bottom income quartile, and, indeed, for that group as a whole, males make up only 43 percent of the total.[41] In Tyler's and Amy's families, there are no gender differences in who attends and finishes college. In Lily's and Carl's families, the women have become a better bet to finish school than the men.[42] And as they get older, Lily is much more likely to go back to school than Carl.

A 2012 study suggests that this further skews marriage markets. The likelihood that a college graduate will marry and that he or she will marry someone with the same education turns out to vary by class. The more advantaged the college graduate, the more likely he or she is to marry and to marry a fellow college graduate.[43] The women who most skew campus gender ratios are the ones returning at older ages, and they may not be looking for a spouse at all. We do not have the data to know, however, whether the age mismatch or cultural differences explain the discrepancy.

Among African Americans and Latinos, in contrast, the gender differences in income shrink, in part because there are fewer minority men in the highest ranks of income producers. For those making $100,000 per year, African-American men outnumber the women only slightly, and looking at the entire group of college graduates working full-time, black women substantially outnumber the men and have only slightly lower median incomes.[44] Latinos are in between, with about twice as many men as women earning more than $100,000 per year.[45] The bleak reports of women outnumbering the men among successful college graduates cloak substantial racial and class differences, differences that are much greater for minority students from lower-income families.[46]

The biggest controversy over the interaction between the changing picture of relationship markets and gender came with the publication of statistics that young, single women were outearning the men in a number of major metropolitan areas, suggesting that women were becoming the richer sex. In fact, the story is much more complicated. Let us take New York City, where endless writers bemoan the prospects for single women in search of happiness. Census data from 2005 looking at the median salaries of twenty-one-to thirty-year-old New Yorkers indicate that the women in fact earn 117 percent of the median male salaries.[47] These figures, however, do not represent national trends. For the country as a whole, women in their twenties make only 89 percent of male full-time pay. Instead, major urban areas differ from the rest of the country because they are more racially diverse and attract a higher percentage of college-graduate women and minority male construction workers than elsewhere. Breaking down the New York figures by race, for example, demonstrates that white women earn 89 percent of the white male rate, close to the 87 percent national norm. Black and Latina women, however, do better vis-à-vis men of the same race than do whites, and do so to a greater degree in New York than nationally. Part of the reason is that women New Yorkers are better educated than male New Yorkers—53 percent of twenty-something women working in New York are college graduates, compared to only 38 percent of the men, with a gap greater for blacks and Latinas than whites.[48] At the same time, the minority men drawn to these cities are often less educated than the women drawn to big city employment, further skewing the effect.[49] And racial differences still matter in marriage markets.[50] In addition, to the extent that cities like New York or San Francisco attract a higher percentage of gay men than lesbians, this can further skew the dating market. Single female college graduates in cities like New York who despair of the choice "between deadbeats (whose numbers are rising) and playboys (whose power is growing)" may in fact face a worse marriage market than similar women elsewhere.[51]

A study that attempts to tease out the market effects finds, intriguingly, that the greater the male income inequality in a city, the lower women's marriage rates at age thirty, even controlling for the number of available men.[52] This makes sense. In a rust belt city like Cleveland, the number of young people with professional or graduate degrees may be too small to constitute a distinct market. The majority of the college-educated will not go on for advanced degrees, and those who do may find that, if they wait, it hurts rather than helps their marriage prospects because a smaller pool of potential mates will be left. In a city like Washington, D.C., however, with a much larger pool of young people with graduate degrees, the effect is different. Tyler, for example, graduated from a good college, got an M.A., landed a secure job, and still didn't marry. By waiting until after he started law school and reached his early thirties, he increased his status and his marriage prospects. We suspect, for example, that if he had not gone to law school, or if had proposed to Amy during his frat boy days, she would have had much less interest in him. And, if he had waited a bit longer, into his mid-to-late thirties, he also would have done just fine so long as he remained employed.

In Cleveland—or Kansas City or Detroit or any number of similar cities—a higher percentage of the population will marry earlier. What the empirical literature shows is that this effect is not just a matter of the size of the city, but also of the level of income inequality in it. In D.C., Tyler entered a different market sector when he decided to go to law school; in Cleveland, those with graduate and professional degrees may not be a distinct enough group to affect marriage patterns. So it could be simultaneously true that high-status men outnumber high-status women in the most elite marriage markets in New York or San Francisco *and* that, for college-graduate women without high salaries or prestigious positions in the same cities, the women in the relevant market outnumber the comparable men.

Income differences acquire greater significance the more they influence mate selection, and income, along with education, have become more important for both men and women. David Buss, an evolutionary psychologist, has tried to measure what men and women find attractive in each other. After years of cross-cultural studies showing that men in most societies rate male and female attractiveness in similar ways, Buss and his colleagues examined how those preferences change over time. At the turn of the twenty-first century, he found that Americans, especially men, increasingly valued their prospective partners' financial possibilities. At the same time, the value that the men placed on their partners' domestic skills plummeted. Love and the importance of physical attractiveness increased in importance for both sexes.[53]

In a more recent study, sociologist Christine Schwartz observes that as "women's labor force participation has grown, men may have begun to compete for high-earning women just as women have traditionally competed for high-earning men." She notes that as men and women both look for high-earning mates, couples become increasingly likely to marry others with similar earn-ing power.[54] Men are increasingly looking for women who will "pull their own weight" in marriage. Schwartz further shows that the greatest changes occurred at the top; that is, the wives of the men with the greatest earnings showed the largest gains in overall income. This is partly because high-earning men have become more likely to marry high-earning women and partly be-cause the women have become less likely to drop out of the labor market after marriage.[55]

Completing the picture is a study from the Brookings Institution's Hamil-ton Project. It shows that marriage rates have decreased for almost everyone—except the women at the highest income levels. The chart depicting the change is stunning. For all men between the ages of thirty and fifty, the percentage married has declined. Even at the top, where income levels have increased sub-stantially, the percentage of married men has fallen, albeit less than for other men. For women in the top 5 percent of the income distribution, however, the percentage between the ages of thirty and fifty who are married has *increased* by over 10 percent while declining for every other group.[56] High-earning (and presumably high-powered) women used to be a turnoff; today they are the prime catches in the marriage market. And, because of competition within this narrow market, they are in the strongest of positions to "put a ring on it."

The result of these changes is a new elite—an elite whose dominant posi-tion is magnified by the marriage market. Over the past thirty years, income in-equality has increased, and it has increased more for men than for women. The Gini coefficient, which measures income inequality, increased by 35 percent for men in comparison with a 19.8 percent increase for women.[57] This means, as demonstrated throughout this chapter, that there are more men at the top (and bottom) of the income spectrum. During this period as well, two incomes have become increasingly important for those who would enjoy middle-class life, and men generally rate women's financial prospects as a more important element in the choice of a partner than they once did. Yet the growth in high-income women, while considerable, has not kept pace with the growth in high-income men. Guttentag and Secord would predict, therefore, that for this demographic (and in today's economy only this demographic) there would be more intense competition for the "right" women. Before we examine how this shapes family norms, let's contrast these developments with the rest of the population.

Gender Ratios and the Disappearance of Marriage

While men continue to outnumber women in elite marriage markets, the same is not true for everyone else. The mismatch between available men and women has been particularly acute in the African-American community—and it is the only group where sex ratios have received sustained attention. As we will see, the mismatch in this market provides insight into the changes in marriage markets outside of the elite, college educated more generally.

Let's start with the numbers. Virtually all researchers conclude that the factors that skew gender ratios have a disproportionately negative impact on the marriage prospects of African-American women. First, the aggregate statistics show a mismatch. In the twenty-five-to thirty-four-year-old population as a whole, the ratio of African-American men to women is 89 men for every 100 women. Whites in contrast have 102 men for every 100 women.[58] These differences reflect slightly lower sex ratios at birth that increase with black men's higher mortality rates. Interracial marriage compounds the effect. In 2008, 22 percent of all black male newlyweds married outside of their race in comparison with only 9 percent of black female newlyweds.[59]

The gender ratios themselves, however, do not fully account for differences in family structure. Scholars, instead, emphasize two other factors with disproportionate effects on African Americans and, increasingly, all poor communities: the disparities between black men's and women's education and employment and the effects of mass incarceration.

Harvard Professor William J. Wilson, who has been calling attention to what is going on in black marriage rates for more than a quarter-century, constructed a "black marriageable male index" that treated only employed black males as "marriageable."[60] In *The Truly Disadvantaged*, he concluded that in inner cities, for every 100 African-American women of a given age, there were only 50 employed African-American men—slim pickings in the construction of a marriage market and a potentially major explanation for the decline in marriage rates. A 2007 report found that only 47 percent of African-American boys graduated from high school in comparison with 69 percent of the girls.[61] The disparities in college graduation rates are greater, with twice as many African-American women as men graduating from college.[62] In the wake of the Great Recession, male African-American unemployment rates were double white rates and higher than those of African-American women.

These problems skew marriage markets even more in urban communities. In many inner cities, more than half of black males do not finish high school. Moreover, the unemployment rate for African-American male high school dropouts in 2004 (near the height of the last boom) was 72 percent in contrast to a 34 percent rate for white male dropouts. The figures for high school graduates were better but only in relative terms. Half of black male high school graduates in their twenties were unemployed in 2004, and these numbers have been rising since the nineties.[63] Taking these factors into account, the Fragile Families Project, which tracks the families of unmarried women giving birth, calculated the sex ratios in a number of American cities and found that, on average, there were only 46 employed African-American men for every 100 African-American women in 2000 compared with 70 to 80 employed Hispanic or white men for every 100 women of those races or ethnic groups in the same communities.[64]

The second factor with a dramatic impact on marriage markets is mass incarceration. One in nine African-American men between the ages of twenty and thirty-four are behind bars at any given time.[65] As many as one-fourth of all black men may spend some time in prison over their lifetimes.[66] Anthropologist and law professor Donald Braman argues that, using sophisticated statistical techniques, mass incarceration accounts for more of the absence of fathers from families in poor African-American communities than gender ratios by themselves and that it is second only to educational levels in predicting father absence. Braman further emphasizes that once incarceration and other variables like education are taken into account, the racial differences in father absence disappear.[67]

These factors have a profound effect on marriage and relationship stability. Some scholars have questioned whether employment alone should determine "marriageability," whereas others have suggested that factors such as incarceration may depress relationship stability because of its effect on increasing children's exposure to abuse, poverty, and other factors that make them less attractive partners as adults.[68] We believe that an important link between the reduction in the number of available men and relationship stability involves the cumulative effect of all of these factors on behavior and culture—and today they describe not just low-income African-American communities, but poor communities more generally.

The Fragile Families Project, which has transformed our understandings of unmarried parenting, has looked at the effect of mate availability on both the transition to marriage and relationship quality outside of marriage and done so for the roughly forty percent of the population who now have children outside of marriage. The project studies unmarried women at the time they give birth and tracks the progress of their relationship with the father of the child afterward. In the nineties, these sociologists attempted to tease out which factor had the greater effect: overall sex ratios or local economic effects that depressed the number of employed men. They found that the number of employed men had a more statistically significant effect than aggregate sex ratios.[69] The majority of the women in these studies have a relationship with the father at the time of the birth, and many of the couples hope to marry eventually, though the majority will break up without doing so. In 2004, sociologists Kristen Harknett and Sara McLanahan observed that their "most striking finding" was that the supply of alternative partners has "a large influence on the parents' decision whether to marry after a non-marital birth or not." In addition, given the significantly lesser availability of African-American men than men of other races, it also explained a large part of the racial differences in marriage rates.[70]

Harknett has produced two additional studies on the topic. One looked at the effect of sex ratios on relationship quality. That study found that markets with higher male-to-female ratios were associated with higher relationship quality:[71] sex ratios were a better predictor than citywide unemployment rates of relationship quality. In a second study, Harknett, together with Arielle Kuperberg, another sociologist, broke down labor market conditions by education. They analyzed how employment opportunities differed by the level of education completed. This study found that strong male labor markets significantly increased marriage rates for men of every educational level and that controlling for labor market opportunities largely eliminated the marriage differences between more and less educated men. Strong female labor markets, in contrast, encouraged later marriages for less educated, non-marital mothers but had little effect on the marriage rates of the more educated mothers.[72]

Taking this body of work together creates a portrait of changing norms, not just an employment effect. Scholars criticized Wilson's original thesis in part because employment patterns could not explain all of the change in marriage rates: the marriage rates of both employed and unemployed men declined.[73] Later scholars have similarly insisted that economics and employment cannot be the answer for the country more generally; the changes must be cultural. These arguments, however, fail to take into account the causal mechanisms involved in the sex ratio thesis: a change in the ratio affects the bargaining that underlies the entire market. That is, as the number of men whom the women in a given community are willing to marry declines, the more desirable men in that market find that they can play the field. They do not need to commit to a relationship to gain sexual access to a woman or to have children with her. Sociologists Kathy Edin and Maria Kefalas found, for example, that when they asked poor women in an inner-city community why their last relationship ended, four in ten blamed repeated and often flagrant infidelities of their partner.[74] The women also enjoy less ability to set the terms within a relationship; Edin and Kefalas found that women cited a chronic pattern of domestic violence as a factor in nearly half of the break-ups.[75] Given this distrust, women prefer men who are willing to spend money on them at the beginning of a relationship rather than save for the future, and men understandably feel that it is difficult to find women who are supportive of men with little or low incomes. The women come to rely on themselves and their blood relatives rather than on the fathers of their children to raise their families.[76] Sociologist Bill Wilson concludes that "from the point of view of day-to-day survival, single parenthood reduces the emotional burden and shields them from the type of exploitation that often accompanies the sharing of both living arrangements and limited resources."[77]

So if greater unemployment—or incarceration or substance abuse—reduces the number of men that women regard as potential long-term partners, the greater the advantage of those men who remain in the relationship market and the more likely the women are to pair temporarily with men they view as questionable partners. This cycle can depress overall marriage rates as well as produce a cultural shift toward greater gender distrust, wariness of commitment, and increased relationship instability;[78] women's comparative scarcity, meanwhile, increases marriage rates, in part because it encourages more responsible and attentive male behavior as the price of access to sexual relationships.

The Fragile Families studies add empirical support for this picture by teasing apart the factors that discourage marriage. These studies indicate that a scarcity of men affects the likelihood of marriage in three ways. First, parents may give up on committed relationships and instead have children with multiple partners. By the time their child is five years old, about half of both men and women in the Fragile Families study had become involved with at least one other partner.[79] This "multipartnered fertility" may interfere with marriage because men tend to be less interested in committed relationships that involve an investment in other men's children. It also makes women more likely to report that a single parent could raise a child just as well as a married parent.[80] Second, mothers who may bear children with "lower quality" men may not be willing to marry such men even if the men are willing to marry them. Indeed, the Harknett and McLanahan study found that the more favorable the marriage market for women, the more likely the mother was to report that her partner was fair and willing to compromise and the less likely she was to report domestic violence.[81] Third, the father, who believes he has ample opportunity to enter into other relationships, may be less willing to commit to the mother, thereby increasing infidelity and relationship conflict.[82] These studies suggest that rather than the marital ideal changing—both men and women continue to regard marriage as an important commitment to someone they regard as a cherished partner—what is changing is the expectation that they will be able to realize that ideal.

Indeed, in these communities, marriage itself continues to represent a serious commitment, but it is not always a commitment worth making. In a study of the impact of marriage on incarcerated men, marriage made it much more likely that the men's relationship with their families would continue. Many of the prisoners' wives explained that they would have left the incarcerated men had they not been married.[83] Marriage thus serves as a commitment-enhancing device,[84] but it also keeps women in relationships that may not be in their best interests. Sociologists Kathy Edin and Maria Kefalas quote one young woman, a white high school dropout who had a child in her teens with a man who, at the time of interview, was awaiting trial:

> That's when I really started [to get better], because I didn't have to worry about what *he* was doing, didn't have to worry about him *cheating* on me, all this stuff. [It was] then I realized that I had to do what I had to do to take care of my son. . . . When he was there, my whole *life* revolved around him, you know, so I always messed up somehow because I was so worried about what *he* was doing.[85]

These studies provide a compelling picture of gender distrust in the poorest urban communities and of the impact of incarceration and unemployment on relationship markets. The results do not just affect those who commit crimes and their loved ones. They produce self-reinforcing cycles. In communities with high unemployment and imprisonment, fewer men are available. With fewer choices, women enter into relationships with men they know are engaged in conduct that may lead to imprisonment, but they become less likely to commit to these men. Men who lack stable relationships, in turn, are more likely to offend—further reducing the available men in the community and further increasing gender distrust.[86] The cycles that link employment instability, incarceration, and the declining number of good jobs and "good men" to gender distrust have been documented in poor communities, but we are just coming to grips with the expansion of similar cycles to the middle of American society.

Inequality, Job Loss, and the End of Men

Every serious scholar who has examined employment emphasizes that what took place in the workplace in the nineties mirrored the changes in the family: both showed improvements at the top and declines at the bottom. Wages increased steadily for those with college degrees or more and stagnated or fell for those with less education. The impact on family stability, though, came less from the decline of wages per se and more from the loss of work.[87] For blue-collar men, pathways into the labor market have become constricted and the availability and stability of work have declined, which, in turn, has affected the number of men who are seen as good marriage prospects.

At the height of the Great Compression, the period of relative income equality between 1945 and the mid-1970s, male leisure time did not vary much by

class; today, it does.[88] Charles Murray documents the changes in employment since 1960 in his prototypical white upper-class community, Belmont,
and in his prototypical white working-class town, Fishtown. In the middle of
the twentieth century, the number of men who worked less than forty hours
a week was low—about 10 percent in Fishtown and 8 percent in Belmont. By
2010, the percentage of men working less than forty hours a week had doubled
in Fishtown, to 20 percent, while it had risen more modestly in Belmont, to
about 12 percent.[89]

Complementing the underemployed are those giving up on work altogether.
In 1970, only about 3 percent of men between the ages of thirty and forty-nine
with a high school diploma or less were not in the labor market compared to
less than 2 percent of men with a college degree. By 2010, those numbers had
risen to more than 12 percent of men with a high school degree or less compared to 3 percent of those with a college degree.[90] Many of those who give up
on the labor market do so because of persistent unemployment. In 1970, white
males in Fishtown between the ages of thirty and forty-nine had unemployment rates that were about 80 percent of the national unemployment rates.
By 2010, the unemployment figures were 130 percent of the national rates. In
Belmont, by contrast, the rates rose from about 10 to 20 percent of the national
figures.[91]

Adding these figures together dramatically reduces the number of men
who are "good catches." Take the 12 percent of men not in the labor force,
add the roughly 10 percent who are unemployed and the 20 percent who are
underemployed and they equal 42 percent of the total. This overstates the
situation a bit, because the statuses may be temporary and many of the underemployed may still be attractive mates, but it also understates the marriage
market problem because these figures include older men, and unemployment
rates are higher for men under thirty. Nonetheless, for 42 percent of men in
their working prime to be unemployed or underemployed is a remarkable
figure; the comparable number in the sixties and seventies would have been
less than 20 percent and, in times of low unemployment, even less. While
the figures for white, Asian, and Latino men are nowhere near the draconian
levels in African-American inner-city communities where the number of
males working full-time may be substantially less than half, in the percentage
of males in working-class communities who can contribute meaningfully to
family income.[92]

These figures demonstrate that work has been steadily eroding for a large
part of the country and that it has worsened since the financial crisis. Since the
crisis, African-American and Latino men have been dropping out of the labor
force faster than women in the same communities. The U.S. Bureau of Labor
Statistics found in 2012 that male workforce participation for the country as

a whole reached its lowest level since the federal government began reporting the data in 1948.[93]

Nor do the employment figures alone capture the impact of the changing economy on working-class communities. As previously noted, employment stability has also decreased for all employees and done so more for the working class than the college educated.[94] Involuntary layoffs have risen along with long-term unemployment. Even before the current recession, the perception of job insecurity had increased. While highly educated workers have responded with a greater willingness to switch jobs, blue-collar workers have found that a layoff likely triggers either longer periods of unemployment or lower wages than in earlier eras.[95] These results can have a cumulative effect on the community well-being and the stability of relationships.

A remarkable book, *The Spirit Level: Why Greater Equality Makes Societies Stronger*, suggests that greater inequality itself makes matters worse. Richard Wilkinson and Kate Pickett, two Brits with backgrounds in medicine and epidemiology, show that greater income disparities correlate with a host of social ills. The authors provide a cross-cultural study that examines the impact of greater inequality across different countries and different states in the United States. Their 2009 study found that greater inequality lowered levels of trust, life expectancy and infant mortality, children's educational performance, and social mobility and that it increased rates of mental illness (including substance abuse), obesity, teenage births, homicides, and imprisonment rates.[96] These factors have a profound effect on community health and family stability. In fact, income inequality had a greater societal impact than poverty rates. The authors report that the United States has higher levels of income inequality than most developed countries and that the higher inequality correlates with higher levels of all of these social ills. Moreover, the higher rates of substance abuse (though not mental illness), homicide, and imprisonment also correlate with inequality measures across the various states and together disproportionately affect men. The result, both because of higher male mortality levels due to drug overdoses and homicides and because of the impact of substance abuse and imprisonment on men's attractiveness as potential mates, further depresses the number of "marriageable men" compared to marriageable women in poor and working-class communities.

Sociologists describe the changes in employment as the disappearance of the center: there are more good jobs and more bad jobs, disproportionately affecting male employees without college degrees or specialized skills.[97] Charles Murray documents how this plays out in white American communities, complementing Wilson's observations that the disappearance of jobs contributed to higher rates of crime and imprisonment in black communities. Arrests for both violent crime and property crime increased steadily in Fishtown from 1960 through the mid-nineties,[98] and imprisonment rates increased even more, from 200 to 1,000 per 100,000 people in the general population in Fishtown from 1970 to 2005. Meanwhile, better-off Belmont, with its higher rates of employment, experienced no increase in either arrests or imprisonment.[99]

All of the indications are that these changes in employment, imprisonment, and community well-being have altered the ratio of men to women in working-class marriage markets and done so in ways that affect overall attitudes toward relationships and marriage. We start with the question of whether couples perceive their marriages to be "very happy." Murray observes that in 1970 about 73 percent of the top income group and 67 percent of the Fishtown group said "yes." Between 1970 and the mid-eighties, those figures steadily declined for both groups as gender roles changed and marital tensions increased. Beginning in 1990, however, marital happiness rose for the affluent, and by 2010, the percentage of Belmont couples who reported their marriages to be very happy was back up above 70 percent. In Fishtown, on the other hand, marital happiness continued to decline steadily, with only slightly more than 50 percent of white working-class couples reporting their marriages to be "very happy."[100]

Perceptions of marital success—along with the class-based changes in divorce and non-marital births—feed back into attitudes toward relationships. When asked whether "marriage has not worked out for the people they know," only 17 percent of college graduates agreed compared with 40 percent of those with only high school degrees and over half of high school dropouts.[101] In the seventies, asked whether extramarital sex is wrong, the less educated were much more likely than the well-educated to say "yes." Among whites, the differences were huge, with 80 percent of Fishtown saying yes in comparison with only 50 percent of Belmont. By 2010, the differences had narrowed, principally because those in Belmont had become much more likely to respond yes.[102]

Other research supports these findings. Looking at all races and asking whether premarital sex is always wrong, the differences between the top and bottom also narrowed. Between the 1970s and the 2000s, both the least and the moderately educated became substantially less likely to say yes, while the most educated women had become more likely to say yes, though by a small margin.[103] The behavior appears to track the change in attitudes. The percentage of women between the ages of twenty-five and forty-four who report having had three or more sex partners over their lifetimes was about the same for all educational groups in 1995. Since then, the number has declined to 57 percent for the most educated and risen to 70 percent for those in the middle.[104]

A similar shift occurred in attitudes toward divorce. In the seventies, approximately half of those with lower levels of education thought divorce should be more difficult to obtain in comparison with only 36 percent of the highly educated. Within the past few years, more of the highly educated (almost 50 percent) thought divorce should be hard to obtain while support for such restrictions fell to 40 percent of the least educated.[105] Marital fidelity corresponds with attitudes toward divorce. As a National Marriage Project study reported, the number of married persons who report extramarital affairs fell slightly, to 13 percent among the most educated, while rising slightly, to 21 percent, for the least educated. The middle was unchanged.[106]

In the seventies, college graduates adopted much more liberal attitudes toward sex and marriage, but in today's insecure, competitive world, elites have adopted slightly more conservative attitudes to match their marriage-oriented behavior. During that same period, white working-class communities reflected the same types of shifts as African-American working-class communities had experienced in the sixties and seventies: they became more skeptical about marriage and more distrustful of the opposite sex. And many justify the decision not to marry in financial terms. Young couples in the middle of the American economic spectrum find living together to be the right choice when the men are doing well enough that they believe that they will be able to marry in the future but not so well that they feel they can marry now.[107]

Sociologist Andrew Cherlin concludes that there is a new pattern for the group in the middle that graduates from high school, but not college, and that struggles economically but is not poor. The new pattern involves multiple cohabiting relationships that often still end in marriage, and it also involves high rates of divorce followed by additional partnerships. He finds that the women most likely to live in multiple cohabiting unions over the course of a lifetime are white women with a high school, but not a college, degree. This group of women has more cohabiting (marital and non-marital) relationships than do African Americans or Latinos with the same level of education or those in all racial groups who graduate from college or drop out of high school. This group also still hopes to marry, and still does marry to a greater degree than high school graduates of other races, but as with high school graduates of all races, the relationships have become more fragile and the non-marital birth rates have continued to climb.[108]

The question sociologists cannot answer is whether this pattern—cohabitation, marriage, divorce, new cohabitation, dissolution, new relationship—is a permanent distinctive pattern for the middle or whether it is a transition point away from more stable relationships altogether.

Conclusion

These results are consistent with the emergence of highly segmented relationship markets built on different norms and gender strategies.[109] For white elites,[110] greater income inequality has increased the number of men at the top. The expansion of this top group of men should increase the competition among the men for the most elite women, giving successful women a greater choice of partners. The result encourages a delay in marriage as both men and women acquire the qualities that translate into favorable matches, qualities that today include investment in both men's and women's education and income and considerable care in avoiding an early birth that would limit future prospects.[111]

Greater inequality also writes off a high percentage of men at the losing end of economic change. Greater inequality has been associated not just with greater long-term unemployment, but also with higher male mortality and imprisonment rates and with riskier behaviors that confer status, such as violence, drug dealing, and infidelity.[112] In the United States, the middle of the income spectrum has historically been stable, marriage-oriented high school graduates. Today, however, the middle seems to be disappearing. High school graduates increasingly look like high school dropouts in terms of divorce and non-marital birth rates. This group is more fluid than the others; it has experienced the most profound changes, and relatively few researchers focus on the center as a subject of study.[113] Yet all indications are that worsening employment prospects—lower wages and work instability—have increased relationship instability and reduced the ratio of attractive men to attractive women.

Even among college graduates, things are not entirely sanguine. College-educated African Americans, for example, have not enjoyed the same decline in divorce rates as college-educated whites,[114] and their non-marital birth rates, which in 1982 were only slightly above that of whites, have increased three- to four-fold. The marital prospects for the most talented African American women have become so bleak that Rick Banks wrote a book, *Is Marriage for White People?* (published in 2011), which asks whether, given the gender mismatch in accomplishments, the most accomplished black women should give up on black men. The good news is that among African Americans in the upper third, gender differences in education appear to be narrowing; the bad news is that this does little to aid the group in the middle (or the poor) where the greatest racially based gender disparities exist.[115]

For whites, the decade when college graduate men as a group enhanced their position in the economy was the nineties. Since 2000, college-graduate income has stagnated. Indeed, since then, college graduates between the ages of twenty-five and thirty-four without advanced degrees, who in the nineties had significantly outperformed workers with less education, saw their income *fall* 9.6 percent.[116] Four-year college may no longer be the ticket to financial security.[117] Only the top 1–2 percent continue to gain. While that group remains disproportionately male, the group's numbers are small. Moreover, since the financial crisis of 2007, unemployment and underemployment have risen for college graduates in their twenties. It is too early to assess the long-term impact of these changes, which have depressed marriage and fertility rates for the country as a whole. It is quite possible that the result will be an even greater concentration of income at the top, even more employment instability, and a worsening picture for the family stability of a larger percentage of Americans.

Remaking Class Barriers: Children and Achievement

When the two of us applied to college, we walked into the SATs without having gone through intensive SAT prep or having read any books on how to ace college testing. We received very little college counseling, and decided on our list of schools by ourselves. We then each wrote our own college essays, and we didn't share them with anyone other than the college admission counselors. Thirty years later, our five children all took some form of SAT prep tutoring. We spent lots of time reviewing their choices of colleges and then even more time reviewing their college applications. Naomi even hired college coaches to help steer her children through the process. June relied on an undergraduate professor friend who had just navigated her own children through the process. We both found the experience daunting.

In late 2012, *New York Times* journalist Jason DeParle documented what happened to three women who graduated from the same high school, one of the few in Texas ranked "academically unacceptable." Angelica, whose mother became a citizen after illegally immigrating from Mexico and acknowledged that her daughter essentially raised herself, enrolled in Emory University; a second became a freshman at Texas State University; and the third began her studies at a community college. But, four years later, none "has a four-year degree. Only one is still studying full time, and two have crushing debts. Angelica, who left Emory owing more than $60,000, earns just above minimum wage in a Galveston furniture store."[1]

In contrast, most of our friends' children who started college finished, though many only after intensive parental involvement arranging a switch of majors when the children, like Angelica, hit a rough patch academically, needed a semester in rehab, or simply had trouble leaving home or breaking up with a high school sweetheart. The new generation of "helicopter" parents does not let go, as our parents did, when children go off to college. Instead, one of our children chastised us because, unlike some other parents, we did not call every day by cellphone, and another felt betrayed when we suggested that he could figure out how to get from the airport to campus without a fifty-dollar cab ride.

The change in families is not just a change in family form. It's a change in the quality and quantity of resources available to children that is associated with family income. The results affect children's stimulation and cognitive development in early childhood, their attachment to and support from the adults in their lives, their feelings of trust and isolation, and their school achievement and community participation. A half-century ago, society marginalized a small group at the bottom that included many African Americans, the rural and urban poor, and other isolated communities. Today, the destruction of community and familial bonds affects a much larger portion of American society and increases the gaps between the top, the middle, and the bottom. The result is the reproduction of class through its impact on children from their first days of life.

Let's look at the numbers. Poor children have access to fewer resources at home and at school, and the effects show. In 1960, the gaps in reading and math test scores among whites of different classes were comparatively small, whereas the gap between blacks and whites was huge. That relationship has changed. Sean Reardon of Stanford University describes this as the "income achievement gap."[2] He looks at test scores from children at the ninetieth percentile of the income distribution and from the tenth percentile and measures the differences. These class-based differences have grown steadily since the late seventies, increasing in each passing decade. So, too, have the gaps among African Americans and Latinos of different classes, though not to the same degree as whites—who have dramatically more wealth at the top of the income ladder. In contrast, racial differences fell substantially between 1950 and the early 1980s. Today, Reardon's income achievement gap is nearly twice as large as the black-white achievement gap and is 30 to 40 percent higher than it was twenty-five years ago.[3] While racial differences persist, class has become the big story in looking at differences in children's educational achievement.

Over the past decade, researchers gained greater insight into the sources of some of these differences. A study published in 2013 indicated that differences in cognitive performance associated with socioeconomic levels appear in children as early as eighteen months and found a six-month gap in both vocabulary learning and language processing efficiency *at age two*.[4] Researchers have long been aware of differences in vocabulary; by age three, for example, children from higher socioeconomic status (SES) families had twice the vocabularies of children from lower SES backgrounds.[5] The newest studies measure not just vocabulary, but processing speed—the amount of time a child takes to recognize a familiar word. These studies find a similar correlation between parents' socioeconomic status and children's speed, which predicts the rate of subsequent language acquisition. Both factors have long-term consequences that correlate with adult performance.[6]

A major source of the differences is the quality of the children's early language environments. Wealthier and better educated parents engaged in dramatically more child-directed speech, providing a more interactive and cognitively stimulating environment, though other factors, such as adequate nutrition, the presence of lead, or parental stress, may contribute.[7] While bad schools can make the differences worse, good schools do not close the gap. So whatever is taking place affects early childhood development. Trips to Europe and SAT tutors may enhance elite children's preparation for college, but they do not explain differences in cognitive achievement. The Head Start program focused on the pre-school years because that is where the largest differences in educational achievement begin—with lifelong consequences.

Reardon further acknowledges that parents' education makes a difference, but it cannot explain what has changed over the past half century. Both in 1960 and 2000, if you wanted to predict how children will do on math and reading tests, you could look at their parents' education. In every decade, the children of engineers do better than the children of carpenters. What has changed is the effect of income. In 1960, the children of a college graduate executive who made $80,000 a year did not do much better than a college graduate teacher who made $20,000 a year. Today the gap between the children of an executive making $200,000 a year and a teacher with the same education making $50,000 a year has increased.

Nor can the gaps be explained by greater income inequality between the bottom and the top in some abstract sense. While the income differences between the middle and the bottom increased during this period, these changes had little effect on children's test scores. The big changes came from increased income inequality in the top half—the gap between the ninetieth and fiftieth percentiles. Ultra-high-income parents are doing something different that affects how their children perform. Tiger mothers like Yale Law professor Amy Chua, an admitted outlier even among high-status parents, really have discovered secrets that allow their children to outperform everyone else. Reardon suggests that high-income parents must somehow be changing how they invest in their children's cognitive development.[8]

Reardon's description matches up with what we have been describing throughout this book. The new upper-middle-class model has enormous payoffs for children—payoffs that re-create class identity. Upper-middle-class parents are more likely to raise children within two-parent families, and both mothers and fathers spend more time with their children than their parents did. These well-off parents, who spend substantial sums on cleaning crews and energy-efficient washers and dryers, devote increasing amounts of their own time and that of carefully selected high-quality nannies, preschool teachers, tutors, sports trainers, and camp counselors to creating activities that stimulate their children's cognitive environment. Well-off families have remade the use of parental energies to invest ever more in children even with two parents in the workforce.

Consider the results of studies that measure the amount of "developmental time" parents spend interacting with their children. They have tried to capture the change in the minutes per day parents spend reading to their children, playing with them, or taking them to sports practice, the library, and ballet lessons. In the sixties and seventies, these results did not vary much by class. High school–graduate mothers spent four minutes a day *more* than college-graduate mothers in activities that contributed to their children's development. The college-graduate dads spent a bit more time than the high school–graduate dads, canceling out the differences among the mothers. Starting in the eighties, both groups began to spend much more time with their children, but the college graduates' increase was more dramatic. By 2010, the differences had grown from a few minutes to more than an hour a day. The younger the child, the greater the differences in parenting time by parents' education had become. College-graduate parents have become much more likely than parents with only a high school education to play patty cake with their toddlers.[9] Perhaps reflecting these differences, a 2013 study found that parents who have attended college felt more confident about their parenting than those who have never attended college.[10]

The same disparities are reflected in differences on spending on children, as figure 7.1 shows. The parents with the most money seek out camps that reinforce foreign language skills, personal trainers who work on Little League techniques, and vacations with their children that range from the Bahamas to the Himalayas. In the seventies, the top-income quartile spent about three times as much as the bottom-income quartile on such activities for their children. Today, it spends nine times as much. In our childhood, working-class and middle-class kids both went to camps and attended after-school activities in their neighborhoods. In the middle-class neighborhoods, the camps might cost a little more and have nicer buses and fancier t-shirts, but the activities were not all that different. Today, the advantages that start in toddlerhood only increase over time. In researching this book, we spoke to an investment banker friend who described the thousands of dollars he spent on tutors, after-school activities, family trips to Nepal, college application coaches, and a private school that made sure all of the teachers' letters of recommendations were in by the end of August. In the public schools that some of our children attended,

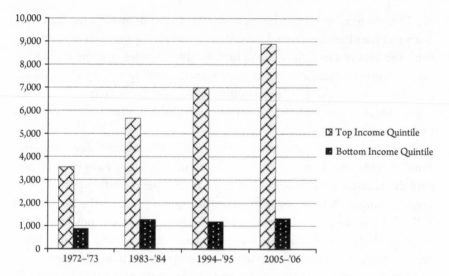

FIGURE 7.1:   Gap in Enrichment Expenditures on Children, 1972–2006 (2008 dollars)
Greg J. Duncan and Richard Murnane, eds., *Whither Opportunity? Rising Inequality, Schools, and Children's Life Chances* (2011).

an overworked guidance counselor was in charge of the process for hundreds of students, many of whom she had never met.

These differences reflect the ability of the upper middle class to combine workforce participation, which increases the family's resources, with active parenting. In 1970, of mothers with young children, 18 percent of mothers with the most education and 12 percent of mothers with the least education worked outside the home. That difference may well have accounted for the fact that high school–graduate mothers spent a few minutes more per day on their children than did college-graduate mothers. By 2000, 65 percent of the more-educated group worked outside the home, but only 30 percent of the least-educated mothers also participated in the labor market. Yet, the more-educated working mothers have increased the time they spend on their children, in part because they no longer also cook dinner, mop the floors, and do the laundry but also in part because they are older and more mature.[11] As Princeton professor Sara McLanahan explains,

> Children who were born to mothers from the most-advantaged backgrounds are making substantial gains in resources. Relative to their counterparts 40 years ago, their mothers are more mature and more likely to be working at well-paying jobs. These children were born into stable unions and are spending more time with their fathers. In contrast, children born to mothers from the most disadvantaged

backgrounds are making smaller gains and, in some instances, even losing parental resources. Their mothers are working at low-paying jobs. Their parents' relationships are unstable, and for many, support from their biological fathers is minimal.[12]

These advantages create feedback loops. The children of women who have a college degree wait to have children until they have assembled the resources that allow them to devote considerable time, money, and attention to their children. The mothers themselves are older and more mature. They are more likely to have jobs that make it easier to combine work and family. Their mature families also are more stable. Working-class women, in contrast, who grow up with less supervision and fewer opportunities, are more likely to become pregnant in their late teens or early twenties, less likely to give birth within marriage, and less likely to respond to an unplanned pregnancy with an abortion.[13] The result builds in greater parental stress from the child's birth.

Sociologists further find that greater income segregation and the community stress that occurs with economic decline affect children's performance. They have discovered, for example, that a higher percentage of children in poor communities have trouble not just with academic but also with attention skills.[14] These children are also more likely to engage in disruptive behavior that affects the academic environment for their classmates. Other studies indicate that community-level events, such as a plant closing or a regional economic downturn, reduce test scores and increase disciplinary problems for children attending public schools in those counties, and the effects occur more quickly for children from lower socioeconomic status families than for their wealthier peers.[15] The worsening problems affect even those children in the same communities whose parents remain employed. Economic decline itself further reduces the resources available for the public schools in these neighborhoods and often increases teacher turnover. Yet researchers find that individual factors, such as budget cuts, have relatively little impact on student performance. Instead, they suggest that "increased stress in families is the primary mechanism through which community job losses influence children's reading and mathematics achievements."[16]

The consequence is not just a divergence in test scores and an end to social mobility. The results of these changes affect basic participation in society. Our college classmates used to talk about the division between the "jocks" and the "brains" in public high schools. The jocks tended to be the guys from working-class neighborhoods; the brains were the children of the suburbs. The jocks dominated the sports teams; the brains led the debate squad. Between 1992 and 2004, however, high school seniors from the bottom income quartile had become significantly less likely to be on high school athletic teams, much less

to play a leadership role. The highest income quartile increased their participation over the same period, snaring a higher percentage of sports' team
captainships. The same thing happened to after-school music, dance, and art
classes. Wealthy tenth graders became more likely to participate; the bottom
quarter of high school students stopped going to these activities. Even church
attendance reflects the growing class disparities. In the seventies and eighties,
church attendance dropped, and it did so in roughly the same proportion for
all children. But beginning in 1990, the rate of religious attendance for high
school seniors whose parents were in the most-educated third stabilized. For
high school seniors in the bottom third, however, church attendance continued to drop. Greater economic inequality has made the top group better off
while depleting the resources of parents in the middle of the economy, with
ripple effects on the well-being and civic engagement of the next generation.[17]

Some of the class differences reflect long-standing cultural divisions about
the proper way to raise children. In *Unequal Childhoods* and follow-up studies,
sociologist Annette Lareau followed a dozen families for about a month, studying their parenting habits.[18] Affluent families, both black and white, engage in
what she labels "concerted cultivation," and children are constantly busy with
soccer practice, piano lessons, tutoring, and other activities. By contrast, working-class and poor families rely on strategies that encourage "the accomplish-
ment of natural growth" in which a child's development occurs spontaneously.
Parents don't chauffeur their children to their carefully planned birthday parties, sports practices, or play dates. Instead, children are responsible for finding their own activities. The overscheduled middle-class children experience
more stress; they are often afraid to disappoint parental expectations. The
working-class children are more independent and feel less entitled. Yet they
lack advocates who help them navigate complicated institutions. A run-in with
a police officer is more likely to result in a conviction on the record than a di-
version program for a working-class teen. With a lawyer, a first offense can be
expunged from the record; without a lawyer, a teen is unlikely ever to have
heard the term.

The same thing is true of school attendance and completion. Too many
cuts in high school may mean no degree for the working-class teen while
upper-middle-class parents negotiate make-up assignments directly with the
principal.[19] Upper-middle-class parents today may hire college application
counselors to help with selecting a school, writing applications, and making
sure their child gets in. The counselors can help find SAT tutors, provide tips
on making sure that harried high school teachers get in the required recommendations, and help craft effective college essays. Working-class students
may be largely on their own. Although the rates of college attendance have
increased for all income groups over the past forty years, the gap in attendance

rates between those at the lowest and highest incomes has remained the same.[20] Unsurprisingly, socioeconomic status correlates not only with college attendance but also with a student's choice of colleges. Students from working-class backgrounds who qualify for admission to selective institutions are much more likely than middle-class students admitted to the same schools to enroll in less selective four-year colleges or in two-year colleges or to not attend at all.[21] It has become significantly harder to manage college applications and financing without parental involvement, and recent state budget cuts are rapidly pushing tuition at what had been affordable state universities beyond the reach of an increasingly larger portion of the population.[22]

These results magnify class differences. Students in the highest income quartile are 23 percent more likely than students in the lowest income quartile to graduate from high school. The desire to go to college does not differ by race or class, but attendance and graduation do.[23] Two-thirds of those students in the upper quarter of the income distribution with at least one college-graduate parent earn a university degree. In comparison, only 9 percent of those in the bottom quarter who would have been the first in their families to do so finish college.[24]

Two generations ago, these class-based differences in culture existed. But the differences in absolute terms were less, and they did not prevent the United States from becoming one of the best educated and prosperous societies in the world. Today, the interaction of cultural differences with family and economic changes *means that children are likely to face even greater inequality in the distribution of resources than their parents, lowering the overall human capital of the next generation.* The strength of the United States—and of democracies more generally—has long been associated with the strength of the middle class. The class-based nature of recent changes in family structure, together with the lack of alternative ways to channel resources to children, threaten the well-being of the middle class in the United States and risk creating a large and unbridgeable gulf between those who can continue to realize the benefits of college education and well-paying, skilled positions and those who, even if they graduate from high school, community college, or technical programs, may continue to see their living standards erode.

This analysis suggests a reinforcing cycle: greater inequality increases the class-based differences in family form, which in turn amplify class-based differences in the cognitive performance of the next generation, which in turn increase overall wage inequality. The result reduces the total, not just the relative, human capital investment in future Americans. Community well-being produces synergistically positive effects; with greater inequality and the disappearance of jobs, we are seeing the destruction of communities and the people within them. The next generation will not do as well as their parents.

The Re-creation of Class

It is time to recognize that family scripts have been rewritten, and they have been rewritten along the diverging lines of gender, class, and culture. Marriage is thriving among higher-income, well-educated men and women who have become more likely to stay together; marriage is dying among lower-income, less-educated men and women, and the marriages they do enter into are more likely to end in divorce. When sociologists lament the "de-institutionalization of marriage," they are in fact describing two long-term forces that affect the ability to realize the benefits of marriage as a universally accessible ideal. The first is the end of male political, social, and economic dominance and, with it, women's greater ability to say "no" to family relationships on onerous terms. The second is the greater ability of well-educated women like Amy to find men like Tyler who make marriage worthwhile and the decreased ability of women like Lily to find men to whom they are willing to commit at all. These shifts in marriage "markets" in turn influence expectations about intimate relationships, decisions to invest in men versus women's earning capacity, and the level of trust parties bring to new relationships. These new expectations interact with the legal changes we describe in the next section to create new social scripts that institutionalize a remade definition of marriage and class-based responses to that redefinition.

Amy and Tyler as well as Lily and Carl are accordingly not just making different choices; they are following different scripts. Amy and Lily now have opportunities to have sex, jobs, and children without marriage, however hard it remains to "have it all." They both have found young men with whom they share emotional intimacy, but both have had that before. Amy is marrying because she has found a young man who adores her and whom she expects to be faithful, to contribute in commensurate ways to the children they expect to have, and to negotiate the tradeoffs involved in moving from one coast to the other, juggling internships in different cities, preserving time for work and study, and trading off domestic chores. Tyler, in turn, not only loves Amy, but recognizes that she is a great catch. He will enjoy greater income and status with her than without her, and he understands that the "price" is a commitment of a different nature from his other relationships. It is a commitment he is happy to make.

Lily, in turn, has given up on finding a man like Tyler, that is, on finding a man she trusts. She has fallen in love before, only to discover that her boyfriend was cheating on her. Carl hasn't been with anyone else that she knows of (at least this month), but neither has he been carrying his own weight. He was supposed to go with her for an ultrasound appointment, but he didn't show up. He borrowed money from her to fix his car and has never paid her back. She isn't confident that he is capable of caring for a newborn, and she doubts he could support her, even temporarily, if she had to depend on him. For Lily, the baby's needs come first, and marriage to Carl is a threat, rather than an asset, in those efforts.

Sociologists persist in calling the new model "soul mate marriage," which they define as "a couple-centered vehicle for personal growth, emotional intimacy, and shared consumption that depends for its survival on the happiness of both spouses."[1] We confess to mystification. What we see instead is a remade model of marriage that Amy, but not Lily, finds possible to achieve. The remade model is not simply an opportunity for "personal growth, emotional intimacy, and shared consumption." It is a model designed to secure pathways to greater investment in children in the post-industrial era. Changing social mores reinforce Amy and Tyler's delight in having found each other and in the shared understanding that their relationship will require interdependence based on flexibility and trust. These same social mores reinforce Lily's conviction that she should not marry a man on whom she cannot depend. She has the child anyway, partly because of her religious beliefs but also because she does not expect to find a better man. She then relies on her own earnings, her family's help, and Carl's occasional contributions to raise her daughter. In doing so, she takes the issue of commitment every bit as seriously as Tyler and Amy; it's just that the commitment she finds worth making is the one to her child.

Shared Power and the Meaning of Marriage

At the core of the older system of marriage was the wholesale subordination of women to men; at the core of the remade marital scripts is the dismantling of that system. Conservative William Kristol observed in 1991 that marriage depended on male power. But, because women were unlikely to come to these conclusions on their own, they must be taught, he concluded, "to grasp the following three points: the necessity of marriage, the importance of good morals, and the necessity of inequality within marriage."[2] Feminist Adrienne Rich had critiqued heterosexual unions in remarkably similar terms a decade earlier.[3] She saw marriage as the product of forces that pressured women into the institution, regardless of how unsatisfying or oppressive women might find the relationship. She explained that women "married because it was necessary, in order to survive economically, in order to have children who would not suffer economic deprivation or social ostracism, in order to remain respectable, in order to do what was expected of women."[4]

Harvard professor James Q. Wilson pointed out in *The Marriage Problem* that the universality of marriage depended at least in part on the subordination of women: of limits in their ability to own property, hold jobs, and raise children on their own.[5] Indeed, Wilson emphasized that "underlying the questioning of marriage was a single core event: the slow emancipation of women."[6]

Family stability, in contrast, has long been thought to rest on socializing women to accept submission to men as part of the natural order, inside and outside of marriage.[7] Women have rarely had the ability to control their own sexuality in the absence of male protection. Mimi Alford, a White House intern during the Kennedy presidency, wrote a book almost a half-century later about her affair with John F. Kennedy that provides insight into the pervasive powerlessness of women. A 2012 news story on the book comments that

> As a girl coming of age in the 1950s, Alford was indoctrinated with the idea that women should accommodate whatever was demanded of them. "I think one of the big messages was: "Be quiet. Don't rock the boat," Alford, now 68, tells *Newsweek*. "The expectation was for you to do a good job, to be liked, to be included—not to ruffle anyone's feathers. If there was a job you were given that you didn't like, you did it." She shakes her head with a rueful grimace; clearly, servicing [White House aide David] Powers [with oral sex] fell into that category.[8]

Jackie Kennedy, in turn, during interviews at the time of her husband's death, indicated that "women should find their sense of purpose through their husbands" and that the old style of marriage is "the best."[9] These messages seem almost shocking today, though the Southern Baptist convention has generated controversy as it continues to hold that the husband "has the God-given responsibility to provide for, to protect, and to lead his family" and that a "wife is to submit herself graciously to the servant leadership of her husband."[10] For almost everyone else, marriage today rests on a different set of scripts.

Critics link the dismantling of gendered marriage to the decline of marriage as a universal designed to align mothers' and fathers' efforts on behalf of their children. Yet the authors who make this argument seem to view it in terms of only two possibilities: a traditional model that follows a gendered script that achieves universality by keeping women dependent or a loose association in which two people remain together only so long as it remains convenient for each of them individually.

We believe that there is a third model, one that views the solo breadwinner and full-time homemaker of the traditional model as anachronisms and that regards shared financial and domestic contributions as the foundation for marriage in the post-industrial economy. This new model rests on a new social script: a script that replaces women's dependence on their husbands with spousal interdependence. The new script assumes commensurate contributions, but it does not distinguish between financial and domestic ones. It eliminates mutually exclusive roles assigned entirely by gender, but it does not assume that men's and women's contributions will be the same in form or expenditure of time. Perhaps most critically, though, it assumes joint responsibility—for both the family's finances and any resulting children. In this script, women have finally become fully autonomous adults. Neither Amy nor Lily has been socialized to look the other way in the face of adultery, and they have a greater ability to leave a violent or abusive relationship.[11] And both agree that marrying is worth it only if they meet a man who is capable of making the new marital script work.

Amy and Lily's autonomy comes from their greater ability to participate in the labor market, and that, in turn, requires more flexible partnership roles. Ironically, the very traits that mark the flexibility and exchange necessary to manage a relationship between equals mark the traits sociologists associate with the "deinstitutionalization" of marriage, the move away from marriage as the central, life-lasting adult relationship. Consider the qualities that Andrew Cherlin selected as the hallmark of the "soul mate" model: (1) Self-investment: Each person should develop a fulfilling independent self instead of merely sacrificing oneself to one's partner. (2) Fluid roles: Roles within marriage should be flexible and negotiable. (3) Honest relationships: Communication and openness in confronting problems are essential.[12]

These traits can just as easily characterize part of the change away from rigid and hierarchal gender roles toward a reintegration of women in the modern market economy. For more egalitarian couples, "self-development" is an important part of a dual-earner model. In the old system, investment in women's education beyond the level necessary to attract the right marriage proposal hurt her domestic prospects. In the new system, such investment pays off in terms of both the ability to land a high-status mate *and* improved prospects for marital stability. Moreover, the ability to move across the country, return to school, take time off, or recharge a career is part of what helps successful couples like Amy and Tyler negotiate the demands of ever more competitive marketplaces.

In a similar fashion, negotiable and flexible roles within marriage are a necessary complement to the move toward families where neither party wishes to be relegated to the powerlessness of the homemaker role. The emphasis on "communication and openness" further aids the negotiation of everyday responsibilities—the tradeoffs necessary to determine which spouse needs to work late on short notice while the other picks up Junior from daycare or takes the car to the mechanic. Paul Amato suggests that the inability to negotiate roles that change because of emerging economic opportunities contributes to divorce as much as if not more in the modern era than does the insistence on assigning roles according to something other than gender.[13] Lily is not marrying Carl, after all, because she does not expect him either to be a reliable wage earner or to do his fair share of the housework.

We accordingly see the traits associated with "deinstitutionalizing" marriage as in fact linked to its reinstitutionalization—but only where the men match up with the women well enough to make it work. The new model is an attempt to respond to the fact that today's women enjoy greater employment opportunities than they once did, and their families depend on the income they earn. The new scripts thus require at least a measure of self-development, coordinated and fluid roles, and openness and effective communication. We think of these new "power couples" as a bit like the Dutch soccer teams of the seventies who practiced "total football." The world took notice when tiny Holland made it to the 1974 FIFA World Cup final based on the advantages of their new system. The Dutch replaced the static positions of defender, midfielder or forward with more fluid roles that allowed players to roam all over the field. The new system required more preparation and better fitness. It also required greater communication and adaptability on the field. Not all players were able to make the transition to the new football model. But no one called it "soul mate soccer."

Popular Support and the New Scripts

Tyler and Amy, not unlike the Dutch teams of the seventies, have not just remade the terms of their own relationship. They also reflect a redefinition of marriage that sets the terms for everyone else. The new marital script has two principal components: both partners are expected to retain the capacity for financial independence and to contribute as needed to the family's finances, and both spouses are expected to share responsibility for child care. Over the course of a lifetime, the partners may switch careers, working hours, and cities, but their relationship is expected to be an interdependent one that becomes more closely intertwined as the relationship deepens.

If there is any part of the new marital script that has won close to unanimous support it is the expectation that married mothers will remain in the labor force. After all, the husbands still get their wives' disproportionate contributions to the domestic side of family life and the second income that often is needed to keep the family afloat. Most spouses, though clearly not all, do in fact work outside the home. In 2004–2005, for example, two-thirds of married mothers did so, and by 2010, 71 percent of all mothers with children under eighteen were in the labor market.[14] A 2012 news poll found that only 2 percent of those surveyed disapproved of a married woman working if her husband is capable of supporting her.[15] Sociologists similarly find that husbands have become more supportive of their wives' jobs and that "the labor force participation of wives had become almost universally accepted in American society by the end of the twentieth century."[16] Indeed, young women have so absorbed these expectations that in 2011 a higher percentage of young women (66 percent) than young men (59 percent) between the ages of eighteen and thirty-four rated being successful in a high-paying career or profession high on their list of life priorities, a substantial change since 1997.[17]

These changes mark a wholesale redefinition of the relationship between home and market—the protected domestic sphere of the nineteenth century and women's roles as mistresses of this sphere is gone. Overwhelmingly, families depend on two incomes, and men and women's relationships are affected by women's ability to be self-supporting. The result certainly increases women's autonomy, and the ability to leave a relationship influences women's bargaining power about the terms of the relationships that endure. But this increase in women's autonomy should not be confused with equality or the dismantling (as opposed to the redefinition) of gendered expectations about family life. In fact, only 16 percent of both men and women believe it is best for their young children if the mother works full-time, compared to 70 percent who believe the same about men.[18] Working full-time and caring for children is challenging (we know), and for those who lack the resources to afford high-quality child care, there is a risk that the children will be shortchanged. Nonetheless, despite a rash of media reports heralding an "opt-out" revolution among college-educated women, and despite the fact that women at the highest and lowest ends of the income scale are less likely to work,[19] the likelihood that a mother will remain in the labor market correlates strongly with her education. According to Census Bureau data, only about 26 percent of mothers with a college degree stay home, while more than 40 percent of mothers lacking high school diplomas are not working. College-educated women are more successful than other groups in combining work and family, in part because they tend to have the resources to pay for child care and other help and are more likely to enjoy flexible working conditions.[20] Despite the barriers created by family-unfriendly workplaces and the high cost of childcare, the percentage of women working full-time has increased steadily and has grown even further since the financial crisis of 2007.[21]

The second part of the new marital script, shared parenting, also has become more widely accepted (even though, here again, the reality does not necessarily match the rhetoric). The Radcliffe Public Policy Center conducted a study in 2000 in which 96 percent of the men and women surveyed agreed that fathers and mothers should share *equally* in the caretaking of children.[22] A *USA Today* poll in the nineties put the number at 88 percent; an academic study, at 82 percent.[23] Time surveys show that fathers have in fact increased the amount of time they spend on child care, but the time spent does not yet (and may never) equal that of mothers.[24] Indeed, women still do more unpaid work than men.[25] Moreover, while the number of stay-at-home dads doubled between 2000 and 2012, that means it went from 0.4 percent of all married couples to 0.8 percent; during the same time period, the number of stay-at-home moms increased by more than 0.4 percent, from approximately 20 percent of all married households to approximately 23 percent.[26] Both increases may reflect the tighter job market following the Great Recession, but they also show the entrenched expectation that women will take on more of the domestic responsibilities than men.

Like the acceptance of women working and shared parenting, joint financial responsibility has become increasingly embedded in public expectations of the nature of marriage. All of these attitudes reinforce the dismantling of sharply differentiated gender roles without necessarily eliminating the expectations that successful men will earn more than their wives and that wives will assume primary responsibility for the domestic sphere. Instead, men and women are subject to mixed messages.

Between 1980 and 2000, both husbands and wives did move toward relatively more egalitarian views of the economics of marriage.[27] The biggest shifts for husbands occurred in the beliefs that the "husband should be the main breadwinner" (54 to 30 percent) and that the "husband should earn a larger salary than his wife" (42 to 24 percent).[28] Husbands' share of housework increased during the same period, with husbands reporting an increase from 29 to 39 percent of the total while wives reported a more modest increase in their husbands' share, from 24 to 30 percent.[29] Nonetheless, about a third of the wives reported that their husbands did half or more of the housework, and the number reporting that their husbands did not help at all dropped from 29 to 16 percent.[30] In addition, almost two-thirds of the couples reported equal decision-making in 2000, a significant increase from 1980. Perhaps most strikingly, while husbands were more likely than their wives to report equal decision-making in 1980, by 2000 the differences in perception largely disappeared—almost the same percentage of husbands and wives reported that neither husband nor wife "has the final word" in family matters.[31]

These changes in aspirations help explain Tyler and Amy's attitudes about their relationship—they each believe they have found someone who will be a true partner, not just in bed, but in managing dual careers, children, and finances. If they both remain employed, Tyler is in fact likely to earn more, but over the course of a lifetime they may cycle in and out of different jobs. The fact that they can both earn a good living gives them more security and greater ability to take risks by going back to school or taking a new position that may not last. Lily, in contrast, has confidence in neither Carl's ability to manage similar decisions nor to defer to her judgment in doing so. For Lily and Carl, commitment means sharing losses without the same cushion Amy and Tyler have. Lily and Amy share similar expectations about the meaning of marriage, but they are following different scripts into childbearing and the organization of resources to support children. These scripts institutionalize class differences.

The New Meaning of Gender Inequality

Today's working-class couples like Lily and Carl have children as a result of often relatively brief and primarily sexual relationships. Harvard poverty researchers Kathy Edin and Timothy Nelson, who have done extensive fieldwork on unmarried fatherhood, observe that one of the reasons these relationships are not terribly stable "is the incredible brevity of most unions prior to conception; young disadvantaged couples who have children together may emerge from the euphoria of the delivery room only to find they have astoundingly little in common."[32]

Of course, the same may have been true of couples in the sixties, but the difference is that they were married by the time they got to the delivery room and embedded in a family system that made divorce hard. The gendered terms of the relationship, moreover, not only prescribed distinct roles; they also accorded power in terms of those roles. In those days, the husband could get a job that paid substantially more than the wife could make on her own, and her financial dependence gave her little choice but to defer to the authority that his income and his gender conferred on him. Consider what is happening to today's relationships between similar couples in a very different economy that frequently provides women with more stable employment than men.

Class and the Dual-Earner Model: The Men

The biggest tensions in managing the new roles stem less from managing women's workforce participation than from the continuing importance of employment success to men's self-esteem and the lack of jobs for them. Difficulty

juggling work and family characterizes most dual-earner families, but difficulty managing the husband's role breaks up relationships. Robert Griswold
wrote in 1993 that "breadwinning has remained the great unifying element
in fathers' lives. Its obligations . . . shape their sense of self, manhood and
gender,"[33] an observation that still rings true today. More recent studies confirm that men and women regard male earning capacity as a critical element
of male status and well-being.[34] "Macho" men find it hard to adjust to wives
who earn more than they do; they often help less at home than do men who
are married to women earning less than they do.[35] Because breadwinning is
integral to their identity, men who are struggling to find work or who have
a comparatively low potential for breadwinning are less likely to get married.[36] A young woman might live with a man who doesn't have a steady job
at decent pay, but she is unlikely to marry him.[37] The men in a 2010 study of
young couples agree that "no matter what the gender revolution prescribes, it
is still paramount for men to earn a living to support their families, which also
implies taking a backseat as a caregiver."[38] Although men have substantially
increased their participation in caregiving, relatively few have assumed roles
as full-time homemakers because of the loss of status that entails, and many
men, who may otherwise identify as co-equal, if not primary caretakers, do
not necessarily accept their wives' role as primary breadwinners. The evolution in family roles, in accordance with women's reintegration into market
labor, does not necessarily involve a complete dismantling of gendered family
responsibilities.

While both men and women continue to value the male breadwinning role,
male income and workforce participation increasingly correspond to class. In
1960, class-based differences in labor force participation were barely detect-
able. In 2011, 90 percent of college graduate males were employed in comparison with 76 percent of male high school graduates and 67 percent of high
school dropouts.[39]

The likelihood that the wife earns more than the husband also corresponds
to class. In families with dual earners, the wife earns more than the husband in
70 percent of marriages in the bottom quintile of families in comparison with
34 percent of wives in families with incomes in the top 20 percent.[40]

The men are often unhappy about these arrangements. Greg McFadden,
thirty-nine, is an actor and stay-at-home dad with a six-year-old child. His
wife, Shannon Hummel, thirty-eight, works as a teacher and as artistic director of a Brooklyn dance company. He comments, "I don't think so much about
gender roles, but I do feel angry and helpless because I can't financially support
the family unit. . . . I'm sick of reading these articles and daddy blogs, about
how 'empowered' men are to be caretakers. Ask them how they feel about not
earning a paycheck."[41]

The story of women going it alone—rejecting marriage to the fathers of their children even if the men are willing—is a story of tough, competent women taking charge of their own lives.[42] But it is also a story of male failure, of the men who will never be able to "drive up in a Chevy and take [their] rightful place at the head of the table."[43] The combination of the two, however, does not typically end with an adjustment of male and female roles into more flexible family arrangements. Studies further indicate that as women earn more money, they do less housework but only until the point where they contribute 51 percent of the family income—then they do more, perhaps to shore up their husbands' fragile egos, a nice example of the conflict between the ideologies of equality and gender roles.[44] The statisticians tell us that the husband's loss of a high-paying job together with the homemaker mom's entry into the workplace to compensate is a prescription for divorce rather than the transformation of men into "mediocre house dude[s]."[45] We have seen this story before—in the Moynihan Report, in Charles Murray's work, in the Great Depression—and in the end, it becomes a story of gender distrust rather than remade terms for companionship.[46]

Dual Earners: The Women's Dilemma

While men and women both accept women's workforce participation, in a 2012 poll, approximately one-third of all women said they would prefer to stay home rather than work outside of the home.[47] Other studies find sharp class divisions in the responses. Asked whether it is "much better for everyone involved if the man is the achiever outside the home and the woman takes care of the home and family," Charles Murray reports that in 1980 over 70 percent of low-income whites were answering yes in comparison with roughly 50 percent of affluent whites. Between 1980 and 2010, both groups became less likely to support the traditional model, with 35 percent of the low-income group still supporting traditional marriage compared with less than 20 percent of affluent whites. The most surprising results, however, occurred over the past ten years, during which support for the gendered model *increased* among low-income whites while it continued to fall for high-income couples.[48]

Paul Amato and his colleagues explain the class variations with respect to the appropriate role of women. Between 1980 and 2000, the percentage of wives employed outside the home rose from 58 to 75 percent.[49] Yet during the same period, the percentage of wives who said that they would prefer "no job at all" increased from 25 to 34 percent.[50] Close to half in both surveys reported wanting part-time work. In 2012, a Pew survey found that the percentage of women who wanted to work full-time went back up to 37 percent during the hard times that followed the financial crisis, but half still preferred part-time work.[51]

Amato explains that employment creates greater tensions for working-class wives. The highly educated often want careers and associate employment with high levels of job satisfaction. Working-class wives, on the other hand, are more likely to be employed because their families need the money and less likely to enjoy their jobs. Moreover, with the women at work, someone still needs to take care of the house and the children. Highly educated mothers who invest in their careers and bear children only after they have become valuable to employers have an easier time staying in the labor force. While the most active parents are likely to give up on the gold ring—the career-capping position that includes ultimate power, status, or income—to meet their families' needs,[52] they have less difficulty remaining in the professional positions after the children arrive than do women with supposedly less-demanding jobs. The U.S. Census Bureau reports that almost two-thirds of new mothers with a college degree or higher receive some kind of paid maternity leave compared to less than one-fifth of those without a high school degree. Moreover, women with less than a high school education are four times more likely to be let go during their pregnancies or within twelve weeks after the birth of their first child than are women with a college education.[53]

Working-class women are thus in a bind. They are more likely to have jobs with no flexibility and no future. Couples with two high incomes use the additional revenue to hire others to assist, but in lower-income families, income that wives earn goes to pay for rent, groceries, and the children's birthday presents. The sociologists suggest that work conflicts more with family life for less-educated women because these couples are less able "to afford services, such as high quality child care, take-out meals, and home cleaning, that help to ease the family burdens associated with dual employment."[54] The result for the wives who worked primarily for money rather than for career satisfaction was greater marital tension[55]—scholars find that marital satisfaction increases when neither spouse cleans the toilet.[56]

The situation worsens even more if the man loses his job altogether. Newsweek reported, relying on the American Time Use Survey, that "laid-off men tend to do less—not more—housework, eating up their extra hours snacking, sleeping, and channel surfing (which might be why the Cartoon Network, whose audience has grown by 10 percent during the downturn, is now running more ads for refrigerator repair school)."[57] Those who place their emphasis on culture insist that neither employment nor wages fully explains the changing American family, and they're right. The causal mechanism that ties the changing economy to the family is the impact on behavior. Laid-off men, who used to make $40 an hour and can find only lower-status positions paying $15 per hour, often do work fewer hours and compensate by doing less, not more housework. Indeed, researchers find that even for those who continue to work, lower levels of job security and the job stress that exists in workplaces experiencing layoffs lead to greater alcohol consumption and higher levels of depression, ultimately producing worse physical health and more workplace injuries.[58] More critically, the employees who live through downsizing are also bad partners—unemployed men are right behind alcoholics and drug addicts as the group most likely to beat their female partners.[59]

Employment instability thus combines with low wages to increase family tensions. The instability often triggers breakups and persuades a higher percentage of the men cycling in and out of dead end jobs to give up on work altogether. At the same time, greater economic inequality tends to correlate with higher rates of chronic unemployment, imprisonment, and violence,[60] increasing the percentage of men whom women regard as unsuitable partners. The women in these communities consequently become warier of men more generally, reinforcing gender distrust and cultural acceptance of shorter-term, more contingent relationships.

The result, as we will explain in the next section, sets up a clash with the new interdependent model of marriage. Working-class women who take on market labor, which they resent, and still perform the majority of homemaking and child care, lose patience with laid-off or slacker husbands. The semi-employed men in turn often take themselves out of the marriage market, either because they believe they cannot live up to the provider role or because the poor behavior that often accompanies the loss of status persuades the women in their lives that marriage is not a good risk.

Bethenny, the young woman in Virginia Beach, explains why she has no interest in marrying the father of her child this way: "Calvin would just mean one less granola bar for the two of us."[61]

* * *

Gender ratios exacerbate all of these factors. Tyler is a good guy with a promising future. He thought that going to law school would better his life, and he recognizes that Amy is in a different class from his other girlfriends. Amy, in turn, chose Tyler to marry because she trusts him and recognizes that he respects her. Carl, in contrast, isn't sure marriage is for him. He likes Lily but feels he cannot live up to her expectations. Once she got pregnant, she put increasing demands on him. She expects him to contribute financially, to help with child care. He sees few prospects for landing the type of job that would make her proud of him and little inclination to spend his days running errands for her. Lily, after all, slept with Carl because she lacks better choices, but she won't seriously consider a longer-term commitment unless he steps up. She is limited in her ability to find men who can meet her expectations, but she does have the power to control access to their child. Carl knows he can always find another woman, and the new women he meets—the ones without children— expect much less from him. They are out for a good time, and so is he. That is an expectation he can live up to.

SECTION III

LEGALIZING INEQUALITY: THE CLASS DIVIDE IN THE MEANING OF FAMILY LAW

When the family changes, the law often helps us make sense of these changes. Sometimes it does so directly—the rules change and couples must adjust to the legal changes. Other times, the law stays the same, but changing social norms alter the meaning of the legal rules. And sometimes, both the law and the norms change simultaneously in ways that reinforce each other. Popular culture often uses the dramatic setting of a trial to capture these shifts. Indeed, we identify the relationship between divorce and changing gender roles with a movie from our youth. We vividly remember *Kramer v. Kramer*, a 1979 film that showed how husband Ted Kramer (played by Dustin Hoffman) struggled to raise his son after his wife, Joanna (played by Meryl Streep), walked out on them. Ted helped us understand what it meant to be a working parent, that fathers too could "mother," and that engaged fathers feared custody presumptions designed to favor women. Even though Meryl Streep remained largely offstage, the subtext of the movie engaged women's changing roles.

Writer Heather Havrilesky reminisces that *Kramer v. Kramer* appeared in the theaters around the same time as her own parents' divorce.[1] Her mother, too, had left, "not so much to find herself (like Meryl Streep's character) as to find a job, something my father (like Dustin Hoffman's Ted Kramer) had strictly forbidden her to do." Heather writes that as a nine-year-old she "didn't understand the larger context of the movie . . . or the fact that, by leaving her kid, Joanna was essentially trying to avoid suicide."[2] She did realize then, however, that the movie, with its focus on divorce, court hearings, and changing parental roles provided a mirror of her own life.

Real-life judges in that time period grappled with the dark side of changing norms that made it possible for women to enter the workforce and for men to play more substantial roles in their children's lives. The courtroom dramas and the decisions that resolved them tried to make sense of the changes. The law ultimately incorporated the insights that came from these cases into new standards guiding shared custody between mothers and fathers. The legal command that identified children's interests with the continuing involvement of both parents following the breakup of a relationship helped the rest of us deal with what was happening around us and forge new norms about family behavior.

The problem for the changes we describe in this book is that large parts of the country, rather than grappling with a common set of changes, are moving in opposite directions. In the seventies, divorce rates rose for everyone. Some (the twenty-something college students of that era) embraced the underlying changes in gender roles. And some rebelled (giving birth to the Moral Majority and the rise of Christian political activism).[3] Some groups experienced the changes earlier: African-American family norms changed more in the fifties and sixties and the white working class would shift more in the eighties and nineties. Yet, with time, women's workforce participation and men's involvement in child care increased for almost everyone. The sympathetic Ted in *Kramer v. Kramer* would look like an ogre if he told his wife today that she couldn't get a job, and Joanna wouldn't need to leave her children to find fulfillment through a career. Moreover, dual-earner white-collar executives and blue-collar machinists with primary caretaker wives both expect to share custody if they end up in court. The law reflected and reinforced the changes of the seventies.[4]

The law cannot do so for the changes of today. It can't because our two couples, Tyler and Amy and Carl and Lily, are moving in different directions. It's not just that they are living different lives, though they are. It's not just that they have different expectations about their relationships, though they do. It is that their emerging norms, the scripts that allow them to make sense of their lives, are moving further apart. For Tyler and Amy, the law still mirrors their experiences. After all, they still married before having children. If, after a few years of marriage and the birth of their children Amy and Tyler were to part, the legal proceedings would be predictable. As a husband, Tyler would automatically be treated as a father. The parties would be expected to split their joint assets. Alimony would be rare, particularly after a marriage of less than ten years. The judge would ask them to list any children born during the marriage and before the court would approve a divorce, it would make arrangements for both parents to continue to be involved in the children's lives. Even if the separation occurred because of substance abuse or an affair, any effort to block the other parent's involvement would incur judicial wrath. When Tyler proposed and Amy accepted, they each did so because they believed that they had found someone they trusted to be a permanent part of their children's lives. If they were to part, the law would reflect that commitment they made to each other as an on-going obligation. Their lives, their relationships, even their disagreements, largely follow the new marital script, one that underlies and is given voice in formal family law decisions.

The same is not true for Lily and Carl. To be sure, the formal law that would be applied to them is the same—but it would apply only if Carl establishes paternity and gets himself to court. Lily, proud of her independence, has no duty to identify Carl as the biological father or to list him on the birth certificate. If after their child is born Carl wants to see the baby, Lily would have no obligation to let him do so in the absence of a court order. Ironically, Carl is most likely to obtain such a court order if Lily gets fed up with him and seeks child support. Then, Lily would be required to cooperate with establishing paternity and Carl would find it easier to insist on seeing the child. Lily, of course, is unlikely to file such an action if she doesn't believe that Carl has any money—a paycheck deduction is much easier to enforce than collection of a judgment—or if she really wants him out of her and the child's life.

In the meantime, Carl is most likely to have any relationship with the child at all only if he keeps Lily happy—contributing financially, offering to help with child care, and staying out of the rest of her life. Lily in turn already distrusts Carl and she will be even less likely to welcome his involvement if she starts to see another man. The courts, if they were ever invited to weigh in on the developments, would disapprove—both of Carl's unreliability and Lily's failure to facilitate his involvement as a father. Yet, Carl and Lily would find it difficult to enforce any court order that resulted, and they have little reason to respect legal decisions that do not reflect their own experiences of family life. Amy and Tyler internalize expectations that childrearing involves two committed parents and plan their lives in order to realize those expectations—the same expectations that underlie court orders; Lily and Carl, however much they admire two-parent arrangements, do not see any way to get there and do not confuse their relationship with the commitments Tyler and Amy have made to each other.

In this section, we explain how legal developments—and the continuing gender wars—contribute to the class divide in family life. The new elite model of family law, which reflects Tyler and Amy's understandings about their own relationship, makes marriage that much more unattractive for Lily and Carl. They achieve a measure of autonomy, an ability to realize relationships on terms of their choosing by staying away from the law. For Lily, the easiest way to keep Carl at bay is to arrange her family to minimize legal involvement. She would be far more inclined to involve Carl if he and the law were to recognize the reality of her parenting: she earns the more reliable income, takes primary responsibility for the child, and calls the shots. To be constructive rather than threatening, anyone else's involvement needs to be on her terms, and so long as the law, which treats both parents as equals, fails to recognize that, she will try to minimize the role it plays in her relationships.

If Amy and Tyler, Lily and Carl end up in court, the subtext of their fights would be the continuing efforts of the courts to rebalance gender power in an era in which women enjoy substantial power to enter and leave relationships but not necessarily forge unions on terms of their choosing. In Amy and Tyler's case, the law reflects the influence of the fathers' rights movement—Tyler would have custodial rights equal to Amy's even if Amy provided more of the care during the marriage. And Tyler is unlikely to pay support, even if his income is substantially higher than Amy's. These results make Amy a bit warier about commitment (and even more reluctant to give up a good job) but less likely to initiate divorce once she does commit. On the other hand, Lily and Carl's relationship is most likely to end not with a court decree, but a decision to stay out of court. This result reaffirms Lily's independence (she is not likely to get much support from Carl in any event), but for Carl it means accepting Lily's control of access to his child. For couples in between, the couples who are most likely to marry, divorce, remarry, and cohabit, the legal picture is murkier and the fight over the relative power of men and women within relationships continues unabated.

We conclude this section with an examination of one of the most divisive issues in family law—an issue at the core of the continuing tensions at the heart of the family. That issue deals with the relationship between sex, procreation, and parenting. When a woman sleeps with a man and has his child, does she owe him the opportunity to assume a parental role? Amy and Tyler enter marriage having made a commitment to parent jointly before they have children. Lily is inclined to limit Carl's participation in their daughter's life, and she is likely to be able to do so.

The most contentious cases are those in which multiple men vie for the title of "father" and have enough resources to have their cases heard. Resolution of these cases, whether they respect women's choices or object to them, will be central to reforging family terms for the increasingly unstable center of American families. Recasting of the bargains, however, cannot occur until there is agreement on the starting point—biology (and thus sex) or function (and thus assumption of a parental role)—for the determination of parenthood. Yet that starting point remains the center of ideological as well as class division. This chapter will explore the role of the law in an era of cultural division. First, it will explain how family law *has* redefined the norms for the college-educated upper third, making marriage more attractive for couples like Tyler and Amy. Second, it will acknowledge the role of the law in continuing to stigmatize those dependent on public benefits. Third, it will show that Lily enjoys greater autonomy when she avoids the law altogether and how the legal system often willingly looks the other way as she does. Finally, this section will explore the unresolved gender conflict that most affects the middle third of the American public. If Lily later marries her new boyfriend Andy and wants him to adopt her child, what should happen to Carl?

9

The Law: Rewriting the Marital Script

The interaction between family law and changing social norms is a two-way street. When norms are stable and uncontested, we don't spend much time thinking about the underlying law; a century ago, for example, few questioned the legal definition of marriage as a relationship between a man and a woman. As norms change, however, attitudes about appropriate behavior clash with the old rules. The process of working through these conflicts, of articulating reasons for legal conclusions, of debating alternative positions before legislatures and the electorate, contributes not only to legal change but also to the emergence of new, broadly shared cultural norms.

In today's world, it is hard to imagine the creation of a new set of broadly shared cultural norms about family life that could apply to both Tyler and Amy and Carl and Lily. Part of the problem is ideological division. We explained in our previous book, *Red Families v. Blue Families*, why the family has become a site of such an intense cultural divide. The "blue" world of big cities, tech centers, and the coasts has embraced a new model of family life. It invests in both men and women, sees family formation as the product of mutual adult decisions, and counsels care in the decision to have a child. The more traditional "red" world of the heartland, rural areas, and the South continues to be more religious. It places greater emphasis on marriage, views family formation at younger ages as appropriate, and public acceptance of non-marital sexuality as objectionable.

The great irony, of course, is that neither group has much trouble with Tyler and Amy. If the two attended law school in Baton Rouge, Louisiana, they might marry a few years earlier, attend church together, and have more children—in part because they could afford them more easily. If the two moved to New York after graduation, they might wait even longer to have children as they work more hours, commute longer distances, and see less of each other. In both places, however, their family lives—their willingness to marry, to stay married, and to be involved in their children's lives—might not differ all that much. What would change are the sports teams they root for and how they explain the values they hold. And therein lies the rub. For while red and blue college graduates live similar lives, what they would prescribe for Carl and Lily differs markedly, and these differences block the emergence of agreement on the law and more widely shared underlying norms.

The blue world would say that both Amy and Lily should be able to form relationships on terms of their choosing. Amy has chosen to wait and to have children with Tyler. More power to her. Lily should be encouraged to make similarly responsible choices through greater empowerment. Comprehensive sex education should start in high school, and contraception and abortion should be freely available. If Lily chooses to have a child, support should be available to help her stay in school and stay employed. If she welcomes Carl—or another partner—into the child's life, she should be encouraged to make the relationship between adult and child stable and ongoing. Above all, state, community, and families should work together to create the circumstances necessary for the child to flourish. If that happens, Lily's and Amy's children are likely to enjoy similar futures.

The red world would applaud Amy and decry Lily's behavior. It would encourage her to find the inner strength necessary to turn her life around. To the extent that Lily struggles financially, the red world would see that as the necessary consequence of a poor decision. To the extent that Lily needs assistance, Carl would be the first choice as a source of support. Providing too much assistance to cushion the impact of Lily and Carl's failings can only, on this perspective, encourage more irresponsible behavior. Their child's suffering is a necessary prerequisite to a better world.

The ideological differences between red and blue might not prevent agreement in a world where most people shared the same assumptions about family life. When Tyler moved from the Midwest to the East Coast, he found that expectations about what made for a satisfying career or a comfortable income changed, but his beliefs about the kind of person he wanted to marry and what made for a good family life did not. And, if ideological divisions did not exist, the courts might find a way to reconcile Lily and Carl's understandings with Tyler and Amy's, either encouraging Lily's autonomy or Carl's authority (and need for responsibility). With both ideological division and class divergence, however, the courts face a daunting task. Both red and blue courts reflect the new elite views about marriage and relationships; they accordingly do not fully understand or approve of Carl and Lily's family decisions. But they fundamentally disagree on how to re-create the pathways to a better life. In the process of these divisions, which include both ideology and class, the law offers little guidance for those who lack the ability to hold good jobs or to provide a stable future for their children.

The Systems of Family Law

If families do go to court, the vast majority of litigants will settle their disputes on their own. As law professors Robert Mnookin and Lewis Kornhauser explained in a classic 1979 article, family law typically does not impose order from above but, rather, provides a framework for adult bargains.[5] They called this "bargaining in the shadow of the law." Couples choose whether to litigate, settle, or stay away from court with an eye on how they expect the court to rule in the event of a final judicial determination. If Amy or Tyler decided to divorce, for example, any settlement they reach outside of court is likely to reflect the fact that a litigated resolution would impose an equal division of the property they accumulated during the marriage and shared custody of any children they might have. Their estimation of the likely judicial outcome affects their bargaining power in private negotiations and, indeed, influences their behavior during marriage. Tyler, after all, having lived through his parents' contentious divorce, is determined to remain involved in his children's lives whether Amy encourages his involvement or not.

In an equally classic set of articles, however, Jacobus tenBroek observed in the early sixties that the law does not act uniformly through such privately controlled litigation. Instead, it acts through "a dual system of family law."[6] In an era in which marriage determined family regularity, the law recognized two family types: a privileged marital family of husband and wife and the children born into that union and a much smaller group of single-parent families produced by death, divorce, or "illegitimate" births.[7] tenBroek observed that the law for the former arose overwhelmingly from private actions arising at divorce, the type of private actions that Mnookin and Kornhauser also described. In these actions, private parties initiate the court action, control the terms of the litigation, and retain the power to settle on terms of their choosing. In an era when the relatively small number of single parents overwhelmingly faced impoverishment, the law, by contrast, imposed order on those outside of a marital unit through a public system of welfare benefits.

The dual system still exists, although the middle—which has historically shared the expectations of the elite—is now caught in between. Over the past quarter-century, a changing society has remade the terms of intimate bargains, first granting women greater independence and expanded participation in the paid labor market and, then, with increased male income inequality, altering their expectations about the terms of intimate relationships.

While institutions such as marriage and parenthood may retain the same basic meaning across different social classes, individual ability to reach the stepping stones into marriage has changed, and decisions about the appropriate ways to organize family life vary by class. As a result, the legal oversight of family formation and dissolution, property division at divorce, and child support and custody arrangements do not necessarily rest on the implicit terms of individual relationships or on what the individuals themselves agree would be a fair resolution of family conflicts. Instead, legal rulings reflect the assumptions of the upper third, reject the contingent arrangements of the marginalized groups who have given up on marriage altogether, and fail to institutionalize the still emerging practices of the middle.

The divergence between top and bottom, between private litigants and those in state-initiated paternity suits, plays out in accordance with the continuing power of the dual system of family law. What is new is the diverging family structures of the American middle—a group too large to be stigmatized or marginalized yet too powerless to ensure that its circumstances command the understandings of the courts. This group still marries more frequently than the poor—and divorces and remarries.[8] This middle group, unlike the marginalized, often does end up in court. It has the ability to bring private actions for divorce, custody, and support, but it does not share in the new elite system that has brought greater stability to family relationships. Rather than assist this group in the articulation of emerging norms that might guide family understandings, the courts fracture in resolving their cases—because at the core of the changing relationships in Middle America is a shift in gender power by women who neither voluntary accede to male preferences nor have the ability to forge new bargains on terms of their choosing.

The new center of American family life involves couples who have not yet given up on each other but who have become increasingly unlikely to make their relationships work. Reconstructing a family law for the center ultimately involves resolution of a deeply divisive issue: does a woman's act of having sex with a man, becoming pregnant, and bearing a child involve an obligation to facilitate his co-equal status as a parent even if he fails to meet the mother's needs or contribute equally to the child's well-being?

Development of the New Marital Script

The new model of marriage and divorce views both the solo breadwinner and the permanent homemaker of the traditional model as anachronisms and regards shared financial and domestic contributions as the foundation for marriage in the post-industrial economy. It implicitly rests on the new social script that replaces specialized marital roles, including women's dependence on their husbands, with spousal interdependence. The new script assumes commensurate contributions, but it does not distinguish between financial and domestic ones. It eliminates mutually exclusive roles assigned entirely by gender, even though it does not assume that men and women's contributions will be the same in form or require the same expenditure of time. Perhaps most critically, though, it assumes joint responsibility—for the family's finances and for any resulting children. In this script, women have finally become fully autonomous adults. It is in some respects the culmination of the last generation's dreams of equality.

The problem, however, is that while egalitarian family law works for couples who in fact make relatively equal contributions to their relationships, it is a bad deal for women at the bottom if it links them to less reliable men, and it muddles the emergence of alternative bargains that might better serve the middle. The model assumes marriage between relative equals who enter their unions with either established earnings or high measures of the trust and the flexibility to manage changing financial fortunes. Hanna Rosin calls the new relationships "see-saw" marriages in which husbands and wives trade bread-winning and homemaking roles in order to take advantage of their mutual opportunities[9]. This new model often describes the unions of the college-educated third, who defer marriage until they achieve emotional maturity and financial independence. These couples, particularly if they marry before their careers are fully established, may trade roles as they move to different cities, work different hours, or acquire additional degrees. It also describes the emerging model for committed gay and lesbian relationships as they deal with the division of responsibilities in the absence of rigid gender roles. It works less well for working-class couples, who accurately see the ideal marriage as requiring a level of financial stability they may never achieve. And with marriage as an increasingly unattractive option for working-class women, the law seeks to impose fathers on wary mothers through child custody and support laws. What family law reforms have failed to acknowledge or shape is the implicit terms of the new lower- and working-class relationships.

Dismantling the Breadwinner/Homemaker Marriage

The legal revolution that dismantled the traditional family is rooted in women's changing status.[10] The re-creation in the seventies of a middle-class family model designed to meet the needs of the post-industrial economy reintegrated home and market and gave women greater independence by ending the omnipresent threat of pregnancy for the sexually active and the formal barriers to women's labor market access. Changes in the status of women set the stage for family law reforms articulating a new marital model.

First, the much-heralded sex revolution resulted in legal guarantees for women's reproductive autonomy. Supreme Court decisions legalized not only abortion but access to contraception. As late as 1965, states such as Connecticut outlawed contraception altogether, even for use by married women within their own homes, and it wasn't until seven years later that the Supreme Court expanded contraceptive access to single adults.[11] In 1970, Congress enacted Title X, which authorized federal family planning funds: it passed unanimously in the Senate and with only thirty-two no votes in the House. Republican President Richard Nixon signed it into law.[12] By the end of the seventies, the Supreme Court extended the right to contraception to minors, holding that it was "irrational" to subject women to the threat of childbirth in order to limit sexuality to marriage.[13] As discussed in chapter 4, in a few short years after abortion and the pill became available, birth rates plummeted, adoptions dropped in half from all-time highs, and the percentage of college-graduate women who were married by the age of twenty-three dropped from roughly fifty to thirty percent. The need to usher women into early marriage to contain pregnancy dramatically weakened, and later marriage became economically important to the creation of the new middle-class model.[14]

Second, the women's movement advocated laws that guaranteed women greater access to educational and workforce equality.[15] While the wage gender gap remains, particularly at the top, anti-discrimination laws together with the expansion of the service sector jobs women have traditionally held ensure women relatively greater access to education and jobs. As noted earlier, women's income has steadily improved over the past half-century, while prospects have declined for every group of men except for the top group of college graduates.[16] The result eliminates much of the coercion that channeled young couples into marriage and kept them there. Women have much greater ability not just to make it on their own as young adults, but also to leave unhappy marriages with children in tow.[17]

Third, the changing status of women set the stage for wholesale family law reforms. Pressure had been building for at least a half a century for divorce reform. When divorce required proving some kind of fault—adultery or "cruelty," for example—couples made a mockery of the law's stringency through divorce mills, based on manufactured proof of fault (in New York, aspiring actresses could be hired to pose with unhappy husbands, supplying proof of adultery) or surreptitious trips to liberal jurisdictions like Nevada.[18] As a practical matter, a couple could, effectively, agree to a divorce if they were willing to lie to the court or go elsewhere. The result brought the law and the divorce courts into disrepute.

When reform finally came, it helped modernize family law across the country, as between 1965 and 1985 every state liberalized the grounds for divorce (Ronald Reagan signed the first pure no-fault divorce statute in California in 1969) and laid the foundation for more equal distribution of property (states could award any property acquired during marriage, regardless of who held title). These reforms came as women's roles within intact marriages also changed. Legally and practically, the husband no longer controlled everything that happened in the home (Naomi's mother-in-law used to greet her husband, when he returned from work, by announcing—without any irony—"The Lord and Master has returned.")[19]

The new marriage model overwhelmingly disadvantaged long-term home-makers who were more dependent on their husbands and less able to prevent divorce or negotiate favorable settlements. The rise in divorce rates thus contributed to the dismantling of the traditional model that emphasized homemaking as a lifelong calling.[20] Women's greater workforce participation, however, combined with the legal changes to make it easier for younger women to walk out on abusive, selfish, or simply insensitive men. Today, almost two-thirds of those initiating divorce are women, often the mothers of young children.[21]

Once the adjustment to the new laws occurred, divorce rates evened out between states with unilateral divorce laws and those with more restrictive terms.[22] Liberalized divorce grounds tend to prompt longer (and presumably more sober) searches for the right mate rather than more starry-eyed soul mate matches; couples in unilateral divorce states tend to marry later than couples in more restrictive states.[23] Moreover, economists Betsey Stephenson and Justin Wolfers report that divorce reform is associated with a 30 percent decline in domestic violence and a significant drop in women's suicide rates.[24] Stephenson concludes that in pure no-fault states couples are less likely to finance their spouse's further education and women are more likely to remain employed during marriage.[25] All of these findings suggest that family changes altered the implicit marital bargain and, at least initially, did so in a way that enhanced women's negotiating power.

Taken together, these changes also dismantled support for wage-earner/homemaker marriages. The ability to divorce without fault increased the vulnerability of dependent wives, and accordingly they became more likely to invest in their own earning capacity. At the same time, the ability to leave gave women more power within marriage and greater protection from violence. As woman have obtained greater power to leave, husbands have become less likely to feel that they can abuse their wives and get away with it. What Andrew Cherlin describes as spouses' increasing search for "personal fulfillment"[26] may also be described as women's ability to object to domestic violence, infidelity, and more prosaic forms of unhappiness.

Dual-Earner Marriage: The New Legal Script

Women's greater equality in turn prompted reforms to a family law code premised on women's intrinsic dependence. At the core of the new marital ideal is *interdependence*—marriage has become an institution that encourages the parties to commingle their assets, share responsibility and decision-making, and create intertwined lives. Simultaneously, however, it expects both spouses to retain their capacity for financial independence after a spilt. These critical changes in family law—equal division of property, support limited to long-term homemakers, and shared parenting—command widespread support. And they correspond to the clearest part of a new marital script. In that script, dual labor market participation is the default norm; full-time homemaker status is a minority arrangement that follows from secure financial and marital status.

The new system began in the nineteenth century, with the Married Women's Property Acts. Before the Acts, husbands owned everything during marriage, including their wives' separate property.[27] At divorce, the women got back their own assets, but the husbands kept everything titled in their names. Since they were typically the only breadwinners, this might mean the house, the bank accounts, and everything acquired over the course of the marriage.[28] The Married Women's Acts gave women control of their own property during marriage, and in some states, they also gave the courts the power to distribute the assets the couples accumulated over the course of the marriage.[29] The trend toward treating assets accumulated over the course of the marriage as subject to division at divorce accelerated with the adoption of no-fault divorce in the last third of the twentieth century. By 1993, every common law state had adopted some version of this system. In practice, if not always by black-letter law, these regimes typically divide the couples' property fifty-fifty at divorce.[30] While the courts retain discretion to consider the parties' respective contributions to the marriage, most courts do not make individualized determinations—they simply presume equal contributions, recognizing marriage as "an egalitarian legal community."[31] The new property regime is an interdependent one.

At the same time that the courts moved toward equal division of accumulated property they also became less inclined to award long-term support following divorce. Historically, alimony served as a form of specific performance of the marital duty of support. That is, men understood that when they married they took on an obligation to support their wives. Under older English law, a couple could not divorce but they could get a legal separation. The husband would ordinarily be obliged to support the wife, but he still got to keep all of the property, his and hers. When the law finally recognized the ability to get a full divorce, that is, a dissolution of the union that allowed the couple to remarry, it also gave the courts the power to order support. That support was something men owed women, not a mutual obligation, and the courts could take into account who was at fault for the breakup in determining amounts.[32]

No-fault divorce made the idea of alimony as ongoing support for an "innocent" wife anachronistic. Women's greater economic independence weakened the gendered claims for alimony, though it wasn't until 1979 that the U.S. Supreme Court struck down an Alabama law that explicitly permitted only women to receive alimony. Divorce reformers sought not just to make divorce easier, but to "end, as far as possible, all personal and economic ties between the spouses" and encourage "both spouses . . . [to] become equal and independent social and economic actors."[33]

Today the rules are gender-neutral. And in many states, fault is irrelevant. Some courts justify spousal support based on the theory that a homemaker spouse lost out on her own career opportunities; others base it on the premise that the parties should share in the marital standard of living for a transitional period after the breakup. Nonetheless, most commentators agree that spousal support is one of the least coherent parts of family law.[34] As a practical matter, this makes it unpredictable, divisive, and increasingly rare.[35]

Consequently, while marriage presumes *interdependence*, the ability to leave marriage carries with it an obligation to retain the capacity for financial *independence*. For example, Kristen and Derek Thomas Berger, a Michigan couple, divorced after ten years of marriage because of Derek's affair. At the time of the divorce in 2008, he made $120,000 per year, and she worked part-time, earning $22,000 per year. The court awarded one year of alimony to Kristen, who had degrees in nursing and dance, to assist in the transition after the divorce. At least as tellingly, in determining the property and child support awards the court took into account Kristen's ability to earn substantially more than her part-time job currently paid. The opinion commented that "it is unreasonable and unprincipled to place nearly 100 percent of the financial responsibility for the children on defendant under these circumstances." The court emphasized that the wife was the one who chose to divorce and that she sought custody of the children. The judge added that "she has a great deal of education and is more than capable of helping to financially support her children. She should not be treated so differently from defendant simply because she wishes at this point to be essentially a stay-at-home mother."[36]

The court expressed a clear expectation that caretaking did not prevent full-time labor force participation and that both parties were expected to contribute to the children's (and their own) financial needs. (And, in direct contrast to the old fault-based system, which would have blamed the divorce on the husband's affair, the court seems to punish the wife for seeking the divorce while it rejects punishing the husband for his infidelity.) Young women with children, who initiate the majority of divorces, rely on their husbands at their peril.[37]

Typical divorcing couples have few assets. And it is rare to award long-term support after a marriage of a few years. Today, the mothers of young children are expected to be economically independent upon divorce, and if they are not so already, then "rehabilitative" alimony gives them a relatively short time in which to do so.[38] While some courts retain the ability to award support after longer marriages, it is difficult to predict in advance whether they will do so.[39] Terry Martin Hekker, a columnist who had celebrated the joys of the homemaker role, provides a particularly poignant example. She describes being handed divorce papers in 2006 after forty years of marriage and comments that

> The judge had awarded me alimony that was less than I was used to getting for household expenses, and now I had to use that money to pay bills I'd never seen before: mortgage, taxes, insurance and car payments. And that princely sum was awarded for only four years, the judge suggesting that I go for job training when I turned 67. Not only was I unprepared for divorce itself, I was utterly lacking in skills to deal with the brutal aftermath.[40]

She insists she would still have married the same man and had children, but she would have resumed her education and begun a career after the youngest started school. The generation coming of age today has gotten the message. Hekker reports that her niece recently insisted that she would remain employed after marriage because she "didn't want to end up like Aunt Terry."

Shared Parenting

In some ways, however, the most dramatic change in family law has been the transition from a legal presumption that mothers should receive custody of children of tender years to a preference for shared parenting.[41] While the commitment to marriage need no longer be permanent—precisely because the husband no longer assumes responsibility for a wife's dependence—the commitment to parenthood is both shared and lasting. A high percentage of the public wants to see fathers more involved in their children's lives. Indeed, when Massachusetts put a proposition on the ballot mandating shared custody, it passed by a vote of 532,716 to 106,521.[42] A study of prospective jurors also found that when researchers presented the jurors with vignettes describing fathers and mothers fighting over custody, the jurors favored granting the child equal time with each parent to a greater degree than the other options.[43]

This makes child support the most important financial division to occur in modern divorce. Divorcing couples are more likely to have children than property, and child support often lasts much longer than alimony. In the traditional gendered system, when courts would routinely award custody of children of "tender years" to the mother, child support awards were typically meager. Instead, they were often tacked onto the spousal support award, sometimes as an afterthought. This meant, as a practical matter, that a young mother who committed adultery or walked out on a less than ogre-like husband could not count on a generous award, whatever the label. After the no-fault revolution, however, child support awards increased in frequency, consistency, and generosity. Had the maternal presumption remained in place, a young woman would be able to leave her husband with the children in tow and receive support through the children's age of majority.[44] As one of us has written elsewhere, this dynamic has made custody battles "ground zero in the gender wars."[45]

The easiest way for an ex-husband to lower child support awards was to seek a greater share of the children's time. And just as more egalitarian gender rules justified the "clean break" at divorce, so too did they justify increased emphasis on shared parenting. The young wife could walk out on the sometimes devastated husband, but she could no longer expect both the children and support.[46]

Law professor Martha Fineman has devoted more than one volume to the change in the law that has weakened women's bargaining position at divorce, particularly through the change from a maternal presumption to more facially neutral rules.[47] Indeed, as law professor Margaret Brinig has shown in an empirical study, women are more likely to file for divorce than men, but they are comparatively less likely to do so if they are unsure they will secure custody of the children.[48]

Shared custody has accordingly become a divorce deterrent for women, and most states have adopted presumptions that favor the continued involvement of both parents following divorce. In accordance with the new legal doctrines, fathers have fought for increasing shares of the children's time both because engaged husbands want the continuing contact and because, with mandatory child-support formulas, the easiest way for a higher-earning parent to lower child support awards is to seek more time with the child.[49] Just as the disappearance of long-term spousal support has reinforced the emphasis on dual incomes, the emphasis on shared custody has encouraged male participation in childrearing.

Elite Expectations about Marriage

These legal changes, though designed to assist the practical role of the courts in overseeing divorce, give voice to expectations about ongoing marriages. The changes in property division, custody, spousal and child support dismantled support for the homemaker role. Marriage changes from a relationship

premised on female dependence to one grounded in principles of interdependence as men and women are both expected to contribute to their families' needs while retaining their individual capacities for independence and
growth. The new system further enshrines parenthood as a mutually assumed
and permanent obligation that survives the adult relationship and includes not
only joint responsibilities to their children but also a duty to foster the involvement of the other parent.

The new model does not just express utopian marital aspirations; it also reinforces the remade gender exchange that underlies the marriages that endure.
The most successful men fear commitment to a woman who, upon divorce, can
claim their greater resources and fear a loss of access to children with whom
they have bonded.[50] Legal changes give these men greater protection within
marriage; the law limits their liability for support and gives them greater control over the children. These changes make marriage less attractive to women,
but elite women can be choosier in a marriage market that favors them.

The legal changes that make it harder for women to initiate divorce and
the change in gender ratios that makes it easier for elite women to find men
worth marrying reinforce the new elite system that keeps men with assets and
women with children married to involved partners. So, too, does the conclusion that high conflict marriages and painful divorces do not serve children's
interests.[51] These changes also reinforce Tyler and Amy's and Carl and Lily's
conviction that marriage is a legal institution not to be entered into lightly. The
new gender bargain on which these relatively egalitarian norms rests does not
reflect working-class realities. The identification of marriage with interdependence and sharing not only fails to express the implicit terms of working-class
relationships; it ties it to a script that assumes two adults making comparable,
if not always equal, investments in the relationship. For those who can manage
neither parity of contribution nor unqualified trust, it makes marriage an impossible bargain.

Imposing Equality on the Unequal

> [He says,] "I'm not working, thems not my kids." If you're not mar-
> ried to the person you say, "They not yours? Hit the door then!" But
> if you're married to them, you say, "Hit the door please?" You know,
> you start nagging and they say, "I'm not going anywhere." . . . You're
> stuck with them just like all the other people stuck with their mar-
> riage and stuff. . . . I think it's best not to get married. Unless you're
> pretty sure that person's going to take care of you.[52]
>
> Divorced mother of four in Chicago, 1987

Amber Strader, 27, was in an on-and-off relationship with a clerk
at Sears a few years ago when she found herself pregnant. A former

nursing student who now tends bar, Ms. Strader said her boyfriend
was so dependent that she had to buy his cigarettes. Marrying him
never entered her mind. "It was like living with another kid," she
said.[53]

Single mother in Lorain, Ohio, 2013

[There's] a lot of legal ramifications when you consider marriage,
bro. See Michael Jordan? He's about to get half taken from him. It's
crazy.[54]

DeMarcus, a twenty-year-old from New York who might
otherwise have married for religious reasons, 2010

Men have long distrusted sharing principles in marriage. Basketball superstar
Michael Jordan's divorce from his first wife is reported to have cost him $168
million,[55] and when Facebook founder Mark Zuckerberg married his long-
time girlfriend (who was enrolled in medical school), pundits commented that
the two *must* have had a prenup, as he would be a fool to risk losing to divorce
the fortune *he* created.

The really new development, however, is the increase in the number of
women who also distrust the legal entanglements of marriage. Twenty-five
years ago, the wariness toward marriage that Bill Wilson documented in the
divorced mother of four living in Chicago was an outlier thought typical of
the African-American underclass and no one else. Today, single white mothers like Lily or Amber echo the same sentiments. Skepticism about whether
marriage is a good thing has become typical of those outside of the top third of
American men and women;[56] although they still want to marry, they are wary
of someone who will take advantage of them. The legal regulation of the family
complicates things further—mandated sharing of assets, children, and lives
can be a threat to those whose lives are unstable and unequal.

The new marital scripts, reflected in the relationships of the upper third and
the legal decisions that give voice to the understanding that underlie them,
simply do not work for much of the rest of the country. The college-educated
third expects dual-earner arrangements, yet it also accepts the interdependence that accompanies modern marriage. It is simultaneously more flexible
in its attitudes toward gender roles and more likely to pair a woman with a
significant income with a man who makes more than she does. The working
class has preferred more traditional and gendered roles but has become less
likely to realize them.

Sociologist Kathleen Gerson found that the coming generation of young
men and women overwhelmingly accepts an egalitarian ideal, but both men
and women feel vulnerable. Women fear being trapped in an unhappy marriage or being deserted by an unfaithful spouse. They accordingly treat work
"as essential to their survival." Men, in contrast, worry more about meeting

the demands of the workplace. They continue to see employment success as central to their self-esteem. If they cannot manage the time demands necessary for the new egalitarian ideal, they want a partner on whom they can rely to manage the home front. Yet poorer men, much like wealthier men, would ideally prefer to marry a woman who carries her own weight financially as well as domestically and is also a "soul mate."[57] Both men and women see the caretaking role as contributing to vulnerability, and both fear spouses who expect to be supported.[58]

While the younger generation as a whole therefore buys into a dual-earner model, they differ in what they see as their fallback options. African-American women top the charts in saying that the alternative is reliance on their individual incomes; the number who opt for self-reliance over a primary breadwinner/primary caretaker division of labor is close to 100 percent in comparison with 80 percent of working-class and poor women of any race and 58 percent of whites (42 percent chose a neo-traditional family arrangement).[59] Gerson quotes a young woman named Angela who explains that she trusted that her marriage would work and that it did not matter if she stayed employed. But she still emphasized that you never know what is going to happen. "I feel like I always have to be ready if my husband leaves me."[60]

This emphasis on independence makes the interdependence of marriage threatening. Marriage *is* a commitment to support and care for the other spouse. Even among privileged women, the threat that a laid-off man might seek spousal support, along with the children and half of the savings, is enough to keep many women away from marriage and the potential of divorce court. A divorce blog observes, under the heading "It's More Frequent Than You Think," that "some litigators find that their female clients had no idea what was ahead when they chose to support their husbands financially and emotionally through most of the marriage out of a sense of obligation and kindness. The idea that they would be asked to continue to do so after the dissolution never occurred to them."[61] Women with lower incomes may not especially fear alimony orders, but they do understand that marriage may require supporting a man from their own meager earnings and a divorce would produce an "equal" division of "their" assets.

These class-based differences in roles affect family stability—and the perceived fairness of divorce outcomes. Law professor Kathy Baker observes that as families have become more diverse, and as scholars call for more contextual understandings of family obligations, the courts have been moving in the opposite direction. Family law provides little guidance on the moral disputes that underlie family breakups, and the courts increasingly impose "formulaic, uniform, and status based" results.[62] Young couples *should* be wary of submitting themselves to a legal system that both lacks agreement on a normative core that fits their lives and fails to recognize that its formulaic default answers do not address the increasing chasm created by class.

Consider what would happen to Bethenny and Calvin, the young couple with a child in Virginia Beach, if they married and divorced. Hanna Rosin described how Calvin talked about the jobs he had had and lost and the ones he was trying to get. Rosin's conclusion was that what Bethenny said she wanted was a traditional model of marriage but that she recognized

> Calvin was not going to drive up in a Chevy and take his rightful place at the head of the table one day soon, because Bethenny was already occupying it, not to mention making the monthly payments on the mortgage, the kitchen renovation, and her own used car. Bethenny was doing too much but she was making it work, and she had her freedom. Why would she want to give all that up?[63]

If their lives continued along the paths they were on at the time of the interview, Bethenny would be the primary wage earner and the primary caretaker. Calvin might provide her with some much needed help with their daughter, and he could contribute financially, if not always reliably. Yet although Calvin could not assume the "head of the family" role, neither was he likely to settle into a subordinate one. If they married and then split, Bethenny could reasonably expect that the courts would equally divide the house, the car, and the bank accounts acquired during the marriage, even if Bethenny had been making the monthly payments on the house, paid for the car out of her earnings, and had put aside the savings for the child's education. The property that comes out of her earnings is "marital," and the courts do not itemize the parties' respective contributions, instead characterizing whatever is acquired during the marriage as a jointly owned total.

In addition, in a changing sign of the times, Calvin might claim joint custody of the child and, if Bethenny continued to earn more than he did, spousal or child support. In fact, young couples like Bethenny and Calvin almost never have to pay spousal support—they simply don't make enough to split their earnings and still have enough left over to take care of a child—but Bethenny could easily be expected to pay child support if Calvin obtained a custody order giving him a significant share of the child's time. Indeed, if Bethenny were to marry Calvin, continue her nursing career, and find that ten years later she was doing well while he was unemployed, Calvin could well receive primary custody and substantial support. The very thought may be enough to persuade her not to marry in the first place. No surprise that Bethenny is not holding her breath in anticipation of a romantic marriage proposal from a man who cannot hold his own in either a financial or a nurturing role.

A 2013 study confirmed that it is not gender per se, but the class-based concerns of those with more to lose that breeds skepticism about commitment. Among those with at least some college, 68 percent of women versus 46 percent of men expect to marry their current partner. The men at this age are on their way up and do not necessarily see their current partners as assets. In contrast, among eighteen- to twenty-nine-year-olds without a high school diploma, 67 percent of men versus 47 percent of women say they expect to marry their current partner. In this group, it is the women who are wary of commitment to men whose promise does not match their own. In both groups, the reluctance to commit increases with the disparities in circumstances.[64] These results correspond to the sex ratio predictions. Ambitious men compete for a smaller pool of similar women; they are wary of women who will not advance their larger ambitions. The women who do not have access to the pool of "high quality" men are reluctant to commit to the remaining group who offer neither reliable incomes nor reliable behavior. The wariness of the elite men and less elite women reflects a shared understanding of what marriage entails: commitment to share one's children and resources. They both conclude that marriage is worth it only when they find a partner who makes that commitment worthwhile.[65]

*   *   *

Legally, the new interdependent ideal makes it appropriate to assume equal ownership of the assets the couple acquires over the course of a marriage, to encourage the parents to share custody after a breakup, and to ask the employed to aid their homemaker spouses. These provisions, however, do not necessarily correspond to the implicit terms Calvin and Bethenny might use to describe their relationship. Their lives do not correspond to the new marital ideal, and the law does not recognize terms that might more accurately describe the exchange between them. Cohabitation—and contingent relationships with few presumed legal ties between adults—may give them a better way to deal with the uncertainty about the direction their relationship will take.

The couples Kathy Edin observes in her study of Philadelphia women describe how they handle these relationships. In a community in which marriage has largely disappeared, the couples still trust the sanctity of the institution. As one woman explained, "I don't believe in divorce, that's why none of the women in my family are married."[66] Other women observed that they weren't ready to get married until they could afford the white picket fence, until the bills were paid *every* month. Men, similarly, were seeking a life partner to whom they could relate as an equal.[67] The men and women did not marry *because* they associated marriage with the new model of equal, interdependent, and shared parenting, not because they rejected it. When Edin asked both mothers and fathers about why, even though they weren't married, they still had children, they responded by letting her know that children gave meaning to their lives. Implicit in the answer was the conclusion that there was no point in waiting for an ideal that they might never realize.

In managing parenting, the unmarried women focus on transactions: the conception of a child, contributions to the house, a night out on the town. The transactions do not necessarily involve long-term commitment, and they certainly do not involve interdependence. Some of the couples manage intermediate relationships. They cohabit. They plan for the future. They even talk of marriage. But the relationship remains contingent. Edin describes one woman, burned by her prior boyfriend's infidelity, who has been together with a new boyfriend for a while. But she does not plan to marry him until she has income and assets of her own. She wants her own stability first. Securing her independence means that she can protect herself if he proves untrustworthy. The prospect of intermingling her life, her finances, her children's future with another requires an exchange she does not trust. His promises are meaningless. His income and behavior are unreliable. She explains that she will not marry now because she does not know "what's going to happen."[68] For the men, as Edin and Timothy Nelson found in a follow-up study, pregnancy and the birth of a baby do make them want to shape up for the sake of the child. Nonetheless, all too often the men become discouraged by unstable employment and obstacles posed by the mother of their children to their assumption of a paternal role.[69]

Commitment requires emotional maturity and confidence about the future.[70] Without that confidence, the dominant legal and cultural model for intimate relationships cannot work.

Shared Parenting: Egalitarian, Patriarchal, or Both?

Women *have* achieved a measure of independence. With greater wariness of interdependent relationships, both men and women can now go it alone. They can live by themselves, chose an intimate partner with no strings attached, live with roommates of their choice, or move back in with mom and dad. Marriage is optional. The same degree of autonomy does not extend to parenting. Although the stigma surrounding single motherhood is dissolving, the law has long sought to protect children's interests by locking in two-parent responsibility for them. The question, however, is where do the two parents come from; that is, which two parents does the law recognize, and how much choice do the adults enjoy in securing parental recognition for their partners?

For conventional couples the answer has not changed all that much. They get married, have biological children, and share responsibility for these children within stable relationships. Recent changes have less to do with family form than with the process of getting to parenthood. Gay or straight, single or partnered, married or unmarried, the financially secure who plan ahead try to build in legal certainty for their parenting relationships of choice. Once they do, both law and modern norms expect them to share custody and support obligations in accordance with the legal designation of parenthood.

The poor, in contrast, have all but given up on marriage. The non-marital birth rate for African-American high school dropouts is 96 percent, and for the poorest of every race relationships have become ever more unstable and multi-partner fertility common.[1] In these circumstances, a monolithic two-parent model is meaningless. Instead, adult partnerships form, dissolve, and reform without any necessary long-term relationship to the assumption of parenting roles. Sociologists who have studied gender distrust among low-income women find that almost all express wariness about men.[2] One study discusses a woman named Angie, who rejected marriage out of hand but who sought

partners who could help her buy things for her house and her children or provide care for her elderly ailing parents. Angie explains:

> I ain't looking for that love shit," she declared. "I need a man to help
> me for a minute, and he's out of my house after that. You see, we got
> to have an understanding. I get what I need, he gets what he needs,
> and it's a done deal. I don't need to know nothin' about how he gets
> what he gets [e.g., acquiring financial resources]. I don't want to know
> nothin' that particular. I'm in control. I run this shit up in here.[3]

By contrast, the study found that those in longer-term relationships have developed "integrated trust." The women who formed these relationships "tended
to enter relationships gradually, placing high value on evidence of their partner's ability to be trusted across multiple domains over time." Angie and even
the group that manages integrated trust undertake parenting through contingent relationships. Harvard's Kathy Edin and Timothy Nelson found similar
mistrust among *men* of the mothers of their children.[4] These relationships are
built on short-term, transactional exchanges about parenting that may or may
not ever develop into anything more permanent. The partners have made no
long-term commitment to each other, and their continued mutual involvement with the child depends on successfully negotiating the relationships with
the other adult. To the extent that the law intrudes into these relationships, it
tends to impose parental status on the basis of biology in ways that may bear
little relationship to the underlying parenting norms.

In between is a working class in transition. Working-class conceptions take
place the same way they did in the old days—in the context of courtships that
tend to be "sexual and brief."[5] These couples may not know each other terribly
well at the time of the child's birth. In another era, they would have married,
and the dependent mother would have stayed with the father so long as he
brought home a paycheck. He could still go out with the boys, and she might
rely more on her relatives than her husband to care for the children, but his
ties to the family would have depended on the strength of his relationship to
her.[6] If he refused to marry her or if they divorced, his relationship to the child
would typically end. In some parts of the country today, these couples still
marry, but those who do also divorce and remarry at high rates. In other parts
of the country, the couples cohabit instead and marry only if they secure employment and a measure of financial stability.[7]

The law fractures as it deals with this group in transition. The courts do not
agree on which legal norms apply to these families, and the norms they do apply
do not necessarily prompt shared understandings in the families subject to the
norms about how to order their own behavior or structure their relationships

with others. The upper third and the middle third, for example, differ in the likelihood of an unplanned pregnancy, assumptions about whether or not such a pregnancy should end in abortion, and norms about the importance of including a non-residential father in the child's life.[8] For the middle third, marriage, if it happens, may or may not involve two biological parents, and the states differ in their willingness to recognize the husband as a legal parent on the basis of marriage alone. Couples who marry, divorce, and remarry may involve one, two, three, or more adults in parenting relationships with the child without agreement among the adults (or the states) as to who counts as a parent and who does not. The term *stepparent* describes an increasingly impor-tant social category; yet, even within the same jurisdiction, courts vary in the extent to which a person designated as a stepparent has legal rights or respon-sibilities with respect to a child.[9] In responding to these changes, class diver-gence combines with ideological division to block the emergence of consensus solutions. "Red" jurisdictions tend to favor doctrines that police women's sex-uality while "blue" jurisdictions are more likely to focus on family function. For the top third, both approaches result in new marital bargains that reinforce interdependence and shared parenting. The middle is caught in the middle of these cultural and class disputes. Consequently, as this chapter analyzes par-enthood, it begins with the law that has facilitated a family law transition to norms of shared responsibility within a committed relationship. It then turns to the more contingent relationships outside of the upper third, where the pre-liminary question of who constitutes a parent is contested, caught up in the process of rebalancing gender power.

Law, Parental Bargains, and Shared Custody

The ever-increasing emphasis on joint custody offers an example of the role of the law in reinforcing the expectations of the upper third. As noted in chapter 8, shared parenting is an integral component to the new marital script for the upper third. Men are expected to play a larger role in their children's lives, and while women are freer to leave unhappy relationships, they no longer control access to the child in the process of doing so. Consider, for example, the case of the Renauds of Vermont.[10] The father and mother shared parenting, with the mother arranging her schedule so that she could take Fridays off to be with the child and the father taking the child to and from day care and also visiting him there during the day. The marriage ended when the child was two, and the father told the mother he was having an affair with a co-worker and wanted a divorce. In another era, the mother would have received sole custody, and the court would have identified the child's interests with the mother's ability to care for him. Today, however, the mother's ability to retain custody depends on her willingness to support the father's involvement. In this case, the mother lost confidence in the father's caregiving because of a combination of concerns about the child's sunburns and worsening diaper rash and suspicions of sexual abuse. After investigators concluded that the abuse allegations could not be substantiated, the court awarded the father, who had not seen the child in months, visitation equal to fifty percent of the child's time and conditioned the mother's continuing custody on her cooperation in repairing the child's relationship with the father.[11]

This case is typical of those that ushered in the new regime. It treats the father's infidelity as irrelevant and views the mother's loss of confidence in the father's behavior as evidence of her lack of support for his parenting rights. Her efforts to limit the father's involvement with the child, with suspicions but not proof of actual harm, threatened her continued custody in spite of her much stronger bond with the child. The courts' insistence on dual parenting, whether or not the mother's concerns about the child's safety were justified, involves a rebalancing of gender authority. In the old regime, a committed mother could not leave a marriage without risking losing custody, but her husband's affair would itself have been grounds to question the adequacy of his parenting. Under the new regime, either party can leave without the courts passing judgment, and joint custody provisions effectively give greater weight to the continued involvement of both parents than to the strength of the child's bond with each parent or the comparative ability of each parent to provide for the needs of the child. The result both encourages and protects fathers' investment in children and counterbalances women's greater autonomy by restricting their ability to leave and take the children with them. Where women enjoy a choice of acceptable partners, it encourages care in the selection of a mate, commitment to the relationship's longevity, and construction of the bridges necessary to make two-parent investment feasible.[12]

Joint custody, which was initially greeted by many courts with some hostility, became increasingly accepted in almost all states, and many jurisdictions have adopted "friendly parent" provisions that support the award of custody to the parent who will best facilitate the continuing involvement of the other parent. Indeed, fathers' rights groups have pressed for a presumption in favor of an equal division of the child's time in all divorces.[13] And joint custody has won widespread public support.[14] In two innovative studies discussed in a 2011 article, the participants strongly preferred joint custody, irrespective of each parent's involvement with the child during the marriage and the existence of conflict between the parents during the divorce. Study participants expressed significant reservations only when one of the parents had instigated the conflict.[15]

Yet, the ability to secure shared custody is an indication of individual male income and power. Joint custody appears to be more common among higher-income parents, parents whose incomes are roughly similar, and cases in which the father has legal representation.[16] A Wisconsin study of custody actions in 2006–2007 found that shared custody, though increasing to approximately half of the custody awards at divorce in the state, ranged from 10 percent of the cases in which the family's income was under $25,000 a year or less to over 60 percent of the cases reporting family income over $150,000 per year.[17] The study, which looked only at court data, did not indicate whether the results reflected the parties' preferences, the incentive for higher income parents to seek more of the child's time, wealthier fathers' greater access to legal representation, or all of the above. Shared custody in paternity adjudications (where the parents never married) remains rarer, though over the ten-year period ending in 2007, sole custody by the mother fell from 97.7 to 90.9 percent of the awards[18] and from 91.9 to 80.9 percent of the cases in which men had voluntarily acknowledged paternity through state-provided procedures.[19] For the upper third, where shared custody is increasingly the norm, the change in custody standards increases the importance of the search for the right partner. Spouses need to be able to coordinate not only dual workforce participation but responsibility for the child as well.

Choosing Fathers: Voluntary Paternity and Unmarried Couples

For college graduates, two-parent relationships arise from planning. They remain likely to marry before they give birth; disputes over paternity are relatively rare. And married parents expect to assume joint responsibility for their children. For others, the determination not only of custody but of parental status may be a product of Jacobus tenBroek's public welfare system.

That system increasingly seeks to ensure two parents for every child without necessarily tying the results to marriage or cohabitation. Federal law encourages the state to streamline paternity procedures.[20] The primary means for doing so is a Voluntary Acknowledgment of Paternity (VAP) signed in the hospital by the mother and father attesting to the man's paternal status. The acknowledgment does not require a paternity test, however, so a mother could lie or could collude with a man who knew he was not the biological father to establish legal parentage.[21]

So long as the mothers and fathers control the process, a VAP provides an effective way to recognize the legal status of unmarried parents.[22] Unlike the court-based adjudications they replace, VAPs require the cooperation of the mother and putative father. They typically are signed either in the hospital or soon after the birth, often the high point of intensity and closeness for the unmarried parents. The majority of these fathers are living with the mothers at the time of birth, and most are willing, if not eager, to acknowledge their relationship to the child. Fragile Families and other studies have found that the more closely involved the parents are prior to the birth, the more likely they are to sign a VAP and to do so within the first month of the child's life.[23] Moreover, at the time of the birth, the men expect to contribute to their children's lives, and those fathers who sign a VAP are more likely to pay support and to stay involved in the child's life if the mother and father part. For unmarried couples, therefore, the paternity procedure corresponds to the couples' expectations about their relationships.

The VAP confirms something the couple is saying to the world: we have had a baby together. Yet acknowledgment of paternity does not necessarily come with fully developed expectations about the parents' continuing relationship. Although the majority of couples who sign VAPs are living together at the time of the birth, they have not made a commitment to each other. If the couples part, as the majority do, there is no legal change in their relationship, unless the mother either seeks public benefits or sues the father for support. If she takes such actions, of course, the father has a basis to seek custody, and in many jurisdictions he may be able to obtain joint custody or substantial visitation even if his involvement with the child has been limited up until the time of the court order.[24] In fact, as the Wisconsin study shows, the likelihood that the father will do so correlates closely with his income.

Imposed Paternity: Child Support Enforcement and the Negation of Private Bargains

At the time tenBroek wrote of a "dual system" of family law, those caught up in the public welfare system were single women who sought support from the expanded welfare state of the sixties. At the core of the system was a central dilemma: women taking care of children on their own were indubitably in need of assistance, yet unless they were widows, the very fact of single parenthood defied the marriage system designed to address the dependence associated with childrearing.[25] The system accordingly stigmatized the available benefits and conditioned them on the mother's cooperation with the state in establishing paternity and securing child support. The ne're-do-well men who presumably had seduced the women and now failed to marry the mothers or support the children were seen as the culprits.[26] The federal system, driven by efforts to minimize costs, has produced a much greater degree of national standardization in paternity establishment and child-support enforcement than in other areas of family law. Indeed, June once defended the Department of Health and Human Services in a case challenging Georgia paternity law.

In 1980, the only way to establish the legal parenthood of an unmarried father in Georgia was for the mother to swear out a criminal arrest warrant in forni- cation and bastardy. It took the prospect of a federal cutoff of welfare benefits to the state to prompt the Georgia legislature to adopt a civil paternity system. Georgia's desire to punish unmarried sexuality gave way to its interest in re- ceiving more federal funds.[27]

Since the sixties, the stigma on single parenthood has waned, but the unpop- ularity of such benefits has not. Clinton-era welfare reform cut cash benefits but provided health care for poor children and subsidized day care important to the mothers' ability to remain in the workforce.[28] What welfare reform did not do, however, was improve the relationships between mothers and fathers. And it could not do so, in part, because while it modernized women's roles, its view of men remained rooted in an older, traditional, gendered model of family relationships. Congressional proponents characterized welfare reform as a measure intended to address "the crisis" in "out-of-wedlock birth" and the first three legislative findings of the 1996 welfare reform act state that: "(1) Marriage is the foundation of a successful society. (2) Marriage is an es- sential institution of a successful society, which promotes the interests of chil- dren. (3) Promotion of responsible fatherhood and motherhood is integral to successful child rearing and the well-being of children."[29] Yet welfare reform has done little to increase marriage rates and significantly more to undermine the parental relationships that do exist.

Unmarried fathers' relationships with their children occur in the context of the contingent relationships they negotiate with the mothers, and every study indicates that the father's continuing relationship with his children depends on how he manages the relationship with the mother. While in other eras, unmar- ried mothers (particularly white mothers) typically did not have a continuing relationship with the father, the more recent studies indicate that at the time of the child's birth, 80 percent of unwed parents are romantically involved, and 50 percent live together.[30] Indeed, even fathers who were no longer with the mothers tended to remain in touch with their children for some period of time. By the fifth year, 40 percent of children had had no contact with their fathers in the past one to two years, 40 percent saw their fathers regularly, and 20 percent were somewhere in between. Black non-Hispanic men were more likely to have maintained contact with their children, to have seen them in the past month, and to have seen them frequently.[31]

The mother's willingness to allow access to the child often depends on the father's willingness to pay for things the child needs, cooperate with the mother, and assist when she needs help.[32] Maureen Waller, like other sociolo- gists, found that the mothers valued fathers' contributions not solely by the dollar value of support contributed, but by such non-economic factors as role modeling.[33] Outside of the formal child custody system, men saw their children's mothers as controlling access. As Kathryn Edin and Timothy Nelson note: "unwed childbearing seems to offer mom, and not dad, all the power: 'it's her way or the highway,' in the words of one father."[34] Indeed, women encourage the greater involvement of the men who contribute to their children, either financially or otherwise, and then often form new relationships if the father does not remain involved.[35]

The formal system of child-support enforcement interferes with these ongoing bargains.[36] The Fragile Families studies found that 24 percent of non-resident fathers paid formal cash support, whereas 35 percent paid cash informally and 44 percent provided in-kind support. Moreover, the dollar value of the informal support was worth more than the formal support. Yet almost no fathers (6 percent) paid both. The mothers accordingly preferred the informal support, which tended to be greater in value, could go directly to the child, and could be tailored to what the father could afford and when he was able to contribute.[37] These informal contributions were more common among couples who had separated recently and tended to diminish over time.[38] Insistence on formal child-support enforcement, on the other hand, tended to alienate the fathers. They often became angry at the mothers. And they became less likely to see the mothers or contribute informally to the children.[39]

Bargains and the Invisible Middle

The middle differs from the top third in that parents are less likely to formalize their relationships, but it differs from the bottom third in that parents are less likely to seek state benefits. Without public benefits, the custodial parents are not compelled to seek support. Many of the non-resident parents, as a Fragile Families study indicates, contribute informally to their children, particularly during the period right after the birth or the breakup. A significant percentage of this group, however, elects a different type of bargain: the custodial parent does not seek support, and the non-resident parent does not see the child. Courts will not often ratify such agreements, even among the elite.[40] Michael Jackson could not persuade the courts to accept his agreement with his ex-wife, Debbie Rowe, for example, to terminate Rowe's parental status in exchange for a release in responsibility for support.[41] Working-class couples more frequently effect such bargains informally—no one seeks support, and the other parent disappears from the child's life.

These results are most common where the parents have never married and never had a close relationship, and they are also likely to occur as more men and women engage in multi-partner childbearing. Studies from the eighties, for example, found that those who sought child-support orders were more likely to have had a longer term relationship with the father.[42] Census data from 2009 provide a detailed look at the reasons custodial parents do not seek child-support orders. Those reasons are listed in the following order:

Other parent provides what he or she can	34.4 percent
Did not feel the need to make legal	32.1 percent
Other parent could not afford to pay	29.2 percent
Did not want other parent to pay	21.2 percent
Child stays with other parent part-time	17.7 percent
Could not locate	16.8 percent
Did not want to have contact with other parent	16.7 percent[43]

These results describe a number of different types of relationships. In the cases where the custodial parent reports that the other parent "provides what he or she can," "did not feel the need to make it legal," or the "child stays with other parent part-time," the parents may have an ongoing relationship of some kind and have worked out support on a cooperative basis. Where the parents do not want contact with the other parent or could not locate the other parent, on the other hand, the relationship may have broken down and the parents may have decided they do not want further involvement with each other.

Consider, for example, the likely denouement of the relationship between Bristol Palin, who became pregnant at seventeen, and her high school sweet-heart, Levi Johnston, who continue to replay their continuing conflicts over the blogosphere. While the celebrity of Bristol's mother, Sarah, as a former vice presidential candidate and governor of Alaska, put the family in an elite class of its own, high school dropouts Levi and Bristol are more typical of the struggling middle of the American spectrum. When their relationship broke down not long after the birth of their son, Tripp, Bristol (who had not yet appeared on *Dancing with the Stars*) worked to provide for their son on her own and sued Levi for support.[44] Levi responded by seeking custody.[45] The litigation became intense, with the parties exchanging charges in the press as well as in court and including attacks on other family members. Levi's contact with the child increased after he and Bristol reconciled; they returned to fighting, however, after Bristol discovered that Levi had fathered another child. On-line tabloids reported (confirmed by Bristol's attorney) that Levi was delinquent in child support, owing tens of thousands in back payments.[46] Despite a court order giving him shared custody, he also rarely sees his son. We frequently see such disputes end with the mother's decision to give up on collecting support in exchange for never having to deal with the father again and the father's acceptance of the implicit bargain as a good one. For this group, autonomy means staying out of court.

The Marital Presumption and Gender Warfare: The Failure of Family Law

We started our discussion of the role of law in family transformation with the idea that the law influences the family primarily by establishing and reinforcing the understandings that underlie institutions such as marriage and parenthood. We have shown how these understandings reinforce the decisions of the upper third to marry while the bottom third, accepting the same definition of marriage, decides it is an institution whose expectations they cannot meet.

In the middle, however, there is less ability than in the upper third to forge satisfactory bargains that take couples into marriage and keep them there, but unlike the bottom, this group has yet to give up on the institution altogether. The middle is accordingly more likely than the other two groups to marry, divorce, cohabit, and marry again, raising children in the context of shifting relationships. At the heart of these new relationships, however, is the question of who calls the shots and on what terms. For the upper third, the choice of a spouse is the choice of a parenting partner, while for the bottom, women often see the fathers as a threat to the children's well-being, and the act of having the child is not an unequivocal commitment to include that person in the child's life. In the middle, this is the subject of a fight. Women in the middle, like the top and the bottom, enjoy increased decision-making power. Men in the middle have more power than the men at the bottom to impose their terms on relationships but not as much as the men at the top to forge deals on terms women find agreeable. The muddle in the middle is therefore a matter of gender power, an issue on the fault lines of the culture wars. The ability of men and women whose children do not receive public benefits to walk away from each other reflects an invisible rebalancing of relationships—the custodial parent acquires freedom from the involvement (and potential control) of the other parent and gives up all support.

The far more visible battle, however, involves those parents who want involvement and are willing to fight to get it. In the custody context, the law is settled: shared custody is available for the asking, and its occurrence tends to be a reflection of a non-custodial parent's willingness to seek it. If paternity is in doubt, however, the selection of the man who counts as a legal parent is a matter of power and of shifting gender norms. Both class and comparative gender power frame the choice of a parent.

The Marital Presumption

In the old days, the marital presumption effected an understood bargain: a woman needed a man to be able to properly raise her children, and the man who committed to the woman through marriage would be the one to receive recognition as a parent. The relationship between marriage and parenthood rested on an implicit bargain. A man who wanted recognition as the father of a child needed to marry the mother. If he refused to do so, he forfeited any right to a paternal role. At the same time, a man who stepped to the fore and married a pregnant woman or stayed married to a woman he knew had "strayed" would be rewarded. The law, through an almost irrebuttable presumption that the husband had fathered a child born into the marriage, would affirm his paternal status and his authority as head of the household. For those couples in the muddled middle, who marry, divorce, have a child with someone else, and marry again, the most intense fights involve the determination of parenthood.

Today, paternity can be established with certainty, so the marital presumption no longer serves to block destructive (and easily manufactured) inquiries into the wife's fidelity. And the relationships, marital or biological, may not necessarily last. Instead, continuing recognition of the marital presumption effectively allows the mother to choose who the father will be. If she stays involved with her husband, then the marital presumption closes in to protect the husband's identification as the father. If, on the other hand, the mother leaves her husband and the child is not born into a marital relationship, biology is likely to determine parenthood. In the era in which the marital presumption arose, a pregnant woman had little real choice in the matter. She needed to secure a father's involvement to be able to raise her child successfully. She could accordingly be expected to accept a betrothal to the child's father, if he offered one, or, as a practical matter, to be grateful to a husband who agreed to forgive her infidelity. Once married, she had little ability to divorce and much to lose from any claim that the husband had not fathered the child.

With reliable paternity testing and the disappearance of much of the stigma associated with women's sexuality, the meaning of the marital presumption has been transformed. Women no longer need to marry or stay married merely because they are pregnant, and in part because of women's greater independence, paternity no longer depends on a man's willingness to marry. Instead, the continued importance of the marital presumption becomes an issue of gender balance, and on this issue the courts provide little guidance—at least at the national level.

The Supreme Court and the Missed Opportunity for Legal Engagement

For those of us who have taught family law for decades, it induces a measure of nostalgia to remember that at one time the U.S. Supreme Court led the modernization of family law, and it did so in the context of cases that involved working-class couples. The cases that dismantled the relationship between marriage and paternity began in 1972 with *Stanley v. Illinois*.[47] Peter Stanley had lived on and off for eighteen years with Joan, the mother of his three children. When she died, the privileging of marriage was so absolute that the state of Illinois treated Stanley's biological children as parentless rather than recognize an unmarried man as a father. The children were placed in foster care. It took a Supreme Court decision for Stanley to acquire standing to object (and to assert a right to the public benefits that came with the children).[48] The Court found that an unmarried father who lived with and supported his children had a constitutional right to try for recognition; the state could no longer base recognition on marriage—or gender—alone. The Court's evolving paternity jurisprudence in subsequent cases[49]—*Quilloin v. Walcott*,[50] *Caban v. Mohammed*,[51] and *Lehr v. Robertson*[52]—suggested that the Court would accord constitutional protection to those fathers who stepped forward to accept responsibility for the child. It appeared that the Court was crafting a functional definition of parenthood that protected the relationships fathers established with their children inside or outside of marriage. The unresolved issue was whether the mother had an obligation to allow the biological father— or any other man—the opportunity to do so.[53]

In 1989, *Michael H. v. Gerald D.* brought the Supreme Court's role in fashioning new family understandings to an effective halt. The case challenged the constitutionality of the marital presumption when the mother and her husband used it to exclude a biological father who had played a role in the child's life. Carole, an international model, bore the child, Victoria, while married to Gerald, a French oil company executive. Blood tests established a 98 percent likelihood that Michael was the biological father, and Victoria called him "Daddy." She and Carole lived with Michael for three months in St. Thomas and for another eight months in California.[54] About the time Victoria turned three, Carole cut off Victoria's relationship with Michael.[55] By the time the case reached the Supreme Court, Gerald and Carole had moved to New York and had two additional children. Victoria had not seen Michael in the intervening five years.[56]

The Supreme Court had the opportunity to complete the articulation of new standards for paternity it had begun in *Stanley*. No justice opined that biology alone provided a constitutional basis for recognition of paternity.[57] Instead, eight of the justices recognized the importance of protecting extant family relationships. They differed, however, on the importance of marriage as an institution versus the recognition of functional parenting relationships, and they differed on the factual question of whether Michael, Carole, and Victoria had ever established enough of a "unitary family"[58] to bar the state from recognizing Gerald, Carole, and Victoria's family instead.[59] Justice Brennan's dissent emphasized that Michael had lived with Carole and Victoria, supported them, acknowledged the child as his own, and sought to continue the relationship. All he lacked was marriage.[60]

In his opinion, by contrast, Justice Scalia, cared more about freezing the meaning of the Constitution in the eighteenth century than the role of the law in developing new norms. He mockingly responded to Justice Brennan that the "unitary" traditional family unit accorded constitutional significance could not be "stretched so far as to include the relationship established between a married woman, her lover, and their child, during a 3-month sojourn in St. Thomas, or during a subsequent 8-month period when, if he happened to be in Los Angeles, he stayed with her and the child."[61]

This discussion—and the competing characterizations of the facts—go to the heart of what makes a modern family and the power balance between men and women. Carole chose to have a child with Michael and to allow him to develop a relationship with Victoria. When that relationship soured, she and Gerald continued their marriage and had additional children. The case raised the issue of what it takes to establish a unitary family and whether a child might benefit from contact with multiple adults playing parental roles. Yet Scalia's plurality opinion relegated these questions to a footnote.

Instead, Scalia's opinion simultaneously disapproved of Carole's sexual behavior and affirmed her choice of Gerald over Michael as Victoria's father. The divided Court upheld the constitutionality of California's marital presumption statute, a statute ensuring that once Carole and Gerald decided to stay together, Michael had no way under state law to establish any relationship with Victoria. The result removed the Court from further consideration of the changing nature of family roles and shut down what had been a vigorous debate among the justices.

Controlling Women

Like the Court, the states have split dramatically on the role of marriage versus biology versus function. Their dispute, however, rests on the issue Scalia failed to acknowledge—women's greater ability to determine the structure of fragile families. At the core of this dispute is a cultural one. Some states effectively hold that when a woman sleeps with a man she consents to his custodial rights to any resulting child. Others accord the mother great ability to encourage or block a parental relationship with a second parent but then protect the resulting family relationship if the mother changes her mind. A third group continues to emphasize the importance of marriage but with difficulty explaining the meaning of marriage absent explicit acknowledgment of the role of gender in the distribution of power.

Two-thirds of the states today reject the marital presumption, but they rarely do so in ways that acknowledge the relationship between their decisions and the impact on gender bargains.[62] Perhaps the most explicit—and intriguing—explanation of this position came from Texas. In a 1993 opinion, the state's highest court observed that the problem with the marital presumption is it "leave[s] this determination of the child's best interest and the definition of family, itself, exclusively to the biological mother."[63] The court rejected a distinction that might depend on which man the mother allowed to develop a relationship with the child and instead ruled that a man's genes could establish his parental standing, regardless of the wishes of the mother or the role of her husband in caring for the child.[64]

Similarly, in other states the marital presumption gives way when the courts conclude that it gives too much power to what they see as undeserving women. In Kentucky, for example, the highest court in the state opined in 2008 that the determination of paternity "is squarely about the legal status of marriage.... The severely wounded institution of marriage in Kentucky surely protects the parties from unwanted interlopers claiming parenthood of a child conceived and born during their coverture."[65] Yet, a mere three years later, the Kentucky court reversed itself[66] to allow biological fathers to challenge paternity. What convinced the court to change its mind were cases like those involving Bethany, her former husband, Trevor, and Andrew, the biological father of her child. The marital presumption would have allowed Bethany, by remarrying Trevor one day before the child was born, to cut Andrew out of the child's life. This was too much for even the Kentucky justices who wished to champion marriage. Instead, the Kentucky Supreme Court quietly overturned its recent decision affirming the marital presumption, concluding that marriage no longer had enough meaning to block the paternity claims of the biological father.[67]

The result of these biologically driven decisions, whether constitutional or statutory, is to give the man who secures a paternity test the right to establish a relationship with the child over the objections of the mother and her husband.[68] These states uphold limits on women's decision-making authority in the name of equal rights for men. Marriage—and the disruption of another parental relationship—largely disappear from the equation.[69] In the context of these disputes, the law neither validates private ordering, which would defer to a birth mother's greater ability to choose a father, nor assists in the creation of a new public consensus about what makes a man a father. Instead, in a majority of states, biology rules but without the court's willingness to directly say that a woman who sleeps with a man owes him the opportunity to be the legal father of the resulting child. The Kentucky Supreme Court, after all, could not agree on the rationale for upholding the

marital presumption in 2008, with the justices issuing a number of con-
flicting opinions, and it did not directly address the interim cases that per-
suaded the court to change its mind later. These cases provide no roadmap
for either husbands like Trevor or spurned lovers like Andrew as to what
makes a man a father outside of his ability to get to court and prove his
genetic lineage.[70]

Women's Agency

There is another way. California leads a different group of states that at least
partially recognize women's ability to determine which partners are able to
establish a parental role. The state supreme court tries to ensure that each child
will have two legal parents, but it places more weight on the assumption of
parental roles than it does on either marriage or biology.[71] The practical result
is to take women's agency seriously. A mother's partner can assume a parental
role only with her cooperation, but once the partner effectively establishes a
parental relationship with the child the mother no longer has the right to cut
off that relationship. Instead, where multiple adults might meet the statutory
criteria to be a presumed parent, California tends to recognize the one likely
to play a continuing role in the child's life.[72]

In making these determinations, California law still recognizes the marital
presumption in addition to a presumption that an adult who welcomes a child
into his household and holds out the child as his own is a presumed father.[73] If
there is more than one presumed parent, the courts choose between them "on
the basis of the weightier considerations of policy and logic."[74]

Suedi was only fifteen when she became pregnant. She had been sleeping with two men, twenty-nine-year-old Anthony and twenty-one-year-old
Gabriel. Although she indicated to both men that each was the father, Gabriel
was not interested in a more committed relationship, so it was Anthony who
moved in with Suedi, accompanied her to childbirth classes, and provided
support during her pregnancy. Suedi cut off contact with Gabriel and eventually married Anthony. When the baby was ten-months-old, DNA tests established that Gabriel, not Anthony, had fathered the child.[75] Which man, Gabriel
or Anthony, should receive legal recognition as the father of Suedi's first
child?

At the heart of the fight between Anthony and Gabriel is the fight to establish a new parental bargain. Suedi, given two men who want recognition
as the child's father, preferred the one who had been there for her; she determined who was willing to step up to the plate well before she determined the
facts of biological paternity. In effect, she treated paternity the way women
always have—she compared the devoted Anthony to the unreliable Gabriel

and picked Anthony as the father. Gabriel, instead, fought for the right to establish the child as "his." Gabriel's approach to parenthood would make childbirth more perilous for Suedi; she would be bound to a man who provided little in return. By contrast, Suedi's ability to secure commitment in exchange for the title "father" makes sex more perilous for Gabriel; he would effectively cede the ability to have a say in the upbringing of his child. The California courts agree that Suedi has the right to choose stability over biology.[76]

Such is the state of the law in middle America today. When Kentucky initially affirmed the validity of the marital presumption, state court judges objected that the result would not advance the sanctity of marriage but, rather, women's power to choose one man over another. The intermediate appellate courts, facing cases like those involving Bethany, who remarried her former husband Trevor one day before the child's birth, almost immediately retreated from application of the marital presumption, and a mere three years later the Kentucky Supreme Court overruled its earlier decision. In the meantime, states like California have expanded the role of function in the definition of parenthood, extending it not only to husbands like Anthony but also to unmarried partners as well. Other states fall in between. At the core of these decisions is a question of autonomy and decision-making power: does a woman who sleeps with a man and bears his child owe him the opportunity to become a legal parent, or does his recognition as a parent depend on his ability and willingness to assume a parental role?

The answer rests on the fault lines of the culture wars—and of class-based family division. As a practical matter, the fact that women give birth allows women to determine which men to allow into the child's life. Tying paternity to an ongoing marriage or to parental function accordingly gives women greater power to determine paternity. Biological definitions of paternity, in contrast, effectively subject women's parenting to the men with whom they conceived the child and do so irrespective of the man's willingness to play a constructive parental role.

The California courts have embraced what the Texas courts rejected, namely, the fact that the marital presumption "allow[s] the mother and her husband to prevent the biological father from ever establishing parental rights over a child."[77] In California, what triggers constitutional protection is neither biology nor marriage in and of itself, but the relationship to the child. This effectively locks in whatever parenting relationships the mother establishes after the child's birth.[78] The result ratifies the parties' decisions, protecting intact relationships without denying the fact of biological paternity and granting the child (and those who establish a relationship with the child) security if the mother later changes her mind.[79]

Conclusion: The Marital Presumption Revisited

Between Texas and California are an array of other results. Utah, for example, like California continues to recognize the marital presumption. But unlike Kentucky, it has worked through the issue of male responsibility. In the Utah cases, the husband who assumes the paternal role after a biological father refuses to do so is a legal father. It does not matter that the marriage does not last, that the mother and the biological father marry when the child is fifteen months old, and that they live together as an intact family. The now ex-husband remains the child's only legal father.

The marital presumption is complex because it involves a series of separate issues. First, will the courts judge men? Utah and California both use function, sometimes tied to marriage (Utah) and sometimes not (California), to determine which man has stepped forward and which has not. Other states, such as Texas, simply give men authority on the basis of biology.

Second, do the states pass judgment on women's sexuality? Kentucky, like Justice Scalia, is more appalled at the mothers' behavior in these cases than concerned about distinguishing between responsible and irresponsible men.

Third, who gets to decide? The upper third locks in a mutual commitment to parenting before the child is born, or in some cases, the prospective parents give up on finding the right mate and engineer termination of a donor's parental rights before conception. Either way, parentage is not in doubt. For the bottom third, the emerging practice is a single-parent phenomenon. While law might impose the biological father on Suedi and Bethany if they did not marry, the mothers would, practically speaking, control access to the child.

In the muddled middle, however, the fight is on. The bio-dads with enough resources to get to court wish to assert parental rights without deferring to the mothers' authority. Like the father in *Renaud*, they believe their right to assume a parenting role does not depend on their relationship with the mother. The mothers, however, who have assumed primary responsibility for the child, want the ability to choose. Like Suedi, they are more likely to pick the more reliable man over the uncommitted one, but they will also choose the man who is better for them whether or not the child has a separate interest in a relationship with the biological father. The problem is that all of the relationships, including the mother's new marriage and the biological father's relationship to the child, have become less likely to last. The judges often disapprove of the behavior of the entire group of seemingly dysfunctional adults. In the process, they provide little guidance for the emergence of norms capable of shaping family behavior. Lily and Carl are largely on their own, and as a practical matter, that means Lily will decide whether or not Carl ever sees the child again, and she will raise the child with relatively little support from Carl or the community.

SECTION IV

REBUILDING COMMUNITY: INEQUALITY, CLASS, AND FAMILY

When we look back through sepia-colored lenses, we think fondly about our childhoods and the entry into adulthood. The period spanned the mid-fifties to the seventies, the period of the Great Compression. We remember our parents' determination that we attend college, something they had found impossible in the middle of the Depression and World War II. We saw doors that had been closed open before us—to obtain university degrees, to enter professions that had refused to admit women or our immigrant forbears, and to combine employment and parenthood. And we sensed then (and are even more sure now) that we were able to realize those opportunities because of the strong support our parents provided us, support that their parents could not provide them and the working class parents of today will struggle to provide for their children.

When we look back as scholars on that period, we see two striking developments that shaped the era that ended in 1980. First, more widespread employment opportunities produced much greater economic security and shrank the wage differences due to education, region and occupation. Postwar America absorbed the immigrants of a half century earlier, and set the stage for the Civil Rights era and women's movement to come.[1] Second, the seemingly strong families of the fifties and sixties represented a brief window in which the middle class model of the industrial era became accessible to the majority of the population just as it was to about to become obsolete. Neither these families, which fueled the increased divorce rates of the seventies and eighties nor the model itself would last, but while it did, the mothers of a higher percentage of American families believed that they could and should focus on their children's preparation for the world to come. Class-based differences in parenting narrowed.[2] The society-wide commitment to equality offered hope that the prosperous society of that era would expand to include those like the racial minorities and rural poor who had been excluded from its benefits. Instead, the economic transformation that followed brought back the inequalities that existed at the height of the manufacturing era and once again made the ability to realize the benefits of a new parenting model a marker of class.

The challenge for the future will be to create a new, more equal society and to do it in the context of the dynamic changes produced by an economy that has valorized competition and hierarchy, eliminated the more secure positions of the industrial era and remade the relative participation of men and women in the new economy. These changes have profoundly affected family structure. Women, whose labor force participation helps fuel the expanded service sector of the information economy, are no longer dependent on men and they can and do demand more than they once did as the price of commitment. At the same time, greater economic inequality stratifies relationship markets: women at the top can find men who meet their terms while other women cannot. The solutions require rethinking the anchors for workers and families in the new era: either we need a greater societal commitment to greater employment security for those who cycle into and out of the increasingly unstable workplaces of the information economy or we need greater societal provision for children whose parents cycle into and out of increasingly unstable relationships. In this section, we explain how both might complement and reinforce each other.

In doing so, we start from the proposition that what will make a difference to Tyler, Amy, Carl, Lily, and their children's futures is simple: greater equality that creates more accessible pathways into the economic opportunities of tomorrow and the stable families children need. Each of their relationships with each other and their contributions to their children are likely to improve if they are stably employed at jobs that pay a living wage, find it easier to retrain and secure new jobs, receive regular raises, and enjoy uninterrupted access to health, retirement and insurance benefits. What will most benefit their children is a similar measure of security in the relationships they establish with the adults in their lives, and in the adults' ability to combine work and childcare, to attend to the children's educational and medical needs, and to do so in ways that improve the children's sense of belonging in communities that value and care for them.

Yet, taking on the issues of economic and personal security will not be easy. First, it requires confronting the sources of economic inequality directly. Technological change and globalization place a greater premium on innovation, expertise, and flexibility at the same time that the creation of winner-take-all corporate cultures produce a short-term focus on profits and earnings and insulate political elites from the concerns of the majority. The combination has reduced public *and* private investment in employees and it rewards select individuals at the expense of institutions and community. We accordingly believe that rebuilding the family requires starting from the top and making the policies that produce inequality visible and morally suspect, reexamining the public-private partnerships that can remake the pathways into employment, making employment itself more flexible by providing other sources of social insurance, and rethinking the role of the public sector in securing job growth.[3]

The second chapter in this section examines the prospects for rebuilding families from the bottom up through a focus on greater support for children from the beginning of a pregnancy into early adulthood. Family well-being reflects both the overall level of societal inequality and reconstruction of the specific infrastructure that unites home and market in addressing children's needs. The long-term changes in women's labor market participation have transformed the role of the family in transmitting resources from one generation to another. The idealized nineteenth-century family responded to the needs of the industrial age by separating home and market and by relying on women's unpaid labor to address the needs of children, the elderly, and working husbands' emotional needs. The contemporary reintegration of the home into the market through women's paid labor and greater reliance on the market to provide domestic services has brought back the nineteenth century disparities associated with class. We propose systematizing the new middle class solutions through greater support for maternal health during pregnancy, early childhood education, and work-family integration. The United States became an industrial power because of the greater investment in children made possible by the embrace of free public education and the empowerment of women necessary to make the education pay off.[4] The country's future in the post-industrial economy similarly depends on rebuilding the infrastructure that supports investment in children from early childhood through early adulthood. The well-being of the next generation should be a matter of national concern.

The third chapter in this section addresses the relationships between sex and children. All societies create expectations about readiness for parenting. Where red and blue elites agree on behavior, as they do with respect to teen sex, progress is possible and, indeed, there has been an encouraging reduction in teen births over the last fifteen years. Where the elites disagree, as they do for those in the late teens and early twenties, less progress is possible, producing widening class-based disparities in the incidence of unplanned pregnancies.[5] In this section, we suggest that agreement on either sex or marriage is unlikely and the focus should change to preparation for parenting. Such a focus would emphasize the importance of employment for both men and women, management of women's fertility as a medical system that begins at puberty and ends at menopause irrespective of sexual activity or marriage, and strategies for the selection of the right partner in creating a child. Just as the rise of industrialization required rebuilding family infrastructures, so too does the rise of the information age require rebuilding the pathways into parentage.

The final chapter reexamines the foundation of family law. It concludes that while the relationships among the adults will be increasingly a matter of choice, the relationship of parents to child is still a matter of public concern. In the new era, defining legal parenthood—inside and out of marriage—takes on increased significance. We accordingly recommend taking greater care in establishing the facts of biological parenthood, creating greater ability to recognize multiple parents who might play a role in the child's life, and protecting the child's interest in on-going functional relationships that may be unrelated to marriage or biology. In the new era, children, too, require a measure of security even as they adapt to new institutions.

Rebuilding from the Top Down: The Family, Inequality, and Employment

Those who study the family face a conundrum: the forces that shape family patterns, the norms underlying intimate relationships, and the possible relational terms between caretaking adults cannot be addressed in any meaningful way by examining the family in isolation. Instead, the story of the family fits within the context of an extensive literature about the importance of the middle class. American history since Thomas Jefferson and almost all of the literature on economic development emphasize the synergistic effects that come from a strong group in the center.[6] This group—English and Brazilian shopkeepers, Jefferson's yeoman farmers, and today's French and Vermont artisan cheese makers, the middle managers of mid-twentieth-century America, and today's nurses, engineers, pharmacists, and office managers—have a stake in strong public and private institutions and serve as a counter to otherwise unaccountable elites. They also supply the investment in the next generation that provides the well-educated workforce that companies increasingly demand.[7]

The inequality that exists in today's society undermines the institutions that strengthen middle-class families and worsens the plight of the poor. We have documented the changing structure of employment that allocates an increasing percentage of societal wealth to a relatively small group at the top, producing fewer stable positions for the middle. Indeed, over the past decade college-graduate wages have stagnated in the same manner as blue-collar wages did in the eighties and nineties. And since the Great Recession, historically stable government jobs have become less reliable.[8]

Strengthening the family accordingly requires rebuilding the foundation of the middle class. Doing so involves addressing the forces that have increased inequality, developing strategies to produce more stable employment paying a living wage, and filling in the inevitable gaps in employment through policies that assist the most marginalized. With full inclusion in American society, most of the gender disparities that skew intimate bargains would disappear.

Inequality and Status Games

> "We may conclude that . . . those males which are best able by their various charms to please or excite the female, are under ordinary circumstances accepted. If this be admitted, there is not much diffi-culty in understanding how male birds have gradually acquired their ornamental characters," Darwin wrote explaining why peacocks (but not peahens) have evolved a long ornamental tail that would otherwise appear to be a disadvantage in movement or in hiding from predators.[9]

Underlying changes in the U.S. economy—and the relationship between employment and family—has been a domestic shift from a manufacturing economy to a service economy caused by a combination of globalization and technological change.[10] Technological change has made it possible to auto-mate many processes, replacing labor-intensive typewriters with easier-to-use PCs, mechanizing harvests, and streamlining factory production. At the same time, the ability to use offshore production diminishes the need for domes-tic labor in manufacturing.[11] Both factors reduce wages—full-time jobs in the service economy pay less than full-time jobs in manufacturing[12]—and weaken labor's bargaining power. Economists today suggest that the beginning of the decline in workers' wages occurred in the fifties and that Moynihan's analysis of inner-city black communities showed the effects of the initial stages of this economically debilitating combination.[13]

Globalization and technological change *do* provide a partial explanation for some of the changes in the nineties in which the returns to those with greater education increased while wages stagnated for the less educated. A growing literature indicates, however, that these forces cannot account for the stagger-ing returns to the wealthiest one percent and the dominance of the financial sector or for the increased gender gap among college graduates.[14] Nor can they entirely account for the rise in employment and benefit instability and the fail-ure of labor to share in the significant increases in productivity over the past twenty years.

Economist Robert Frank has spent an academic lifetime studying inequal-ity. In his 2011 book *The Darwin Economy: Liberty, Economy and the Common Good*, he has a simple, provocative thesis: Charles Darwin was a better econo-mist than Adam Smith. Like Adam Smith, those who are willing to accept the increased inequality of today's economy as the price of progress see the "in-visible hand" of the market as channeling competition for the greater good.

Charles Darwin, in contrast, understood from his study of peacocks' tails that competition might produce considerable rewards for winners without necessarily benefiting the larger group at all. Frank argues that Darwin's insight better describes today's economy than does Smith's, hence the title of his book. We believe it also offers important insights for the relationship between what is happening between the top and the bottom of the American economy.

Frank prefers to explain his thesis through the example of elephant seals rather than peacocks, and we, too, prefer his metaphor. Elephant seals are enormous animals that breed in colonies in Antarctica and along the California coast. The males can be as much as five times larger than the females.[15] Males fight for dominance, and the winners establish harems of forty to fifty females while the loser males lurk at the edge of colonies and rarely breed at all.[16] In a society where male size determines survival and breeding success, being large is a huge advantage—to the individual in competitions with other males. It does not necessarily benefit the group, however. Frank points out that the orca and sharks who feed on the seals prefer bigger, fatter, slower prey. The oversized males occasionally crush the colonies' pups in their pursuit of additional mating opportunities. Increasing size may not necessarily increase long-term prospects for the health and survival of the entire species.

Frank uses his explanation of competition in elephant seal colonies to make a simple point—competition does not necessarily work to the benefit of the group. Instead, some competitions are zero-sum or even negative-sum games. Athletics provides a classic zero-sum competition. If one team wins, another necessarily loses. The net benefit comes from the joy of the contest or the engagement of the spectators. Athletics, however, can also become a negative-sum competition that ultimately destroys the enterprise if left entirely unregulated. If one team can spend more to acquire better athletes, for example, other teams also will have to spend more to stay competitive. But if one team becomes so dominant that the others cannot hope to compete, other teams may give up, or their fans may lose interest. Many leagues impose salary caps for exactly this reason. Unrestrained competition can lead to destructive practices (e.g., use of steroids) that may make participants worse off than if the harmful competition were banned.

In today's society, competition makes even the elite more insecure and encourages the well-off to expend more energy vying with each other and to express less concern for those left behind. Those who emerge at the top of the new, more competitive, system then identify to a greater degree with each other.[17] This has also increased the distance between management and labor. Some scholars suggest that the declining fortunes of American labor have as much to do with executives' competition with each other as with the changes in market forces in the American economy.[18]

Indeed, one of the greatest drivers of inequality almost certainly has been the change in executive compensation. Studies of income inequality indicate that increases at the very top (the one percent or less) are what dramatically skew the results and that the growth at the top largely reflects increases in executive compensation and compensation in the financial sector. From 1979 to 2005, these workers (executives and financial experts) accounted for 58 percent of the expansion of income for the top 1 percent and 67 percent of the increase in income for the top 0.1 percent.[19] Since the Great Recession, things have only gotten worse. The top 1 percent has enjoyed virtually a full recovery, realizing 95 percent of the gains from growth in the years 2009–2012, while the bottom 99 percent was just beginning to recover at the end of that period.[20]

Researchers emphasize that the increase in executive compensation, unlike increases in superstar (think Michael Jordan or Peyton Manning) or professional (think engineers) compensation, are not market driven and do not reflect productivity. As a 2012 study concluded, "CEOs, through compensation committees and inbreeding of boards of directors, have a unique ability to control their own compensation."[21] Indeed, the study explained that one of the factors spurring the growth in pay was contagion: directors who approved pay increases at one institution often went back to their home corporations and demanded pay raises for themselves.

These changes in compensation have not just resulted in increases in executive pay. They have also significantly changed the nature of corporate cultures in ways that ultimately increase the lack of investment in labor. Law professor Lynne Dallas labels the result "short-termism."[22] Executive bonuses came to depend on annual (or sometimes quarterly) earnings or profit statements, regardless of whether these immediate returns resulted in long-term success. Former SEC Chairman Mary Schapiro explained in the context of the financial crisis that, "Many major financial institutions created asymmetric compensation packages that paid employees enormous sums for short-term success, even if these same decisions result in significant long-term losses or failure for investors and taxpayers."[23]

This focus on short-term measures, whether tied to the earnings that justified bonuses or stock prices that increased stock option values, separates executive and worker interests. For example, a company that cut costs through employee downsizing could report higher earnings in the near term that increased stock prices.[24] If the company then found itself with a shortage of skilled employees down the road, the executives who made the initial cuts would not necessarily be around to deal with the consequences or care about the dislocation caused by firing workers and hiring back new ones. Moreover, a narrow focus on monetary incentives may attract individuals more motivated by monetary incentives in the first place and may encourage callousness more generally. Indeed, it appears that the more executive compensation exceeds worker compensation in a company, the more likely the executives are to discount worker interests, according to a study that reviewed actual corporate records and the results of laboratory experiments. In the experiments, subjects were placed in a management role, and those who were told that they would receive high compensation relative to their employees were substantially more likely to fire subordinates than were those who were told they would be paid at a rate closer to that of their subordinates.[25] The results of this incentive structure do not affect just the individual workers subject to the layoffs; they also encourage pro-cyclical policies that increase volatility in the economy more generally.[26]

In this system centered on "individual gain," companies and employees, whether management or labor, stay together only so long as is mutually beneficial; loyalty disappears. The company does not invest in its employees, and the employees are free to jump ship if a better offer comes along. As part of the process, companies purchase more of their goods and services from independent contractors, and some employees become entrepreneurs, starting their own small businesses. If they prosper, the owner gets the profits, but there is little insulation from the ups and downs of the business cycle or the ups and down of the life cycle that come from illness, family emergencies, or unforeseen developments.[27]

The result produces a vicious cycle. Corporate managers, faced with an emphasis on short-term profits and with greater capital mobility to foreign markets, divert more firm assets away from workers and toward share buybacks, increase dividend payouts, and view the corporation as an asset like any other in an investment firm's portfolio.[28] Long-term company health, whether in the form of the quality of its products or the stability of its operations, becomes less important than corporate bonuses, share prices, and dividends that boost the share price, though not necessarily the underlying value, of the asset. The result increases the volatility of both corporate and individual income, and greater insecurity further promotes the focus on immediate gains. If you are not going to be with the company next year, this year's bonus becomes that much more important, and the long-term health of the company fades in importance.[29] Increasing executive compensation is thus linked to the declining share of increases in productivity that go to labor. A 2012 Report by the Boston Consulting Group concludes that many manufacturers have openings that they cannot fill—but only because of their unwillingness to pay a competitive wage.[30] Reporter Adam Davidson described interviewing factory managers who observed what a hard time they had recruiting needed workers—for $10-an-hour jobs. When he asked economists for comments, they replied, "It's hard not to break out laughing"[31] because, as every economist knows, in a competitive market "shortages" exist only because of a refusal to respond to the lack of applicants by raising prices. The managers' comments were indicative of a larger shift in corporate practices, namely, a determination to hold the line on employee compensation even as executive compensation rises.

The result is not, as political scientists Jacob Hacker and Paul Pierson explain in *winner-take-all Politics,* the inevitable product of capitalism, but of a political system that has facilitated the change. Hacker and Pierson observe that since 1978, Republicans have won an extraordinary percentage of close elections and have been able to do so because the U.S. Chamber of Commerce and other conservative fundraisers have targeted political contributions to advance conservative business interests.[32] They argue that the results include lower taxes at the top, fewer regulations, less enforcement, the evisceration of worker protections, and the erosion of the minimum wage. Taken together, they undermine worker ability to form collective units while strengthening management ability to circumvent the control that might arise from either greater shareholder or regulatory scrutiny.

Studies of income inequality show the class and gender impact of these political changes. First, the erosion of the minimum wage has had the greatest impact on the position of working women at the bottom of the economic ladder, increasing the disparities between the 50th and 10th percentiles of female income.[33] Second, the decline in unionization, spurred in part by hostile legislation, accounts for 14 percent of the increase in variance in male wages between 1973 and 2001.[34] These changes, which reduce wages, working conditions, and employment stability, have contributed to a large-scale reduction in labor force participation.[35] The decrease in the permanence of employment and the declining share of corporate earnings that go to workers either through wages or through taxes and public benefits is at the core of changes within the American family.

The Solution: Rebuild the Middle Class—and Strengthen the American Family—through Employment

Rebuilding the family should therefore start with the adults: those at the top of the economy who increasingly hold power to determine the terms on which everyone else is employed (or unemployed) and the basis on which they enter marriage markets and negotiate gender bargains. Starting here we propose a few of the many necessary reforms; these reforms can begin the process of changing the conversation from maximizing profits to maximizing community (and family) health. First, reorient corporate incentives from a short-term focus on earnings to longer-term institutional health; second, rebuild employment and create stable jobs; third, strengthen the social safety net that retrains workers to meet emerging business needs and that separates healthcare, pensions, disability coverage, and other forms of social insurance from employment. These approaches are not mutually exclusive and have significant spillover effects, but they are conceptually, and politically, distinct.

Reduce Inequality through Reforms of Corporate Culture and Executive Compensation

The easiest way to reduce inequality is to reduce top incomes. This could be done through higher taxes, caps on executive compensation, and/or greater regulation of the financial sector.[36]

Reforming executive compensation to better align executive interests with the company's long-term health may be the most critical. Reforms could increase transparency, preclude the exercise of stock options for a period after the executive leaves the company, and include clawback provisions that build in accountability for risks or abuses that may not be apparent at the time of the executives' departure.[37] These relatively minimal reforms might curb some of the worst corporate abuses without fundamentally changing the system.

Farther reaching proposals challenge the premises underlying executive compensation. The reforms that encouraged a higher percentage of corporate compensation to be paid in the form of stock options assumed that the purpose of executive compensation should be to maximize shareholder value, which the market measures in the form of stock prices. Former Federal Reserve Board head Paul Volcker, however, once responded to such an assertion by replying "that is wrong. . . . I'm an economist, the purpose of a corporation is to produce goods and services that serve society period, and that's what you should be paying people for."[38] If we took the approach that Volcker advocated, we would treat corporations as responsible to a variety of constituents, not just shareholders, and those constituents would include employees, consumers, and the larger society.[39]

Corporate consultants and social scientists who study motivation distinguish between extrinsic and intrinsic motivations. Psychologists find that extrinsic motivations, such as short-term bonuses, may affect immediate actions, but they do not change values or long-term behavior. Pay your children to do the dishes and they may become more likely to wash the dinner plates. They do not necessarily become more likely to grow up to be adults who volunteer to help out when they are not being paid. Children who learn to value helping others, whose contributions to the family make them feel good about themselves, are more likely to help out without being asked. Studies of corporate behavior—and the military—find something similar (though psychologists give more weight to these studies than do economists).[40] Merit-based pay, particularly when focused on narrow short-term measures, often divides employees and harms morale. Relatively more equal pay coupled with recognition for high performers and measures that enhance group cohesion have a greater impact on productivity and esprit-de-corps, especially when complex or subjective tasks are involved.[41] In the corporate context, high-performing managers will always receive financial awards, but there is little evidence that outsized compensation, exceeding a 20:1 ratio between CEO and line employees, is necessary to motivate optimal performance.

Focus on Rebuilding Employment

Job creation should be an end in itself. Increasing education may help more people get good jobs, but it cannot substitute for increased employment. In today's market, college-graduate salaries have stagnated, and even skilled workers find themselves subject to the type of layoffs that were once limited to the unskilled.[42]

The lack of good jobs should be a political issue. It has not been partly because at least until recently those most affected are the relatively powerless and in part because of the mistaken belief that the government cannot or should not address the issue. Republican presidential candidate Mitt Romney insisted after all in the 2012 debates that the "government cannot create jobs." Accordingly, the first step in promoting political accountability for the creation of better jobs is better data. Existing reports focus on numbers, not quality. They track overall employment, labor force participation, and unemployment. Reports must also pay more attention to the percentage of gains in productivity that go to workers' wages and to the identification of the number of "good jobs," those that offer stability, promotions, benefits, and flexibility. A renewed focus on employment would also require greater emphasis on growth-oriented economic policies. Conventional economic wisdom emphasizes the importance of consumer spending in stimulating economies and encouraging investment. Almost all (92 percent) of economists agreed, for example, that the Obama Administration's stimulus efforts increased employment.[43] Studies further indicate that a major reason for the lagging American recovery is the decline in state and local jobs as a result of congressional refusal to authorize the type of revenue-sharing and benefit measures that helped spur recoveries from earlier recessions.[44] Austerity in Europe has increased the depth of the recession there, not cured it. Returning to the idea of a full-employment economy should be an important policy objective.[45]

Reform the Minimum Wage to Make Work Pay

Raising the minimum wage would, quite simply, also raise what employees at the lower end of the economic spectrum are paid. Economists agree that subsidies are more efficient than employer mandates, but this is a critical mandate to ensure nationwide conformity and to prevent races to the bottom for wages. The erosion of the federal minimum wage has contributed to the rise in inequality between the fiftieth and tenth percentiles. Economists argue about whether or not such hikes accelerate mechanization and decrease overall employment. The studies produced mixed results, but to the surprise of economists, most show small, if any, effects on employment. Moreover, even if such increases result in some job losses, increased wages would also encourage greater employer investment in more productive workers rather than a rapidly rotating group of shorter-term employees.[46] Job stability increases both productivity *and* family stability.[47]

Subsidize Job Creation and Public Sector Employment

Employment depends on businesses investing in their workforce as well as product development and capital goods.[48] At a time when employees tended to stay with one company for much of their working lives, companies invested more in employees and employees derived more of their identity from identification with the company. One of our relatives who worked as a painter for Ford Motor Co. during the 1960s would never have considered buying a car that wasn't a Ford.

Investment in employee training, which affects short-term earnings, has diminished across the economy and today affects law firms along with firms that hire minimum-wage workers.[49] At the same time, cutbacks in public spending on education decrease training for prospective workers who cannot acquire such training of their own. Technological advances further limit the need for employees with undeveloped or outdated skills. The combined result of these changes is likely to be an ever larger group who will have trouble finding employment and keeping the jobs they do find.[50]

One way to address the issue is to subsidize the wages of the unskilled. The government might underwrite the cost of hiring and training new employees, with rewards for companies that retain the employees on a long-term basis.[51] The principal alternative—and an important supplement—to the subsidization of training within private firms is use of the government as an employer of last resort.[52] Those most likely to be left out of any recovery are the unemployable: those with criminal records, disabilities, histories of drug abuse or mental illness, or limited education and job skills. Moynihan recognized in the sixties that the most disadvantaged could find employment only with a government commitment to increase the number of jobs. Instead, we have seen a wholesale erosion in the number of stable government and private jobs. As the Brookings Institution reported in 2012, for example, decreases in the number of government jobs following the Great Recession has been one of the major contributors to U.S. unemployment.[53]

Flexicurity and a Rebuilt Social Safety Net

Rebuilding families and communities requires rethinking not just the existence of a job that produces a paycheck at the end of the week, but also employment as part of a network that encourages and rewards investment in human capital and that provides security in the event of old age, illness, and disability. The United States once provided both security and opportunities for training and advancement through employment-related systems. "Good jobs," which once included many blue-collar as well as white-collar positions, offered employment security, healthcare, retirement, and other benefits as well as a career ladder with opportunities for raises or promotions.[54]

For family needs that employment might not cover, the stay-at-home wife took charge, providing caretaking stability that complemented employment stability. The division of labor between home and market, coupled with employer-based insurance systems, built in protection for what Martha Fineman calls "vulnerabilities," such as those that come with youth, age, and illness.[55] The stay-at-home wife provided the safety net that cared for sick children, elderly parents, and a temporary second income when necessary to supplement the first.

This system, which combined "good" jobs with gender-defined family roles, is largely gone. While many would say "good riddance," it is important to recognize that the new system provides neither financial nor caretaking security in its place.[56] The families that depend on two incomes or consist of single parents or live far from extended kin may be stretched thin even before illness or calamity strike.[57] Accordingly, we need improved measures that better help families cope with layoffs by developing and supporting their resiliency.[58] In an era in which employment increasingly comes from entrepreneurs, small businesses, and temporary or contract arrangements, the network that ties individuals to education and insurance needs to be rebuilt. Addressing these issues requires rethinking the relationship between work and family and the social safety net that fills in the cracks between them.

The answer begins with reconstructing infrastructure to support stability. While we would like to see more secure jobs, we recognize that in today's economy an increasing percentage of job growth comes from innovative entrepreneurship, new businesses, and a contingent workforce. Temporary or contract employees have grown at three to four times the rate of more traditional employees, and many analysts predict further increases.[59] Contingent and contract employment allows both business and individual flexibility, but developing more flexible workforces that support stable families requires a social safety net that decouples health insurance from employment, unemployment insurance that fills in the gaps between jobs, and an educational system that develops skills well past the point where a student receives a terminal degree.

A first solution to the problem of how to support a more flexible workforce would reconstruct the connections between industry needs and training. European countries, seeking a "third way" between the type of unregulated markets they associate with the United States and the United Kingdom and more top-down labor market regulation common in Europe, have pioneered an approach called "flexicurity." The system accepts the need for greater employment flexibility than European countries have historically permitted while still providing greater security for workers than would be produced by a free market approach. The new system focuses on retraining laid-off workers to meet emerging needs. In Denmark, for example, the flexicurity system helped three hundred of five hundred meatpackers laid off because of a plant closing retrain and secure other jobs within ten months of the layoffs. Another eighty found new jobs as meatpackers, while only sixty continued to receive unemployment benefits.[60]

Accepting flexicurity as a goal can lead to programs that facilitate ongoing employment and re-entry into the labor market by

- allowing workers an extended period of employment benefits, perhaps at a reduced rate, if they to return to school and enroll in a degree-granting program;
- subsidizing training tied to projected industry needs;
- identifying new openings in other parts of the country and facilitating relocation.

A second solution would make healthcare, pension plans, and disability coverage universal and portable.[61] Employer-provided healthcare began in the United States as a way to circumvent World War II–era price controls. In today's employment context, the system massively subsidizes the workers with the highest marginal tax rates and discourages the creation of lower-wage jobs with full benefits. It also creates incentives for American employers to draw on workforces in other parts of the world that decouple health care and employment. While the Affordable Care Act addresses some of the resulting inequities,[62] separating employment and healthcare entirely would provide greater flexibility for employers and greater healthcare security for workers.

Rethink the Government Role in Social Insurance and Transfer Payments

The most successful government programs are not ones that take over private sector functions such as job training but programs that redistribute risk and transfer resources. Social security has been more effective than private pension systems in securing the well-being of the elderly, both in terms of the reliability and universality of the benefits. Less visible, but similarly effective in addressing the combination of financial and family security is the earned income tax credit. The program provides incentives to work and benefits calibrated to family needs. It effectively replaced what used to be known as "welfare" with broad bi-partisan support. Like the tax programs that benefit the wealthy, it is too complex to be reduced to a political slogan—or to fully summarize in this book.

The program, however, does several things that we believe should be models for thinking about families. First, it makes work pay. That is, the benefits are tied to participation in the workforce, which avoids the stigma associated with welfare benefits and contributes to the recipients' sense that they have earned the funds. In addition, because like other forms of tax refunds, the benefits are paid in lump sum amounts, they contribute to savings and planning that aids upward mobility. Second, the program recognizes family needs and provides greater support for children.[63] It thus effectively subsidizes work for those who may have the greatest difficulty combining work and family obligations.

The program's greatest limitations come from the fact that it is not available to the unemployed and it is not geared to address emergencies that may disrupt work. These limitations could be addressed by combining the idea of "tax credits," administered through annual payments that are part of the tax system, with broader notions of insurance to address temporary interruptions in workforce participation, family crises due to the kind of debt triggered by unanticipated emergencies, or other needs. Law professor Sara Greene, for example, suggests using the program to provide automatic enrollment in an program that would create accounts to cover unexpected emergencies. These accounts would operate much like IRAs, with limited provisions for withdrawals, that could be available to cushion family shocks. She observes that today many families use credit cards that way; they charge expenditures only when they absolutely need to, incurring the very high interest rates associated with such borrowing. She proposes restructuring the program to replicate the strategies the better off use to deal with such unanticipated needs. These ideas might be extended to unemployment benefits, a form of social insurance similarly designed to cushion the impact of events that groups find easier to absorb than individuals.

Conclusion

Greater economic security is an essential foundation for family stability. The challenge is how to combine greater employment flexibility with the greater continuity families need. A critical first step is reexamining labor market policies to encourage greater protection for employees. Improved labor markets alone will have a significant positive effect on relationship stability for virtually everyone.[64] The second step, to which we turn in the next chapter, requires helping families take advantage of these new opportunities without shortchanging their children.

Rebuilding from the Bottom Up: Addressing Children's Needs

Jessica Schairer, a single mother who struggles to get by on an income of $25,000 per year, contrasts the lives of her children with those of her supervisor: "I see [them]—they're in swimming and karate and baseball and Boy Scouts, and it seems like it's always her or her husband who's able to make it there," Ms. Schairer said. "That's something I wish I could do for my kids. But number one, that stuff costs a lot of money and, two, I just don't have the time."[1]

Class differences in raising children have grown substantially. First, the sheer disparities in income are greater, and elite families can spend dramatically more on their children than the elites of earlier eras. Moreover, families in the upper third are much more likely to benefit from two incomes, both of which may be higher than those of single mothers like Jessica Schairer.[2] Second, better-off workers often tend to have greater access to paid family leave or greater flexibility in taking time off to drive a child to Little League practice or attend scouting events. Schairer, in contrast, lost a day's pay to take her children on a field trip with their school. Third, the extended families and supportive communities, often dependent on women's unpaid labor, have eroded. If Jessica Schairer can't pay Boy Scouts dues or drive her children to karate practice, the children don't go. As a result, the class gaps in children's cognitive achievements, civic engagement, and athletic participation, and feelings of isolation and loneliness have grown.[3]

To make increased human capital investment in children universal rather than a hallmark of class privilege requires a commitment to provide for all of our children in ways that go beyond what many parents can afford. Nonetheless, the debate over what to do for children, like those being raised by Jessica Schairer, is extremely polarized. Schairer, although she works full-time, qualifies for food stamps and other government assistance. Such benefits have routinely been the target of conservative attacks, including during the 2013 budget fight that resulted in a government shutdown. In Missouri, where 20 percent of children in the state live with hunger, a conservative legislator called for cutting food aid. She observed that hunger "can be a positive motivator," encouraging children to get jobs.[4] In the 2012 presidential election, Republican proposals would have cut food stamp benefits by $2,000 per year per family, massively reduced Medicaid health coverage for families like Schairer's, and raised taxes on the working poor while slashing taxes on those with higher incomes.[5] Many justify the cuts by claiming that marriage would solve the problem; yet, as Schairer observed, she ultimately broke up with the father of her children because he contributed so little to the family.

The wholesale remaking of the pathways to success has dramatic—and drastic—impacts on how we channel support for children. This will require rebuilding the support for children from birth until entry into the workforce through adequate child care, family-friendly workplaces, fallback assistance when children are sick, ability to manage after-school supervision and activities, and increased educational opportunities for lower-income children both before the age of five and after the age of eighteen. The older solution for these issues depended on women's unpaid labor, putting the benefits of domesticity beyond the reach of the working class. Today's society depends on dual-income families who earn enough to pay others to provide child care and "enrichment" activities, again putting the pathways to middle-class life beyond those whose jobs do not pay them enough to secure quality care. Jessica Schairer, ironically, works in a day-care center but not one flexible enough to allow her to devote more time to her own children.

Caring for children involves providing a safe and stimulating environment, overseeing homework and troubleshooting school tensions, supplying nutritious foods and encouraging children to eat them, and establishing the bonding that allows children to feel valued and nurtured. Better-educated parents can bring more resources, emotional and financial, to their children's care. Low-income parenting is simply harder. The most effective interventions are intensive and early; they start with prenatal aid for the mother and continue with efforts to enmesh the family in a supportive community that, for example, allows all children to get to soccer and baseball practices.

The reintegration of women in the workforce requires rebuilding the infrastructure of support for early childhood. Even if greater inequality were not an issue, it would take community efforts to provide for universal preschool just as, a century ago, it took coordinated public and private efforts to ensure universal access to elementary and secondary education. The negative effects of increasing inequality on many communities, which have stretched families thin and increased poor families, isolation from their neighbors and extended kin,[6] makes the reconstruction project that much more critical.

Rebuilding Support for Children

Addressing the re-creation of class from the bottom up means thinking about how we channel resources to children. In a world in which mothers and fathers are likely to be in the workforce, we need to rebuild the networks that promote children's well-being from the time of their mothers' pregnancy forward and that manage work-family gaps and tensions. These policies are critical, regardless of whether the children are born into married, cohabiting, or single-parent households, in constructing the pathways that support children into adulthood.

Maternal Health and Newborn Assistance

New research indicates that malnutrition during pregnancy contributes to adult hypertension, coronary artery disease, and diabetes.[7] Moreover, the mother's well-being immediately after birth has significant effects on newborn bonding, stimulation, nutrition, and physical and emotional health.[8] Childhood poverty is one of the greatest predictors of later health problems; risk factors in childhood, such as poor nutrition, poverty, and less cognitively stimulating environments, having lifelong negative consequences while parental bonding, good nutrition, and full access to healthcare may have positive effects that last a lifetime. Single-parenthood further complicates these risks and increases the likelihood of isolation, lack of support, and depression.[9] Medicaid, for which coverage has been expanded under the Affordable Care Act, can cover some prenatal services, such as supplying vitamins and some prenatal screening, as well as delivery and sixty days of postpartum care. When it comes to other services, however, ranging from counseling and education to support for breastfeeding, coverage varies significantly between states.[10]

In accordance with these findings we recommend improved maternal care. Prenatal healthcare, counseling, and nutrition programs can help identify risk factors, such as inadequate nutrition or potential complications in the pregnancy, and design appropriate interventions. Evaluations of the supplemental food program for pregnant mothers, for example, indicate that the program has generally (though not uniformly) been effective for families at greatest risk of poor nutrition. Regular doctors' visits after the child's birth help provide instruction for new parents, identify health issues, and guide early interventions. Developmental delays, autism spectrum disorders, and problems due to allergies or other illnesses often benefit from intensive interventions at ages when a child's neurological and other systems are still developing.

Post-childbirth home visits can assist with support, education, and nutritional and educational information for new mothers. In New York State, for example, specially trained home visitors targeted at-risk families in an effort to promote positive parenting skills and parent–child interaction, prevent child abuse and neglect, encourage prenatal care and child health and development, and assist the parents in achieving self-sufficiency. The program produced positive results in terms of learning behaviors, and evaluators found that the frequency of the visits, rather than their content or number, was the single most critical component. These visits were intended to provide the kind of ongoing support for new mothers that in earlier eras might have come from extended families.[11]

Early Childhood

The quality of early care has a lasting effect on children's cognitive, social, and psychological development.[12] Longitudinal studies find that children who receive quality child care reap long-term advantages in terms of educational attainment and earnings.[13] Among other effects, at-risk children who don't receive early childhood education that is of high quality are more likely (40 percent) to become teen parents and more likely (70 percent) to be arrested for violent crimes.[14]

Society benefits as well. Economists have estimated that the rate of return on early childhood education in terms of reduced crime and enhanced productivity is 16 percent.[15] Women, who assume the major responsibility for child care, also benefit enormously from reliable and affordable providers.

Nobel Prize–winning economist James Heckman has shown that early interventions focused on the first three to five years of life work but that increased spending on education and later efforts to compensate for early childhood poverty are dramatically less effective.[16] Heckman concludes that biology and neuroscience show "that skills beget skills; that success breeds success; that disadvantage gets embodied into the biology of the child and retards the development of children in terms of their health, character, and smarts."[17] This is one of the reasons why improved overall employment does not necessarily benefit those who were poor to begin with; those who failed to get on the right path in early childhood often lack the skills, habits, and hope necessary to take advantage of later opportunities.[18]

We accordingly recommend the creation of, and subsidies for, high-quality child care. The most effective programs have better trained caregivers and low caregiver/child ratios emphasizing cognitive stimulation and attention to the child's emotional needs and skill development.[19] Subsidization, however, is essential to ensure that such programs are available to the most at-risk children.

Once children begin more formal schooling, programs must include multi-generational interventions. Studies of Head Start find the strongest positive effects at age three from programs that focus on parents *and* children, with a mix of center- and home-based services, often starting during pregnancy. These programs combined services that benefited the children directly with assistance to the parents in learning better parenting skills and in dealing with the parents' own needs.[20] Early childhood education programs provide the greatest benefits to the most at-risk children because their parents are less able to afford such programs, the educational efforts compensate for less stimulating home environments and they assist parents who are the least able to afford high-quality child care ensure appropriate care for their children.[21]

The major objection to such programs is based on studies that indicate that even programs that show large initial gains in student achievement do not necessarily result in lasting differences in test score results.[22] A second objection is cost. State-funded preschool programs cost approximately $5,000 per child.[23] The best studies, however, evaluate the impact across a number of measures, not just test scores, and distinguish between well-designed programs with trained staff and less-effective efforts, finding an effect on social and cognitive development that justifies the cost. Among other benefits, the model programs enhance the individual's earnings and save costs in the criminal justice system.[24] Analyses of universal high-quality preschool indicate that the benefits, especially for the least-advantaged students, outweigh the costs.[25] They also facilitate parents' labor force participation.[26] Parents benefit because many programs encourage their involvement, and their children's more predictable schedule provides certainty for their work schedules.

The School System

Children do not stop growing at age five, and parents still need (and want) to ensure that their children are cared for. Many low-income women, in particular, lose their jobs in the struggle to find reliable before- and after-school care, a difficulty stemming in part from the structure of the school day and the timing of the workweek. The structure of the school day has not changed significantly from earlier eras when women were at home awaiting their children's arrival, and indeed, the schedule still largely presumes that an adult, most commonly a woman, will be available by midafternoon to provide care and supervision of a school-aged child.

Moreover, public schools provide an opportunity to maximize children's futures, to instill values and foster expectations about their later work and family lives. Smaller class sizes in elementary school and intensive college preparation interventions in high school appear to have some positive effects.[27] The highest achieving students in low-income communities act differently from students in high-income communities and are much less likely to apply to selective colleges. Instead, it is their class, rather than their academic accomplishments, which determine their choices of post-secondary education.[28] While approximately one-third of high-achieving students in the lowest income quartile apply to selective colleges, almost 80 percent of those in the top income quartile apply. Some low-income, high-achieving students do apply to selective colleges; what makes them different can, in part, be explained by their knowing more students who are also high-achieving and their increased likelihood of meeting someone from a selective college.[29]

Culturally patterned experiences determine not only achievement but educational aspirations as well.[30] As Duke Professor Stephen Vaisey notes, "we might find it unsurprising that those who grow up poor are more likely to see education as less desirable than mutually-exclusive alternatives, which might motivate them to make choices and pursue life strategies that are socioeconomically disadvantageous."[31] To offset these patterns, a variety of options can support lower-income children and their parents.

To provide greater enrichment for at-risk children and greater support for working parents, children could spend more time in school. This might occur through lengthening the school day. If an earlier start and later ending of the school day is not feasible, then providing more publicly funded after- and before-school programs would similarly contribute to equalizing "enrichment" opportunities available to all children. Some states have already experimented with a longer school day.[32]

Low-income high school students need better opportunities to obtain meaningful information about college choices. This means ensuring that college counselors in smaller, rural schools can provide relevant advising about college options as well as that colleges change some of their recruitment techniques, perhaps by relying on alumni to visit more and diverse schools.[33] Some existing organizations already focus on providing low-income students with information,[34] and their efforts could be expanded.

We're not entirely sure what will help encourage higher education, so this is an area that needs further study. Low-income students pursue a variety of different strategies in making choices about the future, and researchers are analyzing why that is. Certainly, student financial aid programs at colleges make a concrete difference, but not all low-income students have the requisite information and access to take full advantage of these sources.

Post-Secondary Education

Even as more people enroll in college, attendance is skewed toward students from higher-income families (as we saw in chapter 8). Getting that degree is an important step for economic advancement in a new economy (although, as the previous chapter argued, this new economy must have jobs that matter).[35] The tools to implement improved support already exist. Consider, for example, community colleges, which enroll approximately eight million students.[36] Community colleges are a much more affordable alternative to four-year institutions; they have open admission programs and usually are geographically accessible. More than half of all Latino and Native-American college students, and more than 40 percent of all African-American students, are enrolled in community colleges, though blacks, Latinos, and low-income students are less likely to graduate than their white, higher income counterparts.[37] Many community colleges are developing programs that help all students stay in school as well as programs focused on young mothers. Child care centers provide an important service for parents, and some community colleges offer classes to help students think through their reproductive health.

Improving opportunities means attention to the affordability and flexibility of higher education, in ways that affect both men's and women's distinctive needs and life patterns. This means developing policies that focus on the cost of higher education, especially for those who have families to support. Calculation of university expenses for financial aid purposes should include, for example, the cost of child care and medical insurance. Once students enter college, they need ongoing and personalized counseling to ensure that they can meet their financial and family obligations. Students need access to more flexible programs, including community college classes that can be scheduled to correspond to elementary and high school schedules and on-site day care to allow older women to return to school. Some of the most promising developments may be the expansion of online courses and degree programs that make it easier to tailor individual schedules around child care needs. Community college and apprenticeship programs can allow less-skilled workers to return to school to retool their skills or to obtain the education they need to switch jobs or receive promotions. Community college programs tied directly to internships or job placements can help in finding permanent employment.

Providing Workplace Support for Parents: Work–Family Balance

Supporting the next generation means supporting parents. As Sylvia Hewlett and Carolyn Luce summarize their findings, "off ramps are around every curve on the road, but once a woman has taken one, on ramps are few and far between and extremely costly." Although the average woman in their study was out of the labor force for only a little over two years, she lost an average of almost a fifth of her earning power, and those who were out three or more years lost more than a third.[38] In her best-selling book *Lean In*, Facebook COO Sheryl Sandberg argues that women should not leave the workforce to have children before they are actually ready to leave.[39]

In the previous chapter we talked about the importance of "flexicurity," that is, of providing mechanisms to facilitate worker re-entry into the workplace after layoffs caused by plant closings, changing employer needs, and other factors external to the family. Complementing such efforts should be greater workforce flexibility designed to encourage the ability of parents to care for their children while remaining employed. Employees, particularly low-wage ones, may face unpredictable shifts and rigid time requirements. Approximately half of them work a standard workweek, but the other half do not.[40] Even more elite employees may be discouraged from workplace flexibility. Marissa Mayer, president and CEO of Yahoo!, caused enormous controversy—and consternation—in 2013 when, despite trends toward the strategy, she strongly discouraged telecommuting for all fourteen thousand Yahoo! employees.

Seventy percent of children live in households where all adults are in the labor force, which means that these parents necessarily juggle work and family.[41] Caring for the elderly is another stress, with just less than one in five employees providing elder care each year.[42] Half of employees will miss work because of the need to care for the elderly. High-income workers are the most likely to have flexible hours—with high work demands. Low-income workers are the most likely to enjoy some limited subsidies, for child care, preschool, or other benefits, though many of these benefits are cut during tough budget times. In between, however, are many workers who enjoy neither.[43] Hourly workers in most offices, for example, have fixed hours and take time off at their own expense. They have no access to subsidized child care and often no fallback if a child gets sick or needs emergency attention. Some experience pressure to work extra hours; others, like Jessica Schairer, face often agonizing choices between being able to attend a child's field trip or soccer game and making the money needed to feed their families. Others still have no choices; they are fired if they attend to their children's needs or if a babysitter fails to show up.

Top female earners are already the most likely to have access to both unpaid and paid family leave,[44] but increased support helps move the ideal worker model away from delayed childbearing by making leave more routine. It can also increase men's participation in parenting.[45] Moreover, because lower-income women are more likely to be fired or to quit after they give birth, expanded family leave can promote stronger workforce attachment. Some states fund paid leaves through an insurance program financed by employee contributions. California and New Jersey have a paid leave insurance program, financed by employee contributions, that provides most workers with six weeks of partial salary during leaves to care for a new child or a sick family member or domestic partner.[46] Several other states have programs that allow women to use temporary disability insurance to cover a portion of lost wages for leave during and immediately after pregnancy. A few states permit workers to use a portion of their own sick days to care for sick children, parents, spouses, or domestic partners. These leave provisions yield multiple benefits. Women who take leave are more likely to return to work and less likely to rely on public assistance than are those who do not.[47] Workers with paid parental leave are also more likely to return to their employer than are those who lack such leave.[48] When men take advantage of leave policies they contribute more of their fair share of housework.[49]

The benefits are not, of course, just for employees. Employers would save time and resources with reduced turnover rates, and after experience with a comparable program in California, employers overwhelmingly reported either positive or no noticeable impact.[50]

If workforce participation is to be combined with adequate care for children, collective efforts need to ensure that all parents have access to family-friendly workplaces. After all, individuals can rarely bargain on their own to change workplace practices, and in times of high unemployment, individuals often need to take whatever jobs are available. The ability to bargain for flexible hours or working conditions is itself a marker of class. But even if they do seek time off, they may face a "flexibility stigma," in which they are viewed as less serious workers because of their need to leave work for child-related reasons.[51]

Accordingly, we propose a series of different reforms. The first is expanded family leave. Numerous possibilities have been proposed for reforming the current system. These options range from changing the size of employers to require smaller workplaces to provide benefits to expanding coverage to part-time workers or those who have not worked for one full year for the same employer. The most appealing programs provide broad, at least partially paid, coverage. They transform family leave, currently funded solely by employers, into social insurance. In such a system, both employees and employers contribute to a program that is comparable to Social Security in coverage and administration and that might even be administered by the Social Security Administration. Whether it be called Social Security Cares[52] or the FAMILY Act,[53] the basic principle is the same: employers and employees would pay a small portion of their wages to fund a federally-administered paid family leave program. The type and length of leave would remain substantially similar to that currently available under the Family Medical Leave Act (FMLA). Eligibility, however, would be based on the number of quarters worked rather than on the time worked for any individual employer, so employees would remain eligible, regardless of whether they had just begun working for a new employer.

Second, even without extending existing leaves, simply allowing parents to use their own sick leave benefits to care for their children would be a major improvement. More than half of workers do not have paid leave to care for sick children; this is true for less than a third of those with college-plus education and for almost two-thirds of those with high school or less education.[54] Working-class parents should not face a choice between lying and shortchanging their families.

Third, enhancing time flexibility ranges from providing opportunities for compressed workweeks to the timing of shift work.[55] Soliciting employee input into their schedules, providing as much notice of schedules as possible, and allowing employees to trade shifts are examples of solutions that employers can implement without incurring additional costs.[56] While respecting employers' needs for jobs to be done at a specific time in a specific place, such as retail sales, workplace flexibility allows employees to request accommodations in rigid or unpredictable schedules.[57] For someone with an unexpected child care change, or to cover school vacations, flexibility supplements FMLA protections. Some of the creative and advanced flexible work arrangements offered by the Working Mother 100 Best Companies include: the ability to shift start and stop times to accommodate non-work-related responsibilities ranging from commuting to child care to eldercare; compressed workweeks so that workers have more flexibility and longer weekends for family activities and needs; job sharing to facilitate job advancement and family time; and phasing-in programs so that new parents can transition back into work on a temporary part-time schedule.[58]

The college educated have built a new infrastructure that prepares their children for the challenges of tomorrow. We face a choice between assisting the rest of society to catch up or excluding a substantial portion of the next generation from the productive economy of the twenty-first century.

13

Sex, Power, Patriarchy, and Parental Obligation

The price of sex has changed. No longer do good girls—or anyone else—wait for marriage. More than 95 percent of Americans have had at least one sexual relationship before marriage.[1] The availability of contraception has made possible a long search for the right partner or the right circumstances to have children, without completely foregoing some fun along the way.

Yet if gender imbalance has skewed the terms of mating and dating, then the most logical solutions redress the balance. While we have argued that the most effective way to do so is through better employment prospects that affect the ways men and women match up, the other possibility involves resetting the terms of access to sex. There are two ways to do so. Conservatives think of the issue in terms of Lysistrata. They think sex *is* the problem—the social order would be restored if women, like those in Aristophanes' play, just said no to men until they shaped up. Conservatives like Charles Murray certainly believe that sex is a great motivator; if only Lily refused to sleep with Carl until he got and held a job, Murray is certain that Carl would take a dead-end position or maybe two or three or four of them if necessary to gain access to the bedroom. Feminists, too, have argued that women's ability to control the terms of access to sex can reset the terms of sexual bargains; some even fondly recall the Victorian era as a period of empowerment for wives in the boudoir.[2] We have argued throughout this book that women today do have greater power to say no to relationships with men; what they don't have is the ability to set the terms for saying yes to satisfying long-term unions. If women banded together, if they formed a cartel that policed access to sex until men proved more reliable, the balance of power might be reset even without improving male economic prospects.

Liberals object that we have been there and the result is not women embracing sisterhood to say no to men, but the Scarlet Letter. To be sure, the Charles

Murrays of the day do not go out of their way to denigrate women's virtue. Instead, they insist that the solution is to starve their children (by taking away their welfare and their food stamps and their healthcare) and somehow this will shame the men and force them to take jobs that pay the minimum wage of $7.25 an hour.

Conservatives respond that the liberal solution is closer to *Brave New World*. In Aldous Huxley's 1931 novel, natural reproduction has been abolished and sex is a matter of recreation. Huxley's society is happy, comfortable, and soulless, which is how conservatives often portray the sex lives of undergraduates.

In the meantime, the conflict between conservative and liberal elites prevents any realistic assessment of the plight of those who believe neither in the possibilities of abstinence as the solution for a lack of good jobs or contraception as a way to postpone childbearing for the more promising future they do not believe will ever arrive. Central to the realities that inform the class conflict are sex ratios. Enforcing a cartel, whether organized by good Christian women or Murray's Belmont brethren emerging from their gated communities to chastise the ne'er do wells, is difficult in the face of oversupply. Given that "too many women," or at least too many marriageable women compared to the number of marriageable men, is the problem producing the shift in family norms in the first place, cartel enforcement becomes that much more difficult. It's hard to imagine that the working-class women who have become more jaded about relationships will band together to deny sex to men until they become more prosperous and respectful. OPEC, too, after all has a much more difficult time persuading its members to cut supply when prices are falling.

Despite our skepticism, however, we are convinced that sex—having it and understanding it—is critical to the class divide and its potential solutions. Sex, after all, still produces children, and one of the most important sources of class division is the lesser ability of less-privileged women to manage sexuality on terms of their choosing. Nonetheless, the sexual landscape is changing. Although less heralded than other developments, teen sex has declined—decreasing the number of teen births as well. Instead, inopportune births have moved into the early twenties.[3]

We believe that the most promising strategies look beyond sex itself to what sex produces. Concern about children and the need for better preparation for childrearing is the moral claim that has some hope of commanding widespread support. We argue below that the better strategies focus directly on supporting parenthood and enhancing women's autonomy. Both using the pill and managing sex require support. Both tend to be more effective when prospective parents have hope for a better future. Ultimately the point for both those who advocate waiting until marriage and those who advocate waiting for maturity is preparation for the most challenging responsibility most of us will ever face—parenthood. Recasting the issue of family formation in terms of readiness for parenthood rather than sex offers some hope of agreement on the policies necessary to remake the foundation for family life.

Teen Sex and Class Translation

Those who see greater sexual restraint as the key to renegotiating family ties have been cheered by the drop in teen sex. Fewer children are conceived in the back seat of a Chevy—or a Kia. Between 1988 and 2010 an increasing number of teens reported that they were still virgins. For unmarried females between the ages of fifteen and nineteen, the number who had ever had sex has fallen steadily from 52 to 43 percent. For unmarried males, the figures are even more dramatic, falling from 60 to 42 percent in the same period.[4] One of the largest drops occurred for adolescents whose parents had some college education.[5] Former Harvard professor Mark Hauser mentioned in a talk at the Gruter Institute for Law and Behavioral Research that a survey of incoming Harvard freshman reported that only 15 percent were not virgins. The audience guffawed, but most studies find that the most successful teens live it up only *after* they get into Harvard.

For these trends to have significance for family creation, however, they need to correspond to new pathways into adult relationships and to do so in ways that make sense not just for the college-educated elite, but for those who do not attend college. In fact, the circumstances that produce these changes—elite agreement, class translation, and balanced high school gender ratios—do not carry on beyond graduation. Nonetheless, the drop in teen sex and the even more dramatic drop in teen births is something to be examined—and cheered.

In looking at why these changes have occurred, we see few comprehensive studies. In an era of budget cuts, federal authorities fund few studies with "sex" in the title, so we are left to speculate. There are, however, a number of clues.

First, adults are in agreement. Not many approve of 15-year-olds having sex.[6] We assume that those who do either do not have children or never emerged from their own drug-hazed adolescence.

Second, religious groups emphasize teen abstinence, a message that reaches deeper into the working class, at least for those who attend religious services. Texas professor Mark Regnerus found that those teens who went to church at least once a week and reported that religion was "very important" to them were significantly more likely to still be virgins. Reporting that religion was "fairly important" or attending church regularly but less than once a week had a smaller impact. While church attendance declines with worsening economic prospects, those in religious communities who reinforce their belief and behavior tend to defer the beginning of sexual activity.[7]

A third reason reinforcing the no-sex effect may have been the AIDS epidemic, particularly in the nineties. It increased support for both abstinence and condom use. Studies do find that the use of multiple means of contraception (e.g., the pill and condoms) explains some of the drop in pregnancies. The effect of greater abstinence, in contrast, is largely limited to fifteen- to seventeen-year-olds—the group that has had the sharpest decline in sexual activity.[8]

A fourth reason may be gender ratios. High school girls are still more cautious about sex than boys, and the percentage of boys reporting sexual activity outnumbers the percentage of girls so reporting through the teen years, though the differences narrow as teens get older.[9] As a practical matter, this means that the number of boys seeking partners outnumbers the number of girls.

Finally, the Great Recession may have made teens warier of early pregnancy, and attention to sexual abuse seems to have had some effect in protecting younger teens; fewer report involuntary sexual activity, though the decline was greater for boys than for girls.[10]

These figures indicate something remarkable in our study of intimate relationships—trend lines moving in the same direction for red and blue elites and, to a lesser degree, the winners and losers of the modern economy. The results proceed from the combination of elite agreement and the translation of elite norms holding the line on sexual activity into behavior that affects less well-off as well as elite groups.[11] While those who favor abstinence for religious reasons and those who simply are not ready express different reasons for their behavior, the change in behavior can be mutually reinforcing. The high school years have become a bit more sexually conservative for most groups.

The Twenties and the Hook-Up Culture

The drop in teen sex cannot have much impact on marriage or non-marital birth rates unless it continues into the twenties, and there is little evidence that it does. Instead, the new patterns push the beginning of sexual activity and family formation a little further into adulthood, and here the relatively small class-based patterns in the teen years become a much starker divide.

Sociologists Mark Regnerus and Jeremy Uecker report that 84 percent of those between the ages of eighteen and twenty-three have already had sex.[12] Yet, there is no consensus on whether this is morally right. In 2012, while 59 percent of Americans believed it morally acceptable for unmarried adults to have sex, 38 percent believed it was morally wrong; in contrast, only 7 percent

believed it was morally acceptable for married people to have affairs.[13] Moreover, while Regnerus and Uecker found that both men and women take
seriously the line between voluntary sexual activity and rape, women continue
to report high levels of actual or attempted sexual assaults, particularly during
their younger years.[14]

If objections to unmarried sex have declined, men's and women's preferences still differ. Women continue to have much less interest than men in a
one-night stand, and women still hope to get something—resources, commitment, good behavior—as the price of agreement.[15] Yet this "market" economy
produces an ironic result. The men with the fewest resources have the most
partners. While male college graduates report sleeping with an average of five
women each, those who graduate from high school claim an average of 7.4
partners, and twenty-two-year-old high school dropouts state that they have
slept with 8 to 9 women.[16] It's possible, of course, that these numbers reflect
willingness to boast, and they almost certainly reflect the length of relationships. High school dropouts may have more partners because the women in
their relationships dump them more quickly. Even so, the numbers suggest
that, at least while they're young, the men do not have trouble finding willing mates. Regnerus and Uecker conclude, "If historically men were willing to
work for sex—that is, earn the attentions of a potential partner by displaying
commitment, life skills, and/or a promising trajectory—the modern man certainly doesn't have to."[17]

The larger problem with trying to extend sexual abstinence into the twenties, however, is a lack of agreement on either the purpose or the means of
achievement. In high school, the only true agreement on goals is parental focus
on escorting their offspring safely through graduation. For religious teens, the
ultimate objective is marriage. For secular teens, the goal is admission to the
right college or achievement of the maturity necessary to make appropriate
adult choices. For blue elites, in particular, too immediate an emphasis on
marriage can get in the way of career objectives. As Hanna Rosin observed (in
a chapter she subtitled "Single Girls Master the Hook-Up"), ambitious college
women approached their love lives like "savvy headhunters."[18] Like their male
counterparts, they conclude that relationships take time they don't have. The
hook-up doesn't have to. While men and women do differ in a number of ways,
both see premature commitment as a threat to a promising life but do not view
recreational sex in the same way. Abstinence is not part of the picture—but
avoiding childbirth is, and contraception is a way of life.

"Red" college students increasingly defer sex as well, though not as much
as students in more liberal parts of the country. And conservative college
women delay sexual activity to a much greater degree than do liberal women.
Regnerus and Uecker report that 40 percent of conservative college women

between the ages of eighteen and twenty-three are still virgins in contrast to only 16 percent of liberals. The figure rises to an astounding 63 percent for white, conservative, religious never-married students or college graduates between the ages of eighteen and twenty-three.[19] The sociologists explain that the association between religiosity and sexual restraint involves the intersection of politics, religion, and class. Religiously devout college students who are political liberals are much less likely to abstain from sex than are political conservatives. Yet conservative white males who do not attend college are "among the most sexually active of all emerging adults," even if they are moderately religious.[20] Abstinence—or at least public commitment to abstinence—appears to have become a marker of elite red college student identity, even as it has largely disappeared for everyone else. Like the Regnerus and Uecker study, other research confirms that for some college students, abstinence is part of the price of membership in evangelical Christian groups on university campuses.[21]

The secular left, in contrast, has less of a problem with sex than with efforts to control sex. Liberals distrust conservative efforts to promote abstinence only and to restrain sexuality, first, because they do not agree with the religious foundation for the beliefs, second, because such efforts almost always reinforce gender stereotypes and result in greater restrictions on women and, third, because they have a disproportionately negative impact on the poor. The Guttmacher Institute reports, for example, that between 1994 and 2006 the unintended pregnancy rate grew by 50 percent for women below the poverty line. During the same period it fell by 29 percent for higher-income women. Moreover, whatever the sexual behavior of conservative elites, Regnerus and Uecker find that the number of virgins among unmarried conservative women between nineteen and twenty-three who are not in college falls to 16 percent. While that is still higher than the numbers of abstaining liberal women who don't attend college (6 percent), it suggests that neither conservative nor religious beliefs in themselves are likely to reverse the effects of less-favorable marital prospects.[22] Conservatives like to point out that many women who become pregnant either didn't use available contraception or became pregnant anyway. The other side of the coin, however, is that women who see no point in using contraception also see no point in abstaining until marriage, especially since marriage has become an ideal they do not expect to realize.

These developments create a cultural chasm between elites *and* a class gap in behavior. Elites do not have a single path into two-parent families; both abstinence and religious values and deferred commitment accompanied by the pill can successfully lead to stable relationships later in life. Neither approach, however, automatically translates into equally effective efforts for the less successful. And the conflict between the religious right and the secular left makes it less likely that new consensus-based norms on sexual conduct will emerge. In the absence of either agreement on shared norms or similar circumstances that produce a convergence in behavior, the gap between elite and non-elite patterns is likely to grow.

It is time, therefore, to address the relationship between sex and children directly. Conservatives view sex as "sacred" because of its relationship to pro-creation. Their insistence on the connection reinforces the opposition to abortion and wariness about the public embrace of contraception. Liberals insist on the importance of contraception and the continued legality of abortion precisely because they view childrearing as a critical (indeed, sacred may not be too strong a word) undertaking. We consider whether there is any common ground in the approach toward children, and we believe there is—the need to care for those we produce. Before we get there, however, we address the role of abortion in keeping these groups apart.

Abortion, Single Parents, and Childbearing

Abortion, even more than sex itself, is the fault line in the culture wars over family values. To the right, it symbolizes the lax morality that seemingly encourages non-marital sex; to the left, it represents women's freedom to live lives not circumscribed by unending childbearing. Abortion, then, involves fundamental differences about religion, morality, and the organization of life. It has become an important political issue because of, not in spite of, such differences.[23] That is, as the major political parties have become ideologically aligned, the Republican party has used the all-or-nothing nature of the abortion issue to lock in the religious right as a reliable part of its base.[24] Since 2000, moreover, more and more of those who embrace the "conservative" label have also endorsed anti-abortion policies, even if they are not religious or do not belong to a religion that opposes abortion.[25] Studies further show that anti-abortion legislators are more opposed to abortion than their constituents.[26] Accordingly, agreement on this issue is not possible.

It is nonetheless important to recognize the practical significance of abortion. For blue elites, it is essential to holding the line on non-marital, teen, and other inopportune births; for red elites, it simultaneously increases the opposition to non-marital sex and lessens opposition to unmarried parenthood. For both, it sharpens rhetorical divisions even as it should lead both to embrace greater support for struggling parents.

The women's movement has always emphasized that the objective ought to be to make abortion safe, legal, and rare, and this underlies the approaches most likely to decrease abortion rates. First, an impressive empirical literature shows that the jurisdictions with the most systematic provision of contraception have the lowest abortion rates, and the systematic use of contraception ought to be the first objective.[27] Second, there should be recognition that the availability of abortion makes it possible to hold the line on the pregnancies that derail women's educational opportunities and life chances. College Christians should, of course, be free to emphasize abstinence if they choose. We wish them well. But it is important to recognize the difference between abstinence as a marker of membership in what is effectively the elite private club that Christian groups on some campuses have become and abstinence as social policy. Indeed, teens who promise to remain abstinent are as likely to have premarital sex as those who don't, and when they do become sexually active, they are less likely to use various forms of birth control.[28]

It takes different kinds of motivation and discipline to remain abstinent than to use the pill, and extending such policies across the class divide is improbable. So anti-abortion efforts, especially when coupled with opposition to public subsidization of contraception, amount to class warfare. They take away an important tool that allows poorer women to avoid destructive teen births. The children of college-graduate women, who overwhelmingly grow up in stable two-parent families, continue to outpace the children of other women in part because abortion for them remains safe, available, and rare.

After the publication of our last book, *Red Families v. Blue Families*, Ross Douthat wrote in the *New York Times* that our description of the new "blue" model for middle-class life works in promoting stable, two-parent families but that it could never become universal because it depends on abortion.[29] Religious and cultural conservatives remain convinced that contraception is not foolproof and that abortion is unthinkable; therefore, a combination of birth control and later marriage cannot be the basis for an acceptable family strategy. Our would-be defenders rushed to the blogosphere even before we saw Douthat's column and made the points we would have made at the time. The college-educated elite in fact have fewer abortions than any other group. They do so because they are the group that has most effectively embraced contraception. Yet in the months following Douthat's column, we concluded that he was at least partially right. Looking only at what happens to those who have unplanned pregnancies, the likelihood that the pregnancy will end in abortion varies with income and education, and a very high percentage of the pregnancies of the most elite groups do end in abortion—the more highly educated abort a higher percentage of unplanned pregnancies than do those with less education.[30] For women in the highly educated group, abortion remains available and important to affirming the right family values, a necessary element of the successful effort to hold the line on non-marital births. If the college educated elite were to "preach what they practice," as Charles Murray suggests, the importance of abortion would be part of the sermon. Accordingly, no compromise is possible on the legality of abortion.

Ironically, the willingness to abort appears to be correlated with optimism about the future; it is important in holding the line on teen births among poor women as well as on non-marital births for college students. As two economists found, greater income inequality in a state—particularly the gap between the middle and the bottom—is strongly correlated with high teen birth rates. In looking for the explanation, the study found that the rates of unplanned pregnancy were about the same in the more equal and less equal states. What explained the differences in the birth rates was the willingness to abort. Even after controlling for such factors as the political climate in the state and the population's degree of religiosity, the economists found that economic inequality had a lot to do with whether teens gave birth or waited until they were better prepared for parenthood—and abortion was the method they chose to secure the result.[31] Mothers who do not hold out much hope for either a good job or a satisfying marriage go ahead and have the child. The acceptability of abortion accordingly does not in itself explain the increase in non-marital births; indeed, the study attempted to control for that. Instead, higher abortion rates turned out to be a sign of hope rather than despair. In predicting both teen birth rates and the willingness to use abortion because of the unacceptability of the birth, optimism about future employment and partnership prospects is a critical factor.

For conservative religious elites, the conviction that contraception is unreliable and abortion is unacceptable contributes to the emphasis on abstinence—and, as a practical matter—a growing acceptance of non-marital births. The 2012 Republican Party Platform stated:

> We renew our call for replacing "family planning" programs for teens with increased funding for abstinence education, which teaches abstinence until marriage as the responsible and expected standard of behavior. Abstinence from sexual activity is the only protection that is 100 percent effective against out-of-wedlock pregnancies and sexually transmitted diseases, including HIV/AIDS when transmitted sexually.[32]

Insisting that abortion is unacceptable, however, contributes to the erosion of the stigma against non-marital births. To be sure, conservatives would prefer marriage before childbirth. In the face of anti-abortion fervor, however, they have become much more willing to tolerate, albeit not provide economic support to, the single mother who refuses the "easy way out." While traveling in rural Indiana at 4 a.m. in late 2012, for example, one of us listened in fascination as a mother and daughter proudly described the nineteen-year-old daughter's decision to have her rapist's child because she had embraced "the culture of life."

Outside of the elite, an anti-abortion stance similarly reinforces the acceptability of nonmarital childbirth. Kathy Edin and Maria Kefala observed that the young women they studied often mentioned their opposition to abortion in deciding to raise an unplanned child, but did not think marriage necessarily followed a pregnancy.[33] The young working-class couples they studied are certainly not abstinent, but their moral beliefs help justify the decision to have the child. Marriage, in contrast, depends much more on their perception of the reliability of the father. Today, no one is saying to the young woman who was raped that the decision to keep the child depends on her ability to arrange a marriage.

The irony is that both religious elites, who emphasize abstinence and have their children within marriage, and secular elites, who place little weight on marriage per se but overwhelmingly rear their children within two-parent families, value careful preparation for childrearing. Yet they fundamentally disagree on how to get there and what the fallback measures are. Liberals have long championed women's ability to make their own decisions and believe that the best way to encourage women to make the right decisions for themselves and their children is to enhance women's emotional, physical, and financial well-being.[34] In this context, abortion is a personal choice, one that the government should ensure is available to any woman with the government paying for those who cannot afford it on their own. Liberals simultaneously champion women's autonomy in decision-making and focus on putting in place the supports—jobs, access to contraception and abortion, subsidized health and child care—that encourage good decisions.[35]

Conservatives place more emphasis on morality—avoiding non-marital sex, condemning abortion, encouraging marriage—but forgive those who stray so long as they come back to the right values. Outside of the culturally explosive issue of abortion, the two positions differ more in terms of their rhetoric than in their conclusions about single parenthood. Today, both conservatives and liberals view single parenthood as an acceptable second choice, preferable to abortion for conservatives and preferable to constraints on women's decision-making power for liberals. If, as a pragmatic, political decision, we change our focus from how the pregnancy occurred to the acceptability of the non-marital mother raising the child, we see a remarkable degree of overlap. This common understanding should then provide the basis for increasing support of nonmarital parents—or at least for the children they have been encouraged to raise. The question then becomes whether they can be in agreement on encouraging children to be born in more promising circumstances.

Preparation for Parenting

Our previous book critiqued abstinence-only efforts and found them wanting. We then compared marriage promotion campaigns and found more to like, though recent studies cast doubt on their effectiveness, particularly outside of white middle-class couples.[36] Here we explore the possibilities for family education efforts focused on parenting. In doing so, we recognize that any degree of cultural convergence is difficult and unlikely. We nonetheless try to distinguish between elite ideological divisions (e.g., emphasis on traditional marriage vs. emphasis on acceptance of diverse family forms) and class behavioral divergence (marriage before children is no longer attractive to many members of the working class, whereas it remains typical for the elite). We accordingly focus on where red and blue elites might agree, notwithstanding political differences, on better family formation practices; unlike marriage, becoming a parent is not limited by class. Parent education involves techniques that need not be controversial—create stimulating environments in early childhood, learn how to breast feed, teach parents how to interact with a newborn, and so on. They are more likely to work because parents are more motivated to care for their children than teens are to avoid sex, and they are more likely to be accepted because of the cultural convergence on support for parenting.

Childrearing Is an Important Obligation

We have emphasized the deep divisions that exist about the appropriate pathways into parenthood. Where there is less disagreement is on the importance of the children who result.[37] Today, moreover, young adults look at parenting as separate from adult relationships. In 2010, for example, Pew Research found that 52 percent of those between the ages of eighteen and twenty-nine said that being a good parent is "one of the most important things" in life. In comparison, just 30 percent ranked having a successful marriage as that important. In 1997, in contrast, 42 percent of respondents in the same age range said that being a good parent was one of the most important things in life while 35 percent said the same about having a successful marriage.[38] In the intervening years, parenting had become more important and marriage less so. Focusing on parenting itself may thus have relevance both for those who value marriage as essential and those who do not. While not everyone may feel it is important to become a parent, the value of parenting to children is not controversial.

Preparation for Parenting Includes Education and Employment

Childrearing is tough. We know, and every new parent finds out quickly. The arrival of a newborn is often overwhelming, and it takes substantial economic resources to manage a child from infanthood through adulthood.[39] The financial preparation can take a number of forms, but increasingly it requires the workforce participation of both men and women.

Men's workforce participation remains largely a given. Men expect to work, prefer to work, and find that employment increases the likelihood of marriage and of opportunities for other relationships. Women's workforce participation is a more contentious issue. A 2012 Gallup poll showed that for women, workforce participation is at least in part a partisan issue. Asked whether they would ideally prefer to stay home and care for the family, Republican women are more likely than Democratic women to say yes, with 57 percent of Republican women and only 37 percent of Democratic women expressing a preference for the domestic role.[40] In contrast, Democrats are more likely than Republicans to prefer to work outside the home by a margin of 59 to 37 percent. Some of the differences may reflect age (older women are more likely to be Republicans than younger women) and race (African-American women, who are more likely than whites to be Democrats, are also more likely to be in the workplace). Nonetheless, it suggests that Republicans and conservatives place greater emphasis on traditional gender roles.

The reason we don't believe that the partisan divide on this issue is a deal breaker for parenting education, however, involves the combination of class and the question of second choices. Conservatives recognize that for women to be able to play a domestic role there needs to be a breadwinning partner. If there isn't, the women need to work. Charles Murray accordingly argued in the eighties that unmarried welfare recipients could transform themselves into the "deserving" poor by seeking work.[41] Then 2012 Republican presidential candidate Mitt Romney echoed those sentiments, stating that he wanted to increase the work requirement. Romney observed that "I said, for instance, that even if you have a child 2 years of age, you need to go to work. And people said, 'Well that's heartless.' And I said, 'No, no, I'm willing to spend more giving daycare to allow those parents to go back to work. It'll cost the state more providing that daycare, but I want the individuals to have the dignity of work.'"[42]

Liberals, who remain skeptical of welfare reform, are nonetheless more likely to view mothers' employment as appropriate and to applaud state aid in assisting mothers in obtaining employment. Moreover, for poor women, employment tends to enhance relationship prospects as well as the ability to provide for children—poor men expect their partners to be breadwinners.[43]

Preparation for parenthood should therefore emphasize the importance of being able to work if needed. Both men and women should prepare themselves to obtain employment that can support a family.

Choosing the Right Partner Contributes to Relationship Stability

Picking the right partner is critical for marriage, but it is also important for single parents. The Pew Study reports that 93 percent of men want to marry a woman who is a good mother, and 91 percent of women want a man who is a good father.[44] Both sexes also want a partner who is caring and compassionate and puts the family ahead of everything else. And both men and women agree on these qualities well ahead of other factors. In addition, effective marriage classes encourage students to look for the warning signs of domestic violence, learn how to keep the lines of communication open, and insist on mutual respect.[45]

Studies further show that women who are choosier about the fathers of their children, whether or not they marry, tend to have more stable relationships. Linda Burton et al., for example, in the study we discussed in chapter 10, explored the role of selectivity in relationship stability.[46] The study found that many intimate relationships today are characterized by "quick entrees, partners gathering little evidence about trustworthiness, limited interdependence, and an emphasis on partners meeting specific immediate needs."[47] The expectation that men will earn at least as much as women is changing more slowly than the opportunities for women to earn as much as men. Men and women are unlikely to trust each other if they have to earn that trust only by living up to unrealistic (and outmoded) expectations about what it means to be a good partner.[48]

Given our analysis of the way men and women match up, we recognize that the payoff of pickiness for Amy is a lot higher than it is for Lily; Amy, after all, enjoys better odds of finding a partner who will be an asset in raising her children. Yet, Burton finds that the level of selectivity varies within as well as across communities and often does so as a result of childhood experiences. The marriage education classes we found in states like Utah emphasized factors that can be taught, such as recognizing the warning signs of domestic violence. The best advice, however, may be to slow down: about the choice of partner, the initiation of intimate relationships, and certainly the openness to pregnancy.

Contraception Is Part of Long-Term Relationships

June, in her Catholic high school, once participated in a debate about the church's position on birth control. Midway through the debate, she realized that her opponent couldn't imagine that a married woman might want to use contraception. After more than fifty years of marriage and five children between us, we have a hard time imagining an otherwise fertile married woman who would not.

However much the Christian right advocates abstinence before marriage, we suspect that few advocate abstinence within marriage. And although the Catholic Church continues to oppose all artificial means of contraception, almost all married couples, including most Catholics, use it.[49] So we see information about contraception as an important part of preparation for childrearing, inside or outside marriage.

In looking at the health of children, an important factor for the most vulnerable is the birth of a second child close in time to the first. The second child taxes even the best prepared parents' energy and resources. For women who have a first child in their teen years, in poverty, or as single parents, avoiding the quick birth of a second child contributes to the well-being of mother and child.

We accordingly see no necessary contradiction between comprehensive family planning and marriage promotion. Indeed, we see the two as intricately related. Contraception can be presented as something couples contemplating marriage should plan for. And it doesn't hurt to give them the necessary information before the engagement.

Moreover, as we explained in *Red Families v. Blue Families*, the poorer a woman is, the more likely she is to have her high school sex education class as her only source of information about birth control at the time of her first sexual encounter—and the more likely she is to be currently enrolled in abstinence-only classes. We think depriving young women of accurate information about contraception and childbirth is inexcusable, and providing that information is an important corrective to the growing class differences in family formation.

Finally, one of the growing class differences in contraceptive use involves timing and motive. We increasingly hear from our friends and our students that the word is out that the pill makes periods more regular and eases the severity of menstrual cramps. Indeed, WebMD insists that oral contraceptives can reduce cancer risk, eliminate acne, lighten monthly bleeding, control PMS, and make periods less painful.[50] We leave to others the truth of these assertions. We note only that adolescents who see doctors on a regular basis are often advised to start on the pill shortly after puberty for precisely these reasons. For these girls, the pill is part of a rite of passage. It marks the beginning of adulthood. It becomes a daily ritual. It is separated from the beginning of sexual activity, perhaps for as long as a decade.

It is time to recognize that effective contraception, for the married and the unmarried, is a system that should be extended to all girls at the time they reach puberty. Its meaning—whether connected to physical maturity, marriage, or sexuality—can be adjusted to local customs and cultures, but its importance to women's lives should not be overlooked or shortchanged.

The Birth of a Child Does Not Change Women's Life Scripts

We were on a panel with a Catholic priest not long after Bristol Palin announced that she and her child's father, Levi Johnston, had renewed their engagement. He seemed to think that marriage provided an important answer. We explained that our advice to her was exactly the same after the birth of the child as it would have been before. Stay in school, invest in your own earning capacity, and avoid the birth of a second child too soon after the birth of the first. We also explained how marriage was unlikely to be a panacea and could be a trap. At the time, Bristol was struggling to get a GED and to hold a low-paying job. For many women in her circumstances, marriage holds out the promise of being able to quit school or work and stay home with the child. The conventional wisdom used to be that the birth of an additional child would help cement the father's commitment to the family. None of that holds true today.

As Bristol quickly discovered, Levi was unlikely to be a reliable dad. He hasn't held a steady job, gotten his high school degree, or remained faithful (though we have no insight into his subsequent marriage to someone else). The likelihood of marriage lasting in the face of any of these facts is small. And if marriage were to mean trusting in Levi's earning prospects rather than her own, it would be a mistake. Marriage might in fact strengthen the relationship between father and child. And if it worked, all three would be better off. Yet making it work almost certainly depends on two-parent contributions to the family's finances and developing a greater degree of cooperation and trust. Given the uncertainties that underlie young men's earnings and today's families, the best advice to young mothers is that marriage is not a substitute for investing in yourself. Young men already realize that the lack of a job may mean the lack of a family life; the part they need to learn is how to win over the woman and children of their dreams on the basis of something other than a paycheck.

*   *   *

14

The Death of Family Law—And Prospects for Its Rebirth

Family has long been tied to dependency—the reliance of women on their husband's income and the importance of marriage in providing for children and their caretakers.[1] The rise of more autonomous women, who *can* thrive on their own earnings, and the decline of marriage—both as the institution for organizing sex and as the exclusive way to provide for children—have rocked family law to its core. While women have won a measure of autonomy, the system still cannot rubber-stamp private agreements that leave dependent parties bereft. And adult relationships have become so varied in their understandings that it is no longer possible to think of them as following a single script. As a result, the core of family law—as a system that provides default terms to guide adult relationships when the parties fail to agree, that guides young couples into a single institutional framework for their relationships, and that imposes societal norms (for better or worse) on those who stray—no longer can or should serve the same purposes. What remains, as something more than the expression of adult agreements, is the family law that regulates parentage, custody, and child support. Protecting children's needs requires something more than leaving matters to their parents.

Central to this transformation is the move away from a single model of the family as a married, heterosexual couple raising their biological children. Indeed, we are not sure that couples know what they're getting into when they move in together, have a child together, or even plan to marry. Nothing about these relationships implies agreement that Amy will cook (Tyler is definitely better at that) or that Carl will take out the garbage (in fact, Lily routinely did so when they were living together). Even if we ignore marriage itself, Tyler and Amy, as lawyers with two incomes, almost certainly do not share the same assumptions about their relationship as struggling parents Lily and Carl. If, after ten years together and two children, Amy left Tyler, should he have to pay support if his law firm job pays twice as much as the local judgeship she was thrilled to get? Should Carl's parental rights be terminated if Lily wants the man she latter marries to adopt the child? Amy and Tyler have not thought about such things (unless they took our family law class), and Lily and Carl would almost certainly disagree on the right outcome if another man came along. Even the U.S. Supreme Court struggles with such issues, as it issues divided opinions and sends the matters back to the states.[2]

The Limits of Family Law

What the law cannot do is impose a one-size-fits-all model for family relationships. It tried, in an era in which almost all adults were married, only poor women worked outside of the home, and leaving a marriage could only be done based on fault. But consider what might happen today if Amy and Tyler divorce, Tyler earns twice as much as Amy, and Amy has become involved with someone else. A court would need to decide child custody, child support, property distribution, and alimony issues. First, when it comes to the financial issues, Amy has the same opportunities for employment as Tyler. Supreme Court Justice Sandra Day O'Connor graduated third in her class from Stanford but found that no law firm would hire her. This is not true for Amy. Thus child support, alimony, and property distribution do not need to address dependence or protect the public fisc. Amy, after all, was able to leave Tyler *because* she is self-supporting.

Second, we might assume that Amy earns less because she took on more of the childrearing responsibilities, and indeed, women continue to spend more time on childcare than men do, even if men have somewhat closed the gap.[3] Yet, women who remain employed full-time do not pay the same income penalty as do women who take time off, and men who, like Tyler, make time for their children earn lower wages as well.[4] If Amy were a stay-at-home mom, she would clearly have suffered an earnings loss because of her family responsibilities. It is really hard to know, however, how much of the income difference between Amy and Tyler reflects her decisions to plan the children's birthday parties, arrange dance lessons, and attend more of their soccer games, and it is even harder to determine how much a court should inquire into the causes for the income disparity.

Third, men and women still make different choices about occupations (more men become engineers, more women become pharmacists) in part because of assumptions about family responsibilities.[5] But how much of Tyler's decision to represent high-tech start-ups versus Amy's acceptance of a judicial appointment has anything to do with gender or family? We can cite the statistics (30 percent of the federal judicial and 40 percent of Obama judicial appointees are women),[6] but it is hard to conclude that Tyler should support Amy when she has landed a prestigious position that pays more than enough to allow her to support herself. Untangling gender, family obligations, and random circumstances in particular cases is impossible. Complicating things further is the fact that Amy chose to leave. Tyler is crushed. In another era, Amy would be the villain for breaching her marriage vows. Today, the courts in the state in which Amy and Tyler are living have declared that fault is irrelevant.

These factors make it hard to develop fair and generally applicable rules. Moreover, the combination of the gender wars (feminists vs. fathers' rights groups) and red versus blue ideological division make it even harder to get it right. Legislatures and courts have concluded that case-by-case judgments create too much uncertainty and potential for political backlash. The result is a move away from discretion. While a judge used to determine support and custody in accordance with his judgment of the parties' needs (and we do mean "his"), the states have moved toward more mechanical fifty-fifty divisions of property, child support equations, and alimony guidelines precisely because of a lack of agreement in the midst of changing gender roles.[7] Indeed, the courts in deeply divided states, such as Alabama, have responded to the lack of agreement about what should happen in these cases by withdrawing from the normative debate—they decide cases on their individual facts and do not issue written opinions that provide guidance for future cases in the most hotly contested areas of family law.[8]

Class divisions complicate things further. The top group of men still overwhelmingly marry women who earn less than they do;[9] the upper third includes both homemakers happy to rely on their spouse's income and high-earning women eager to stay in the labor market.[10] The middle group of women, in contrast, are more likely to be in the labor market because their families need the money, and when they do earn more it is likely to be because they are supporting spouses who are un- or underemployed.[11]

Tyler makes more than Amy for reasons that are typical of college-graduate marriages; even within the legal profession, he has made different employment choices. Carl and Lily are unlikely to marry for the same reasons that make his income unreliable. If they did marry, they would be likely to divorce during a period in which Carl was out of work and Lily could no longer stand being the primary caretaker, sole breadwinner, and Carl's cheerleader. At that point, Carl, like Amy, would be earning less than the other spouse, and Carl, like Amy, may well have spent more time with the child, at least in the period just preceding the divorce. Should Carl and Amy receive comparable relief? We don't think so, but teasing out the reasons is complex and depends on an analysis of their contributions, both financial and caretaking, to the marriage.

Practically speaking, courts rarely award more than transitional support in these cases. As we argue below, this may not be a bad thing, even if it is not always fair or ideal. Instead, the challenge for family law becomes, first, how to lock in the bargains that benefit children and, second, how to do so in ways that take into account the balance of power between men and women in different circumstances. To do this, courts need some discretion to address differing circumstances (even though we recognize that judges inevitably exercise discretion in accordance with their own limited and often biased worldviews).

The Rebirth of Family Law

The debate over family values—and their legal expression—proceeds as though financial and child custody laws are independent of the power framework in which the rules are to be implemented. We have argued throughout this book that they are not. Instead, the rebirth of family law as something that is useful and reflects actual needs and practices requires a model of how lovers and parents might redefine their relationships in such an era.

At the core of that model lies a vision of what creating new gender bargains ultimately requires. The universality of marriage rested on the wholesale subordination of women, and many, particularly from the right, believe it still does. On an all-male Fox news panel—in 2013—conservative blogger Erick Erickson opined that the increasing number of women who are the primary breadwinners supporting their children (40 percent) was a downright repudiation of nature itself. He explained:

> When you look at biology, look at the natural world, the roles of a male and a female in society, and other animals, the male typically is the dominant role. The female, it's not antithesis, or it's not competing, it's a complementary role. We as people in a smart society have lost the ability to have complementary relationships in nuclear families, and it's tearing us apart.[12]

In other words, the problem with the family is that women no longer defer to their "lords and masters."

At the same time, in relationships where women are both the primary breadwinners and the primary caretakers, they often receive little in return. These women do have the increased societal status that greater earnings offer. These greater earnings, however, while they are attractive to potential partners, do not necessarily produce any greater measure of deference or power within the home. We have argued that this is true in large part because they have fewer potential matches with reliable and respectful men than do more elite women. If lower-income men responded to their partners' higher income by saying "yes dear, yes dear" a little more often, we could imagine more stable relationships. We do know wonderful partnerships where the wife earns more than the husband, where each partner cycles in and out of the work place, and where the man has taken on more of the childcare, cooking, and shopping. The places where we see this most often, however, are on university faculties and self-selected progressive strongholds. We also see many working-class couples trade shifts in order to minimize child care costs and home care costs. What we don't see, however, is many women staying with otherwise healthy men who can't manage either to hold a job or clean the house.[13] University of Florida law professor Nancy Dowd has written eloquently that the same male hierarchies that shortchange working-class men also enshrine traditional indicia of male status;[14] many studies find that the man who does not earn more than his female partner is *less* likely to clean the house than one who does.[15] Indeed, those men who face few attractive job opportunities often experience the greatest pressure to perform traditional male roles. Those who do not attend college are significantly more likely than those who do to report that it is a problem if the wife earns more than the husband, and the wife is more likely to cut back on her hours if the additional income would exceed her husband's.[16] The gender revolution that has accepted women into the workforce has not produced a generation of homemaking men, nor does it seem likely to do so any time soon.[17]

We can easily imagine a different future, and the previous chapters described how we might get there. We believe that both men and women, even those raised to defer to the male "lord and master" in the relationship, can develop and accept equal partnerships, and of course, many couples would prefer them. The more difficult issue is what to do about the present; a present in which the existing relationship terms that are readily available persuade too many parents not to invest in their children. Bracketing the question of whether the dismantling of gender roles will ever be possible, we believe it makes sense to focus on the parenting partnership, to ask what allocation of power best increases the odds that adult resources will flow to children. The answer lies in a family law system that counters the impact of gender ratios to facilitate more constructive relationship terms.

Doing so requires accepting, at least implicitly, the consequences of class differences in opportunities and power. In the upper third, women do enjoy reasonable prospects of finding the "right" man, and the men eager to pair with the "right" women are willing to commit and invest in the resulting children. These relationships tend to be stable, in part because the greater availability of men makes lasting bargains possible and in part because the men in the upper third continue to enjoy more power in society and within the relationships after children are born.

This is true whether or not couples marry.[18] American *marriages* are less stable than European cohabitations; the instability rather than the lack of the ring is what affects children. It is possible to celebrate adults' greater freedom to craft relationships with however many partners they choose and still be concerned that an adult walking out on a partner may deprive their child of a parent, a companion, and a provider. The challenge for family law is to affirm parental commitment to children at a time when the communities and the institutions that have historically done so are in disarray. We propose that family law attempt to do more systematically what it has always done for elites: lock in parental bargains that benefit children, nudge parents toward greater acceptance of the responsibilities that go with parenthood, and help forge new understandings, whether express or implied, that promote family stability. This does not require dramatic changes in the current system applicable to dissolving the adult partnership relationship, but it has more of an impact on parenting relationships.

Property and Support

First, for those who are married, the existing system, in recognition of marriage as an interdependent commitment, appropriately requires equitable, if not equal, property division. Shared property regimes protect the investment of the spouse who contributes more to the children and the other spouse's career. We can easily imagine cases where equal division is not appropriate; yet in a world without agreement on what those cases are (the GE executive who made millions or the school teacher working a second shift to care for her two children and laid off husband?), we believe that equal division should be the preferred solution. Given the ability of the sophisticated to insist on premarital agreements, it does not deter marriage. In the majority of cases, there is not enough property to dispute (half of divorcing couples have net worths under $80,000),[19] and in the few cases where the result is unfair (our harried school teacher, perhaps), the courts should have discretion to adjust the form of the award (through a lien on the house, for example, that requires a split in the proceeds only after it is sold). Tyler and Amy would therefore split their house, car, and bank accounts without too much inquiry into who earned more or who did more child care.

Second, the existing clear distinctions between married and unmarried couples with respect to property ownership make sense. Non-marital couples have deliberately chosen their status. Lily is unlikely to marry Carl unless she believes he will contribute as much as she does, and while, like most unmarried couples, they are unlikely ever to have enough property to dispute, women like Lily would be at a substantial disadvantage if their intimate relationships could give rise to claims that offset child support or create questions about title to her bank account. Rather than extend rights in any wholesale way to unmarried couples,[20] we would keep open the type of equitable claims that arise when one partner contributes to the other's house or business.[21]

Third, we believe that long-term spousal support should be limited to (a) long-term marriages, (b) with a substantial difference in income, and (c) decisions made during the marriage (such as full-time homemaking) that contributed to the differences. The move toward rules in these areas provides greater certainty and definitive recognition of the existing dependency of long-term homemakers. The idea of support is tied to older notions of either women's intrinsic dependence or the assumption that gendered income differences reflected a natural or at least preferred division of family responsibilities. Today, courts award alimony in only 15 percent of all divorces, and most of these awards are transitional in nature.[22] While alimony does benefit the one-in-five wives who have no income,[23] younger women increasingly find that they need to retain their income capacity because of their families' finances, and more than two-thirds of women in the bottom quintile of family income earn as much as, or more than, their husbands.[24] Long-term support seems inappropriate, however, to deal with either what should be public responsibilities, such as illness or involuntary unemployment, or personal preferences, such as a judgeship rather than a private law firm partnership. Spousal support at the top, while sometimes appropriate, tends to reinforce gendered divisions of responsibilities, and spousal support at the bottom is largely irrelevant. In the middle, however, it often seems unfair for those men whose wives make the decision to call it quits and for those women whose income is their children's principal source of support.

These changes confirm the long-term trend toward treating adults as autonomous individuals responsible for their own well-being. To complete the picture requires examining the obligations that the law should continue to impose. These responsibilities require consideration of the relationship of parents to children.

Parenting and Child Support

Remaking the agenda starts with identifying who the legal parents are and what their obligations are to their children. Existing law assumes that biological progenitors should have a relationship with their children,[25] but it has failed either to replace the marital presumption with new institutions that

serve children's interests or to lock in bargains that make it more likely that
two parents will be involved. Doing so requires taking into account the power
dynamic that underlies relationships. For college graduates, that dynamic continues to depend on the role of formal institutions in both giving fathers rights
(e.g., shared custody, particularly after divorce) and allowing women to establish single parenthood (sperm donors). These institutions make parenthood
certain and counter women's increasing ability to leave unhappy relationships
with fathers' greater ability to maintain a relationship with the children. Encouraging parental relationships for those unlikely to marry or to ever go near
a sperm bank is another matter.

We accordingly begin with the question of who the parents are, that is, who
receives legal recognition as an adult with the ability to seek custody and to
become liable for child support. A new system must acknowledge biology yet
recognize the strength of established relationships, taking seriously women's
agency in welcoming a partner into the child's life. Such a system offers the
most hope for encouraging bargains that advance children's interests.

The first step, acknowledging biology, requires reconsideration of paternity.
We have argued elsewhere that mandatory paternity tests at birth could establish the genetic tie, giving notice to the adults that they should base their
relationships on truth and intentionality rather than falsehoods.[26] Today, the
costs of DNA tests have fallen sufficiently (and pre- and post-natal testing for
other purposes are becoming common) such that it would be relatively easy
to encourage providing these tests at birth, for married as well as unmarried
couples, allowing exceptions only where the two parents agree they will never
be able to contest each other's parental standing.[27]

We recognize, however, many potential objections to mandating such tests.
First, the drive to establish paternity has overwhelmingly come from those
who would penalize unmarried parents, primarily through the type of counterproductive child support efforts described in chapter 10. That is obviously
not our goal. In fact, we see no point in forcing new mothers to name men
who have no interest in the child, multiple partners who will not be involved
in the child's life, anonymous donors, or violent, abusive or otherwise danger-
ous men. Second, while we view paternity tests as most appropriate to confirm
the biological contribution of men who want recognition as fathers, we do not
wish to create additional barriers to recognition where the intended mother
and father are in agreement. Third, we view the legal establishment of paternity as giving men who can gain access to the legal system greater ability to
secure time with the child, and thus greater power over the mother, whether or
not this is in the best interest of the child.

Given these concerns, we believe efforts to secure paternity testing should
be tied to (a) the consent of both parties, (b) subsidization of the cost of the

tests, and (c) appropriate background law on the rights and obligations of parents. We think parental bargains should reflect the truth of paternity, but we oppose the use of this information to bring back shotgun parenting.

Consequently, the necessary complement to greater recognition of the facts of biological parenthood is the development of systems that lock in parents' commitments to children on the basis of their assumption of a parental role rather than on biology or marriage per se. Imagine, for example, that Lily, the unmarried mother we described at the beginning of the book, enters into a new relationship with Andy, a great guy who takes over the father's role. Carl, the biological father, did not support Lily during the pregnancy and has seen the child only a few times since. Insisting that Lily identify him and help him establish paternity would allow him to interfere with Lily's efforts to care for the child (and certainly with Lily's new relationship with Andy) without necessarily inducing him to contribute anything to Lily or the child. Moreover, under this coercive system, even if Andy then lives with Lily and the child for several years, becoming, for all practical purposes, the child's father, he would have no ability to insist on a continuing relationship with the child if his relationship with Lily ended. Instead, Carl will remain the only second parent, even if he makes little effort to see or support the child; Andy can achieve a secure parental status only through an adoption that terminates Carl's parental rights.

Moving away from bright line judgments about parenthood to discretionary ones would allow courts to choose among Lily, Carl, or Andy. Yet, making such choices is difficult in an era of political division over cultural values and a judicial move toward rules (the "father" has a right to shared custody) rather than standards (the child's relationship with the person who has acted as a parent should be protected).[28] Moreover, discretionary standards often empower judges to impose their personal preferences on the parties. Many judges, for example, would identify with Carl and uphold his rights to a role in the child's life on the basis of biology alone.[29] Other judges would be less forgiving of his failure to marry Lily or provide support for her and the child.[30]

Complicating matters further is the involvement of more than two adults in the child's life on an ongoing basis; what if both Carl and Andy are involved with the child even though only Andy is involved with Lily? Several states now recognize more than two parents who may play a role in the child's life.[31] Adoption of such statutes is often motivated by the desire to reinforce families of choice, where, for example, a lesbian couple and a biological father wish to raise a child together. Such statutes, however, might also apply to biological parents and stepparents in heterosexual relationships. In the majority of jurisdictions that limit the number of parents to two, Andy would have to replace Carl permanently and via legal substitution in order to acquire parental status.

If it were possible to recognize three parents, however, the courts could acknowledge Andy's parental role without terminating Carl's status as a parent. Yet, giving all three—Lily, Carl, and Andy—custodial rights at the same time would be daunting in the best of circumstances. The poorer the family, the more likely Lily and her relatives are to be the most stable influences in the child's life; the better off Lily becomes, the more likely she is to form a long-term, stable relationship with someone like Andy.[32] If that doesn't happen, if Lily's relationship with Andy proves to be as brief and as unstable as her relationship with Carl, Carl may more likely be the one to step forward at some future date if the child needs him. But none of this is predictable at the time of the child's birth.

It is therefore time to acknowledge the potential involvement of multiple adults in a child's life in ways that balance the role of biology, established relationships, and healthy environments. Indeed, some states, including California[33] and Louisiana,[34] have developed legal rules to manage the multiple adults who may cycle in and out of a child's life (the two states differ significantly in their reasons for doing so, however).

First, California and Louisiana recognize multiple adults who *may* obtain the legal status of parenthood without a requirement of equal rights or responsibilities for all of them. In California, an individual can become a presumed parent through the marital presumption or by welcoming the child into the household and holding out the child as one's own.[35] Both categories require assumption of parental functions. Louisiana recognizes "dual paternity," allowing the courts to acknowledge the parental status of both a husband and a separate biological father, though it has recently limited the ability of the unmarried, biological father to assert paternity after the first year of the child's life.[36] We believe that both biological and functional parents (whether married or not) should be seen as "potential parents" identified by their connection to the child within the first two years of the child's life but that there is no need to decide among them or to assign any rights or responsibilities until the need arises. If Lily were living with Andy, for example, no court action need be taken unless Lily and Andy break up, Lily seeks child support from Carl (or Carl seeks child custody), or Lily and Andy decide that Andy should seek to adopt the child. Only at that point need the court address which of the three parents is entitled to recognition.

Second, when making that decision on custody rights, established relationships should trump biology alone. This means recognizing a person who has established a bond with the child and contributed to the child's support rather than a person asserting parentage on the basis solely of the biological tie without any functional relationship. In other words, a person becomes a parent by satisfying the following three requirements: (1) assumes a parental role, with the express or implied consent of the initial legal parent, (2) encourages the child to accept the adult as a parent, and (3) lives with the child either in the custodial parent's home or separately (for at least 50 percent of the time) over a period of at least two years.[37] If Lily and Andy were to separate when the child was three after two years of living together and the child recognized Andy as her father, we would give Andy (but not the absent Carl) the ability to seek shared custody in accordance with the best interest of the child. If, on the other hand, Lily and Andy broke up because Andy abused Lily or the child, Carl would be the only father to receive recognition. If, however, Carl had remained involved in the child's life and Andy had a closer parental bond with the child as well, we would keep open the possibility of the continuing involvement of all three, but we would not favor a presumption that ties with all three are necessarily in the child's interests.[38]

Third, when it comes to financial obligations, we would treat the non-custodial biological parent as a guarantor, even in the absence of an established relationship. That is, so long as someone else has assumed the second parent role or the custodial parent is not asking for support, no support could be ordered. If, however, the custodial parent needs support, the biological parent remains potentially liable so long as his parental status has not been terminated. Thus, if Andy and Lily split when the child is three, Andy seeks no continuing relationship with the child, and Lily seeks support three years later because of a financial emergency, Carl (but not Andy) would be liable for support.

Fourth, the courts should, of course, retain the ability to determine custodial rights in accordance with the child's best interest and the ability to encourage healthy environments. Shared custody does not work where the parents are at war with each other, and violent and abusive conduct, such as child abuse, should continue to be disqualifying.

Fully implementing such a system requires reconceiving state support for children altogether; the existing measures have little to do with replacing the old Aid to Families with Dependent Children–type of support that was supposed to come from an ideal father who has "abandoned" his children. Current law imposes support orders on men with little ability to pay and disregards in kind contributions, which may be the only form of support a man can provide—and which also may serve to promote his own feelings of contributing to his child's growth. The one circumstance where child-support enforcement does make sense is where the father has a steady job and deserted the family. This is the circumstance in which the mother is also most likely to want a support order.

We propose an end to state insistence on counterproductive child-support enforcement as a condition of state aid of any kind to custodial parents. Instead, we would use the resources spent on such efforts to assist children directly. This means giving greater priority to enforcement efforts on behalf of the many custodial parents who welcome aid in enforcement, giving fathers who contribute in kind greater recognition for their efforts and disentangling state assistance for children from misleading images of deadbeat dads in an era when unmarried fathers are often contributing to their children and mothers are frequently the ones who decide to end the relationship.

Remaking the Place of Family Law

What skews dissolution decisions today and makes intimate relationships of all kinds more perilous is the erosion of the social safety net and the lack of support for childrearing. The principle of insurance rests on spreading risk. A larger group of people can bear the costs of an unanticipated illness, disability or temporary unemployment following an economic downturn better than a single individual. Yet, most families are too small to bear these costs on their own without wiping out the resources of the group.

The upper third of the country enjoys a robust (and often invisible) insurance system that includes employer-provided health care and disability benefits, flexible jobs with paid sick leave, and the resources to hire nannies and home health care workers that fill in the gaps. Much of the rest of the country still relies on family members to take up many of these functions. We have yet to face squarely what that means in a divorce where the wage-earner is leaving a spouse who cannot find a job because of illness or an industry downturn. Nor have we honestly addressed the consequences of using child support rather than public funds to provide medical care for a sick child when that means, sometimes literally, taking food out of the mouths of the other children the non-custodial parent is supporting. Family law in these circumstances can take away from Peter to pay Paul but it cannot create healthier families or strengthen communities. A stronger social safety net would make it easier to focus on the marshaling of resources necessary to provide for the next generation.

In today's world, we are in the middle of rebuilding our understandings of how the family relates to the larger society. The increase in inequality masks a long-term readjustment of the relationship between home and market. The elimination of the subordination of women and the redefinition of the relationship between the adults from dependents to equals requires reconsideration of the role of the family. We see the families of tomorrow as sources of investment in the future—in children's capacity as adults. The erosion of the community for a large part of the country, however, threatens interdependent relationships across the board. An adult with limited income who cares for an unemployed, ill or simply unproductive spouse risks the already strained resources available for children. In such a circumscribed world, it is hardly surprising that many find marriage to be an institution that they cannot afford. The building of the family requires expanding the numbers of adults who can participate in full and meaningful citizenship. Only then can interdependence become a source of strength rather than a threat that robs the future.

Ironically, one of the most promising developments likely to prompt the rebirth of family law is the growing recognition of same-sex couples. The evolving law that governs same-sex couples will need to take a fresh look at the balance between financial and domestic contributions to marriage free from the confines of gender stereotypes, and consider the nature of parental relationships outside of heterosexual reproduction. We suspect that these reassessments of family obligation will increasingly result in the recognition of multiple parents who play important, but not necessarily equal roles in children's lives. Same-sex couples often involve a biological parent, that parent's partner, a donor, and sometimes the donor's partner in the children's lives. Working through these arrangements may create new models for including former spouses, cohabitants, and step-parents in ongoing relationships. Similarly, we suspect that notions of dependence and interdependence may take on new meaning when freed from gendered expectations about spousal roles. Reconsidering family obligations through the perspective of family relationships may ultimately help reunite the different classes of family law.

For the future, we hope the law adapts to the changing structure of the American family, recognizing the multiple ways that fathers can support children without direct financial contributions, acknowledging the dependence and interdependence that marriage creates, and recognizing the significance of the primary caretaker. Fundamentally, this requires recognizing and respecting women's increasing autonomy. Our social understandings and law are still somewhat in flux on these issues, our social scripts still are not completely settled, and instead of playing a divisive and coercive role, the law can play a supportive role.

* * * * *

Conclusion

As we said at the beginning of the book, the story of what has happened to the American family is simple: the economy has profoundly affected family structure. Explaining just how the economy has done so, however, is not at all simple. The first step is analyzing the redistribution of power among men and among women, showing how it changes the terms of intimate bargains. The second step is exploring just what this means: it locks in new agreements at the top that benefit children but makes such agreements impossible in the middle and virtually irrelevant at the bottom.

The redistribution of power started with the redefinition of the relationship between home and market. Women's wholesale entry into the labor market over the past half-century has enhanced most women's position in society. Earning their own income gives women greater ability to say no to a relationship or a marriage proposal, to leave an unhappy union, and to raise children without marrying. Women's willingness to commit to a relationship, much like men's, therefore depends to a much greater on the ability to find the right partner. Women at the top have become increasingly likely to find that partner, and it has become more difficult for women outside of the elite because of what is happening to men.

The increase in inequality among men took place after the wholesale change in women's roles, and greater inequality changed both male societal power and the way men and women match up. Over the past thirty years, only the men at the top have seen their incomes increase—all other men have lost ground. With more good jobs and bad jobs, the jobs in the center have disappeared, disproportionately affecting the heavily male middle manager and skilled blue-collar ranks. The result is increased political and economic power for the top men and less power for those on the losing end of the changes, who find themselves increasingly marginalized.

The change among women has taken place on different terms. Over the past thirty years, almost all women—except for high school dropouts—have seen income gains. Women's educational achievements have outpaced men's, placing more women in well-paying positions that depend on schooling and skills, such as pharmacists and office managers. More women in the middle, without college degrees, hold relatively stable, if less well-paying positions, such as healthcare aides, cashiers, and clerical workers, and they are more likely than men to seek additional education if their economic prospects sour. Only poor women have lost ground.

These changes among men and among women affect the way that men and women match up and their ability to craft relationships on mutually acceptable terms. At the top, both men and women have gained in contrast with other men and women. The men's overall gains, however, are greater than those of the women. They have secured a larger percentage of the overall gains in income, and they have gained in their ability to set the terms of political discourse. At the same time, however, more steeply banked male hierarchies intensify the competition among men for the highest-status women; the ability to land the right partner matters more in an era of greater male inequality. Top men therefore report more wariness than do top women in their willingness to commit to a particular partner, but they remain willing to marry the right person.

The secret to why marriage works for this group is that it combines greater male societal power with greater female power to choose among potential partners and a legal structure that locks in their commitment to children. Top men face two kinds of risks if they marry and divorce: loss of control over the assets associated with their higher earning capacity and loss of access to the children in whom they have invested time, resources, love, and affection. The law has changed to protect elite men from both types of risks. It has made it easier to enforce one-sided pre-marital agreements, dramatically limited the availability of spousal support, and adopted a preference for shared parenting that guarantees men with the resources to go to court a for significant share of their children's time—and a reduction in child support if the men exercise their parental prerogatives. The result has remade marriage along seemingly more egalitarian lines for the principal benefit of the top men who continue to out-earn their wives.[39]

The puzzle becomes why top women still marry on these less-favorable terms. The answer in part is that the women still appreciate the opportunity to marry a man who makes more than they do.[40] Women in the college-graduate upper third marry because the men still have a lot to offer, and the men still commit in part because the law protects their investment.

In the middle, in contrast, the women have gained ground in terms of their societal power relative to other women and to comparable men. This means that the women have the greater independence that comes from their earnings, but it also means that they have fewer "good" male choices, men who reliably contribute in a way that lives up to a partnership model. These women should, like the men at the top, be wary about marriage, and they are, but unlike top men, they have been unable to make marriage a better bargain. They, too, face the risk that they will have to share their income, but unlike top men, the women in the middle are unlikely to enter into a pre-nuptial agreement and fear, to a greater degree, the need to share their limited resources during marriage. Moreover, the shared-custody reforms the top men helped engineer in order to secure their interest in children work to the disadvantage of the women in the middle. As a result, women in this group acquire greater power by not marrying.[41] Without marriage, men have no claim to the woman's earnings and, when it comes to parenthood, they must sign a voluntary acknowledgment of paternity (which requires the mother's cooperation) or engage in what may be, for them, an expensive and time-consuming paternity action that will be difficult to enforce. While the law does not ratify the greater societal power that allows women to control access to their children, it looks the other way as they exercise that power. And in a world in which women enjoy greater practical control over childrearing without greater legal recognition, the women have greater incentive to lie and cheat about paternity.

At the bottom, men and women have lost ground in society. Their interests are largely unrepresented in the political system, and they enjoy less support than they once did from community and extended families. Men in this group have long been marginalized, and today, they face even greater challenges from chronic unemployment and mass incarceration. Family law continues to be driven by state interventions to protect the public fisc and has become pointlessly punitive. In an earlier era, the stigmatization of the poor at least served to enhance the solidarity between the top and the middle. In today's world that solidarity is gone. As a result, the law purports to reinforce family precepts that no one follows, particularly when it comes to child support. The men at the bottom are not deserting the women and children; the women are often throwing the men out. The men are not necessarily deadbeats, living the good life while their children suffer. Instead, the men often do contribute in ways that the law fails to recognize. Men's wages are not indispensable to family life; women in the middle and at the bottom often earn more than they do. If the law were to impose the emerging norms of the middle on the bottom, it would ratify women's control of family life. Such a system would support a woman's ability to set preconditions for a partner's involvement with her children and then accept the consequences of female choice. The current system reflects only the experiences of the top.

Family law—and society more generally—faces a dilemma: ratify the results of fundamentally different power balances in the top and the middle through different legal systems for people with different statuses or ratify the practical effects by continuing to look the other way and pretending that differences do not exist. The only way to bring these groups closer together is to change the circumstances that have driven them apart. If society provides more equal opportunities for women as well as men at the top, for men as well as women in the middle, and for all three groups on something closer to a level playing field, a single system of family law might emerge. Until then, the focus should be less on the adults than the children whose lives are being short-changed by growing societal inequality.

The larger issue that underlies this book is the role of inequality in society more generally. The idea of "equality," viewed in the abstract, is a subject of political division. We like to joke, how many hierarchs does it take to change a light bulb? Two, one to order the other to do what it takes to get it done. How many egalitarians does it take to change a light bulb? Can't happen; one would have to rise above the other to complete the task. In chapter 3, we explained that these attitudes underlie attitudes toward the family. Liberals, who tend to be egalitarians, wish to respect all families; they blame family flaws on the system. Conservatives, who are more likely to see hierarchy as inevitable, if not divinely ordained, blame poverty on individual flaws, including the failure to marry. Indeed, in a metastudy of political attitudes, psychologist John Jost characterizes these differing views on political orientations:

> Conservatives consider people to be inherently *unequal and due unequal rewards*; liberals are *egalitarian*. Conservatives venerate *tradition* and—most of all—*order* and *authority*; liberals believe planned *change* brings the possibility of improvement.[42]

Jost concludes that the prevalence of "liberal" preferences, such as openness to change, versus "conservative" ones, such as tolerance for inequality, is a major factor in political loyalties and the party realignment that has taken place over the past thirty years.[43]

The Yale Cultural Cognition Project posits that individuals view empirical data—"Is global warming real?" "Does gun control increase individual safety?"—through cultural lenses in which the observer interprets new information by aligning it with preexisting beliefs. Thus, when political scientist Larry Bartels looked at responses to a question about whether inequality was due to the fact that "some people just don't work as hard," he found that the answers had more to do with individual ideological orientation than with information about inequality.[44] Self-described conservatives were much more likely than self-described liberals to answer yes and the differences were greatest among the best informed. More than 70 percent of conservatives with the "most information," based on a composite measure that included educational levels and self-reports about staying current on public affairs, answered that inequality reflected the fact that some people worked harder, in comparison with less than 20 percent of the liberals with the most information. When Charles Murray blames family breakdown on poor men's laziness, he is thus hewing to a traditional conservative approach that has shaped elite dogma for centuries.

Given the polarization in views on the reasons why inequality exists, we have no illusions about the prospects for consensus on solutions. We don't think we'll be able to convince Charles Murray that poverty is not due to laziness. But the lack of consensus should not result in paralysis. We believe—and we believe we have demonstrated in this book—that inequality explains much of the shift we have seen in the family even as the shifts in the family contribute in turn to greater inequality. We also believe for this and other reasons that greater inequality is destructive in itself as the economic winners identify less with the losers in the new economy, and the greater concentration of wealth makes elites less accountable in ways that contribute to the destruction of community.

We nonetheless conclude that it is not necessary to resolve the age-old question of whether economic inequality per se produces the harms. Instead, we have tried to focus on the causal links that exacerbate the effects of inequality. Much of the valorization of steeply banked hierarchies and winner-take-all compensation systems produces a short-term focus that is easier to game; to the extent it does not lead to healthier institutions or greater productivity it should be suspect for reasons apart from its impact on the family.

In similar ways, if changing family structure reflects a larger set of societal changes that inevitably makes families less stable, this does not justify the failure to address inequality among children. With the rise of nineteenth-century industrialization, access to privately funded education became both more important and more unequal as the urban well-to-do could attend great universities while the urban poor had little choice but to send mothers and young children into the factories. It took a century to universalize access to secondary education and the resistance to school spending and child labor laws energized left-right and North-South ideological splits similar to those of today. Yet the emergence of the United States as the best-educated country in the world also made the country an industrial powerhouse.

Children's cognitive development, education, and training will be even more important to the workplaces of tomorrow and an impressive literature demonstrates that early childhood education has a bigger payoff on children's development than later interventions. These proposals should not be thought of simply as remedial measures necessary to combat the effects of greater inequality, even if they perform that function; instead, they should be seen as part of the infrastructure that supports children in a reorganized economy. Just as parents' roles changed to facilitate the investment in children necessary for the industrial era, so too are parental roles changing to support a new pattern of investment for the information era. Tailoring this investment to the needs of the new economy and universalizing access to the benefits that result requires thinking of childrearing as a societal undertaking. Just as productive society requires roads, schools and bridges, so does it need institutions that integrate work and family and prepare parents to meet the rigors of childrearing.

An important part of that infrastructure is the legal system. Family law establishes minimum parental obligations to children and in the process it helps to coordinate adult behavior. To do so effectively, however, it has to start with a determination of who the legal parents are and recognition of the circumstances that allow them to play a constructive role in their children's future. Economic and political changes have made it possible to allow women to join men as fully autonomous citizens in the new system; the challenge for family law is to provide a just foundation for redefining parental connection to children.

Family law, however, will ultimately succeed in doing so only if it is part of a societal reconstruction. The solutions to the destabilization of the family are inextricably linked to the rebirth of a social community that provides stable employment for every able adult, enmeshes new parents in community networks that strengthen their ability to care for their children, and treats every child as a valued member of the society of tomorrow. To accomplish these tasks, however, to truly rebuild our families, requires first building a more equal and more just society.

NOTES

Introduction

1. Richard Wilkinson & Kat Pickett, *The Spirit Level: Why Greater Equality Makes Societies Stronger* (New York: Bloomsbury, 2009).

2. Andrew J. Cherlin, *The Marriage-Go-Round: The State of Marriage and the Family in America Today* (New York: Vintage, 2009), 168–169; Andrew J. Cherlin, "Between Poor and Prosperous: Do the Family Patterns of Moderately-Educated Americans Deserve a Closer Look?" in *Social Class and Changing Families in an Unequal Society*, ed. Marcia J. Carlson and Paula England (Stanford, CA: Stanford University Press, 2011), 68–84.

3. Wilkinson and Pickett, *Spirit Level*.

4. The *New York Times* indicates that 30.4 percent of those over the age of 25 held a college degree in 2012, an all-time high. Richard Pérez-Peña, "U.S. Bachelor Degree Rate Passes Milestone," Feb. 23, 2012, *New York Times*, www.nytimes.com/2012/02/24/education/census-finds-bachelors-degrees-at-record-level.html. That figure rose to 33.5 percent of Americans ages 25 to 29, up 24.7 percent in 1995. National Center for Education Statistics. Catherine Rampell, "Data Reveal a Rise Among College Degrees Among Americans," June 12, 2013, www.nytimes.com/2013/06/13/education/a-sharp-rise-in-americans-with-college-degrees.html (citing National Center for Education Statistics).

5. Catherine Rampell, "Where Do You Fall on the Income Curve?" Economix blog, *New York Times*, May 24, 2011.

6. Nicole Stoops, "Educational Attainment in the United States: 2003," Current Population Reports P20-550 (Washington, DC: U.S. Census Bureau, June 2004), www.census.gov/prod/2004pubs/p20-550.pdf.

7. National Center for Education Statistics, "Fast Facts: Dropout Rates" (Washington, DC: National Center for Education Statistics, 2012), www.nces.ed.gov/fastfacts/display.asp?id=16; Statistic Brain, "High School Dropout Statistics," www.statisticbrain.com/high-school-dropout-statistics (last viewed May 17, 2013).

8. U.S. Census Bureau, "Income, Poverty and Health Insurance in the United States: 2011—Highlights, www.census.gov/hhes/www/poverty/data/incpovhlth/2011/highlights.html.

9. See generally Larry M. Bartels, *Unequal Democracy: The Political Economy of the New Gilded Age* (Princeton, NJ: Princeton University Press 2008).

10. John Parker, "Burgeoning Bourgeoisie," *The Economist*, Feb. 12, 2009, www.wichaar.com/news/295/ARTICLE/12328/2009-02-20.html (the middle class has historically been view as "people who are prepared to make sacrifices to create a better life for

themselves"); Susan Pace Hamill, *A Moral Perspective on the Role of Education in Sustaining the Middle Class*, 24 ND J. L. ETHICS & PUB POL'Y 309, 311 (2010); Lawrence Stone, *The Family, Sex and Marriage in England, 1500–1800* (London: Harper & Row, 1977), 22–95 (contrasting class attitudes toward children, with the landed classes investing heavily in children, the lower middle class emphasizing discipline, and the lower classes viewing them as nuisances).

11. Les Christie, "America's Smartest Cities," *CNN Money*, Oct. 1, 2010, www.money.cnn.com/2010/10/01/pf/college/Americas_brainiest_cities/index.htm.

12. For an insightful discussion of the class culture gap in America, see Joan C. Williams, *Reshaping the Work-Family Debate: Why Men and Class Matter* (Cambridge, MA: Harvard University Press, 2010). Williams draws a further distinction between what she describes as the "stable" working class versus the "hard living types." The stable group distinguishes itself from the hard living types and the poor in the same communities in terms of their discipline, values, and commitment to doing the right thing. The hard living types, in contrast, are more likely to have problems with substance abuse, to have trouble holding a job, and to cycle in and out of relationships. In another era, both groups might have had similar jobs and similar incomes buoyed by the demand for blue collar labor in the middle of the last century. Today, both groups are downwardly mobile, but the distinctions between the "hard living" class and the poor are rapidly disappearing, while the "stable" living types may be hanging on to a somewhat better life. In the stories we tell in this book, these distinctions may also involve gender—the women in this group have become more likely to be the ones hanging on to stable jobs and greater discipline in their personal lives while the harder living men lose ground.

Chapter 1

1. The characters we describe are a composite of people we know. All of the individual pieces of these stories have occurred to someone we spoke to, but no single person we know has experienced all of the facts exactly as we have described them here.

2. Elizabeth Waldman, "Labor Force Statistics from a Family Perspective," *Monthly Labor Review*, December 1983, www.bls.gov/opub/mlr/1983/12/art2full.pdf.

3. Adam Looney and Michael Greenstone, "The Marriage Gap: The Impact of Economic and Technological Chang on Marriage Rates," Hamilton Project Paper, Feb. 2012, www.hamiltonproject.org/papers/the_marriage_gap_the_impact_of_economic_and_technological_change_on_ma.

4. See, e.g., Charles Murray, *Coming Apart: The State of White America, 1960–2010* (New York: Random House, 2013), 156.

5. See Sara McLanahan, "Diverging Destinies: How Children Are Faring after the Second Demographic Transition," *Demography* 41, no. 4 (2004): 607, 617; Kay Hymowitz, Jason S. Carroll, W. Bradford Wilcox, and Kelleen Kaye, "Knot Yet: The Benefits and Costs of Delayed Marriage in America," National Marriage Project Report, 2013, 8, http://nationalmarriageproject.org/wp-content/uploads/2013/03/KnotYet-FinalForWeb.pdf.

6. Hymowitz et al., "Knot Yet," 8, fig. II.

7. Hymowitz et al., "Knot Yet"; compare fig. IIA with fig. IIB and fig. IIC.

8. For different views on these developments, compare Hanna Rosin, *The End of Men and the Rise of Women* (New York: Penguin, 2012), 3–4, with Mark Regnerus and Jeremy Uecker, *Premarital Sex in America: How Young Americans Meet, Mate, and Think about Marrying* (New York: Oxford University Press, 2011), 122.

9. W. Bradford Wilcox and Elizabeth Marquardt, eds., "When Marriage Disappears: The New Middle America," The State of Our Unions: Marriage in America, 2010, 57, fig. S3, http://stateofourunions.org/2010/SOOU2010.pdf.

10. Murray, *Coming Apart*, 166.

11. Wilcox and Marquardt, "When Marriage Disappears," 40, fig. 16.
12. Wilcox and Marquardt, "When Marriage Disappears," 29, fig. 8; 30, fig. 9.
13. See Hymowitz et al., "Knot Yet," 8, fig. II.

Chapter 2

1. See, e.g., James Q. Wilson, *The Marriage Problem: How Our Culture Has Weakened Families* (New York: HarperCollins, 2002).
2. Diana B. Elliott, Kristy Krivickas, Matthew W. Brault, and Rose M. Kreider, "Historical Marriage Trends from 1890–2010: A Focus on Race Differences," SEHSD Working Paper no. 2012-12, 2012, 15, www.census.gov/hhes/socdemo/marriage/data/acs/ElliottetalPAA2012paper.pdf.
3. Daniel Patrick Moynihan, *The Negro Family: The Case for National Action* (Moynihan Report) (Washington, DC: U.S. Department of Labor, Office of Policy Planning and Research, March 1965), www.dol.gov/oasam/programs/history/webid-meynihan.htm.
4. The Family Leader, "The Marriage Vow," July 7, 2011, www.thefamilyleader.com/wp-content/uploads/2011/07/themarriagevow.final_.7.7.111.pdf
5. Linda Burton and M. Belinda Tucker, *Romantic Unions in an Era of Uncertainty: A Post-Moynihan Perspective on African American Women and Marriage*, 621 ANNALS AM.ACAD. POL.& SOC. SCI. (hereinafter ANNALS) 132 (2009).
6. Moynihan Report, chap. 2. Massey and Sampson observe that: "[I]n the context of an emergent black power movement, Moynihan's emphasis on humiliated black men could not have been less timely, and in the context of a coalescing feminist movement, his pairing of matriarchy and pathology could not have been less welcome. Young black militants and newly self-aware feminists joined in the rising tide of vilification, and Moynihan was widely pilloried not only as a racist, but a sexist to boot." Douglas S. Massey and Robert J. Sampson, *Introduction: Moynihan Redux: Legacies and Lessons*, 621 ANNALS 6, 9 (2009).
7. Scholars, however, continue to debate whether the principal purpose of the Report was self-promotion, political advantage, or policy development. See, e.g., James T. Patterson, *Freedom Is Not Enough: The Moynihan Report and America's Struggle over Black Family Life from LBJ to Obama* (New York: Basic Books, 2010), 22.
8. Doris Kearns Goodwin, *Lyndon Johnson and the American Dream* (New York: St. Martin's, 1991), 211.
9. Thomas Meeham, Moynihan of the Moynihan Report, *New York Times*, July 31, 1966, www.nytimes.com/books/98/10/04/specials/moynihan-report.html; Patterson, *Freedom Is Not Enough*, 1–4.
10. The Report concludes: "The policy of the United States is to bring the Negro American to full and equal sharing in the responsibilities and rewards of citizenship. To this end, the programs of the Federal government bearing on this objective shall be designed to have the effect, directly or indirectly, of enhancing the stability and resources of the Negro American family." Moynihan, *The Negro Family*, chap. 5: "The Case for National Action," www.dol.gov/oasam/programs/history/moynchapter5.htm.
11. A great irony is that few of his vociferous critics had actually read Moynihan's report. One wonders, for example, whether critics who claimed Moynihan was racist had read even the first page of the report, where it was claimed that "the racist virus in the American blood stream still afflicts us." Massey and Sampson, "Introduction: Moynihan Redux," 9.
12. William Ryan, "Savage Discovery: The Moynihan Report," *The Nation*, Nov. 22, 1965, 380–384.
13. Adoph Reed Jr. & Julian Bond, "Equality: Why We Can't Wait," *The Nation*, Dec. 9, 1991, 733.
14. Massey and Sampson, "Introduction: Moynihan Redux," 14.

15. Massey and Sampson, "Introduction: Moynihan Redux," 13; see also Frank R. Furstenberg, *If Moynihan Had Only Known: Race, Class, and Family Change in the Late Twentieth Century*, 621 ANNALS 94 (2009) (restating Moynihan's argument in terms of the intersection of race and class).

16. Massey and Sampson, "Introduction: Moynihan Redux," 13 (emphasizing how the right, then and now, treats family instability as a cause of poverty while Moynihan treated it as a consequence of macrostructures such as employment and poverty).

17. Moynihan Report, "Introduction." http://www.dol.gov/oasam/programs/history/webid-meynihan.htm.

18. Moynihan Report, chap. 2.

19. Moynihan Report, chap. 2: "The Negro American Family," available at www.dol.gov/oasam/programs/history/moynchapter2.htm.

20. Massey and Sampson, "Introduction: Moynihan Redux," 14.

21. Moynihan Report, chap. 3: "The Roots of the Problem," available at www.dol.gov/oasam/programs/history/moynchapter3.htm.

22. Moynihan Report, chap. 3.

23. Moynihan wrote further: "There is, presumably, no special reason why a society in which males are dominant in family relationships is to be preferred to a matriarchal arrangement. However, it is clearly a disadvantage for a minority group to be operating on one principle, while the great majority of the population, and the one with the most advantages to begin with, is operating on another. . . . Ours is a society which presumes male leadership in private and public affairs. The arrangements of society facilitate such leadership and reward it. A subculture, such as that of the Negro American, in which this is not the pattern, is placed at a distinct disadvantage." Moynihan Report, chap. 4: "The Tangle of Pathology," www.dol.gov/oasam/programs/history/moynchapter4.htm.

24. Bruce Hayden, commenting on Dave Kopel, "Freedom Is Not Enough: The Moynihan Report and America's Struggle over Black Family Life—From LBJ to Obama," the Volokh Conspiracy blog, May 17, 2010, www.volokh.com/2010/05/17/freedom-is-not-enough-the-moynihan-report-and-americas-struggle-over-black-family-life-from-lbj-to-obama/#comments.

Chapter 3

1. *Wall Street Journal*, Oct. 29, 1993, A14.

2. Charles Murray, *Coming Apart: The State of White America, 1960–2010* (New York: Random House, 2013), 156–158 (divorce rates), 160 (white non-marital birth rates), 159, 167 (concentration by class).

3. Murray, *Coming Apart*, 167.

4. Murray, *Coming Apart*, 153.

5. Indeed, at the end of a book that Murray limits to whites, he reports, to "his surprise," that expanding the analysis "to include all Americans makes hardly any difference at all" (269). So why limit the discussion to whites?

6. Murray emphasized the rise in crime in African-American communities in *Losing Ground* and in his 1993 editorial predicted that white communities would follow suit. Charles Murray, *Losing Ground: American Social Policy, 1950-1980* (New York, Basic Books, 1984, 1994). His 2012 data show that arrests for violent and property crimes did in fact increase dramatically in white working-class communities between the mid-seventies and the early nineties but leveled off between 1998 and 2007 (193). Murray argues (see appendix E)

that the arrest rates in fact reflect increases in white criminal activity rather than simply higher arrest rates overall, but he attributes the drop in crime to higher levels of incarceration without examination of possible alternative explanations (194). Murray's larger point, however, is convincing: the class-based differences in criminal behavior and arrests increased between 1960 and the mid-nineties.

7. Tim Murphy, "What's Hurting White America? It's Not the Welfare State," *Mother Jones*, April 5, 2011, www.motherjones.com/mojo/2011/04/whats-hurting-white-america-welfare-state-charles-murray.
8. Murray, *Coming Apart*.
9. Murray, *Coming Apart*, chap. 11.
10. *Wall Street Journal*, Oct. 29, 1993, A14.
11. Murray, *Coming Apart*, 188.
12. Murray, *Coming Apart*, 175.
13. See, e.g., Robert J. Samuelson, "Employers Lack Confidence, Not Skilled Labor," *Washington Post*, May 5, 2013, www.washingtonpost.com/opinions/employers-lack-confidence-not-skilled-labor/2013/05/05/757340c8-b411-11e2-9a98-4be1688d7d84_story.html.
14. Charles Murray, "Why Economics Cannot Explain Our Cultural Divide," *Wall Street Journal*, March 16, 2012, http://online.wsj.com/news/articles/SB10001424052702304692804577281582403394206. See also Courtland Milloy, "Charles Murray and Shiftless Lazy Whites," *Washington Post*, April 24, 2011, www.washingtonpost.com/local/charles-murray-and-shiftless-lazy-whites/2011/04/24/AFmC0beE_story.html. ("'In the 1990s, why would you have larger numbers of white males leaving the workforce when jobs were everywhere?' Murray asked. 'A different attitude towards work, a fundamental change in the norm, that's what I have identified'"); see Murray, *Coming Apart*, 181.
15. Murray, *Coming Apart*, 178.
16. Murray, *Coming Apart*, 218. Although, in contrast with *Losing Ground*, *Coming Apart* involves relatively little discussion of government benefits, focusing primarily on the growth in disability benefits, he nonetheless insists that welfare "plays a big role" (222).
17. Murray, *Coming Apart*, 181.
18. Murray, "Why Economics Can't Explain Our Cultural Divide."
19. Murray, "Why Economics Can't Explain Our Cultural Divide."
20. Johann Hari, "Man Made Disaster," *New York Times Book Review*, Sept. 9, 2011, citing Thomas Keneally, *Three Famines, Starvation and Politics* (New York: PublicAffairs, 2011).
21. See, e.g., lead editorial, *The Times* (London), Sept. 22, 1846, http://xroads.virginia.edu/~hyper/SADLIER/IRISH/Notfamin.htm (taking the position that the potato blight was a "blessing" and an opportunity to reform the Irish character). *The Times*, like Murray, insisted that the real problem was the Irish and that there was plenty of work available in Europe if only the Irish were willing to take the jobs.
22. This is true of those who criticize Becker as well as those who do not. See, e.g., Shelly Lundberg and Robert A. Pollak, "The American Family and Family Economies," *Journal of Economic Perspectives* 21, no. 2 (2007): 3–26, www.ssc.wisc.edu/~walker/wp/wp-content/uploads/2012/09/LundbergPollak2007.pdf; Betsey Stevenson and Justin Wolfers, "Marriage and Divorce: Changes and Their Driving Forces," IZA Discussion Paper no. 2602 (Feb. 2007), www.econstor.eu/bitstream/10419/34065/1/543741710.pdf.
23. Andrew J. Cherlin, "The Deinstitutionalization of American Marriage," *Journal of Marriage and Family* 66, no. 4 (2004): 848–861, www.casamariposa.org/Prop8/Attachments/DIX0049.pdf.
24. Gary Becker, A Treatise on the Family (Cambridge, MA., 1981).

Chapter 4

1. George A. Akerlof, Janet L. Yellen, and Michael L. Katz, "An Analysis of Out-of-Wedlock Childbearing in the United States," *Quarterly Journal of Economics* 111, no. 2 (1996): 277, 279, quoting Lillian Rubin, *Worlds of Pain* (New York: Basic Books, 1969).

2. Hanna Rosin, *The End of Men and the Rise of Women* (New York: Penguin, 2012), 3–4.

3. James Q. Wilson, *The Marriage Problem: How Our Culture Has Weakened Families* (New York: HarperCollins, 2003).

4. Mona Charen, "Blame the Sexual Revolution, Not Men," *National Review Online,* Oct. 28, 2011, www.nationalreview.com/articles/281490/blame-sexual-revolution-br-not-men-mona-charen.

5. Akerlof et al., "Out-of-Wedlock Childbearing," 277.

6. Akerlof et al., "Out-of-Wedlock Childbearing," 308.

7. See *Planned Parenthood v. Casey,* 505 U.S. 833 (1992).

8. Wilson, *Marriage Problem,* 156.

9. Akerlof, et al, "An Analysis of Out of Wedlock Childbearing." See also Wilson, *Marriage Problem,* 282, 308–310.

10. Rickie Solinger, *Wake Up Little Susie: Single Pregnancy and Race before Roe v. Wade* (New York: Routledge, 1992).

11. They further assume that working-class women who do not attend college are ready to begin childbearing at earlier ages and are therefore most likely to "want" accidentally conceived children. They acknowledge, however, that mothers who give birth outside of marriage are least likely to plan either contraceptive use or pregnancy. Indeed, they quote the 1982 National Survey of Family Growth to the effect that mothers of children born out of wedlock in 1970 reported that "19 percent were wanted at the time; 65 percent were mistimed or neither wanted nor unwanted; 15 percent were unwanted." The statistics indicate that these women are not "choosing" childbearing in any conscious sense. Instead, they are part of a system that no longer either deters non-marital sex or produces marriage on a universal basis. Economists, however, believe in "revealed preferences"; that is, they assume that a woman who has a child "wants" that child. Akerlof et al., "Out-of-Wedlock Childbearing," 280.

12. See Rosin, *The End of Men.*

13. Claudia Goldin and Lawrence F. Katz, "The Power of the Pill: Oral Contraceptives and Women's Career and Marriage," *Journal of Political Economy* 110, no. 4 (2002): 730–770.

14. Claudia Goldin, *The Long Road to the Fast Track: Career and Family,* 596 ANNALS AM. ACAD. POL. & SOC. SCI. 20 (2004), http://scholar.harvard.edu/files/goldin/files/the_long_road_to_the_fast_track_career_and_family.pdf.

15. Goldin and Katz, "Power of the Pill," 749.

16. W. Bradford Wilcox and Elizabeth Marquardt, eds., "When Marriage Disappears: The New Middle America," *The State of Our Unions: Marriage in America,* 2010, 56, fig. S2, http://stateofourunions.org/2010/SOOU2010.pdf.

17. Betsey Stevenson and Justin Wolfers, "Marriage and Divorce: Changes and Their Driving Forces," *Journal of Economic Perspectives* 21, no. 2 (2007): 35.

18. Stevenson and Wolfers, "Marriage and Divorce," 35.

19. Although by the 1980 census 91 percent of women college grads in their fifties had married—in comparison with 97 percent of those with high school degrees or less. Adam Isen and Betsey Stevenson, "Women's Education and Family Behavior: Trends in Marriage, Divorce and Fertility," NBER Working Paper no. 15725 (Feb. 2010), 7–8, www.nber.org/papers/w15725.pdf.

20. Isen and Stevenson, "Women's Education and Family Behavior," 21.

21. Indeed, the age gap between men and women at time of first marriage shrank over the course of the past century and stayed largely the same between the mid-seventies and 2000. Stevenson and Wolfers, "Marriage and Divorce," 27–52, 31.

22. See W. Bradford Wilcox and Elizabeth Marquardt, eds., "When Baby Makes Three: How Parenthood Makes Life Meaningful and How Marriage Makes Parenthood Bearable," *The State of Our Unions: Marriage in America,* 2011, 27, fig. 10, http://nationalmarriageproject.org/wp-content/uploads/2012/05/Union_2011.pdf.

23. Sara McLanahan, "Diverging Destinies: How Children Are Faring after the Second Demographic Transition," *Demography* 41, no. 4 (2004), fig. 6.

24. Valerie K. Oppenheimer, "A Theory of Marriage Timing," *American Journal of Sociology* 94, no. 3 (1988): 563–591.

25. Jason DeParle, "For Poor, Leap to College Often Ends in a Hard Fall," *New York Times*, Dec. 22, 2012, www.nytimes.com/2012/12/23/education/poor-students-struggle-as-class-plays-a-greater-role-in-success.html?pagewanted=all.

Chapter 5

1. As British economist Alison Wolf tartly observes, "The likelihood of an economy structured for the convenience of mothers with children is vanishingly small, whether at the pinnacle of the job pyramid or down below." Alison Wolf, *The XX Factor: How the Rise of Working Women Has Created a Far Less Equal World* (New York: Crown Books, 2013), 256. She notes also that women "think about children more and from much earlier on" than do men and that "'path dependence,'" in which "once you have started down [the] path, where mothers have the larger childcare role," it becomes more difficult to "upend things" (254).

2. See, e.g., Nancy Polikoff, *Beyond (Straight and Gay) Marriage: Valuing All Families under the Law* (Boston: Beacon, 2008).

3. The focus of our analysis of marriage markets is heterosexual couples because the analysis of heterosexual marriage markets is far more developed than that for same-sex couples.

4. Kevin Fasick, "Gals' Date Fright: Not Enough Guys!" *New York Post*, Dec. 29, 2011, www.nypost.com/p/news/local/gals_date_fright_not_enough_guys_jgxBNJtU-vu9arN7K1kawFM.

5. Hugh Wilson, "The Places Where Women Outnumber Men," MSN Him, Jan. 28, 2011, http://him.uk.msn.com/sex-and-dating/articles.aspx?cp-documentid=155889273.

6. Jos. J. Schall, "Evolutionary Biology: Sex Ratios Writ Small," *Nature* 453 (May 29, 2008): 605–606, www.nature.com/nature/journal/v453/n7195/full/453605a.html.

7. Marcia Guttentag and Paul F. Secord, *Too Many Women? The Sex Ratio Question* (Beverly Hills, CA: Sage, 1983).

8. Guttentag and Secord, *Too Many Women?* 185.

9. Guttentag and Secord, *Too Many Women?* 24–27.

10. Guttentag and Secord, *Too Many Women?*

11. Guttentag and Secord, *Too Many Women?* 27.

12. Guttentag and Secord, *Too Many Women?* 28.

13. In a cross-cultural study of the impact of sex ratios, later sociologists found the following:

    > Our results suggest that an undersupply of women, combined with men's overwhelming structural power, leads to high marriage and fertility rates and low rates of divorce and illegitimacy. But high sex ratios also serve to delimit and constrain the roles women occupy. Hence, where women are in short supply, their levels of literacy and labor-force participation are low, both relative to men in their own society and to women in low-sex-ratio societies. Their suicide rate, relative to men's, is also high.

    Scott J. South and Katherine Trent, "Sex Ratios and Women's Roles: A Cross-National Analysis," *American Journal of Sociology* 93, no. 5 (1988): 1096, 1112.

14. Guttentag and Secord, *Too Many Women?* 29.

15. Guttentag and Secord, *Too Many Women?* 30.

16. Guttentag and Secord, *Too Many Women?* 85. Jill Hasday suggests that other practices within the Orthodox community may have produced the gender imbalance (private communication, April 1, 2013). Guttentag and Secord observe that there has been no suggestion of infanticide. Empirical efforts to test the hypothesis have involved small numbers and mixed results. Olivia Judson, "Is It Really All in the Timing?" Opinionator blog,

New York Times, June 14, 2006, www.opinionator.blogs.nytimes.com/2006/06/14/
is-it-really-all-in-the-timing.

17. Denmark, for example, has a high female-to-male ratio (1.06), matrilineal lineages, multiple female heads of state, a high divorce rate—and most notably for a society in which women have power—readily available, publicly subsidized childcare. We do not want to overstate the amount of power women have in that society, however. Although Danish women have the highest employment rate in Europe, they still earn less than Danish men, and a significant portion of the difference cannot be explained by differences in hours or education. See Cecilie Wehner, Mia Kambskard, and Peter Abrahamson, "Demography of the Family—The Case of Denmark," unpublished report, University of York, n.d., www.york.ac.uk/inst/spru/research/nordic/denmdemo.PDF; European Working Conditions Observatory, "Women and Men in the Danish Labour Market," Ministry of Employment Annual Report (last updated March 24, 2011), www.eurofound.europa. eu/ewco/2011/03/DK110302SI.htm.

18. We do wonder about the effects of colonialism and other forms of racial oppression. Women held power among the Bakhari, after all, only because of colonial interference. Some argue, usually pejoratively, that communities with female-headed households are "matriarchies," with women holding social power. Guttentag and Secord did not see such communities, however, as part of a female dominated society. Indeed, we see these households as examples of women's autonomy (women can say "no" to bad terms with men) but not power over men.

19. Guttentag and Secord, *Too Many Women?* 190.

20. Scott J. South & Katherine Trent, "Sex Ratios and Women's Roles: A Cross-National Analysis," *American Journal of Sociology* 93, no. 5 (1988): 1096, 1112.

21. South and Trent, 1097. They also predicted that female depression and suicide rates would be higher.

22. South & Trent, *"Sex Ratios and Women's Roles,"* 1100–1101.

23. South & Trent, *"Sex Ratios and Women's Roles,"* 1108.

24. South & Trent, *"Sex Ratios and Women's Roles,"* 1108.

25. Josh Angrist, "How Do Sex Ratios Affect Marriage and Labor Markets? Evidence from America's Second Generation," *Quarterly Journal of Economics* 117, no. 3 (2002): 997, 1033.

26. Emily A. Stone, Todd K. Shackelford, and David M. Buss, "Sex Ratio and Mate Preferences: A Cross-Cultural Investigation," *European Journal of Social Psychology* 37, no. 2 (2007): 288, 294.

27. Ran Abramitzky, Adeline Delavande, and Luis Vasconcelos, "Marrying Up: The Role of Sex Ratio in Assortative Matching," *American Economic Journal: Applied Economics* 3, no. 3 (2011): 124, www.aeaweb.org/articles.php?doi=10.1257/app.3.3.124.

28. Abramitzky et al., "Marrying Up," 136. There are also two possible explanations for the decrease in the age gap. The authors observe that with fewer men, women would tend to marry later so that more older women would be available. But it is also possible that men who had been through the war may have preferred women closer to their own age (148–149).

29. Mark Regnerus and Jeremy Uecker, *Premarital Sex in America: How Young Americans Meet, Mate, and Think about Marrying* (New York: Oxford University Press, 2011), 122.

30. Regnerus and Uecker, *Premarital Sex in America*, 123.

31. Regnerus and Uecker, *Premarital Sex in America*, 124.

32. See Richard Wilkinson and Kate Pickett, *The Spirit Level: Why Greater Equality Makes Societies Stronger*, repr. ed. (New York: Bloomsbury, 2011).

Chapter 6

1. Kay Hymowitz, "Will Women Marry Down?" *Daily Caller*, April 18, 2011, www.dailycaller. com/2011/04/18/will-women-marry-down/#ixzz1nu8g7hwW.

2. Ralph Richard Banks, *Is Marriage for White People? How the African American Marriage Decline Affects Everyone* (New York: Penguin, 2011), 99.

3. Denise I. Smith and Renee E. Spraggins, "Gender in the United States," (n.d.; last updated Jan. 14, 2013), www.nationalatlas.gov/articles/people/a_gender.html.

4. Smith and Spraggins, "Gender in the United States."

5. For a provocative discussion of the impact of gender imbalances on African Americans, see Banks, *Is Marriage for White People?*.

6. See, e.g., Donald Braman, *Doing Time on the Outside: Incarceration and Family Life in Urban America* (Ann Arbor: University of Michigan Press, 2007), 84–90.

7. Alex Witchel, "Anne Heche Is Playing It Normal Now," *New York Times Magazine*, July 31, 2009, www.nytimes.com/2009/08/02/magazine/02heche-t.html?pagewanted=all.

8. Christine R. Schwartz and Robert D. Mare, "Trends in Educational Assortative Marriage from 1940 to 2003," *Demography* 42, no. 4 (2005): 621–646.

9. Schwartz and Mare, "Trends in Educational Assortative Marriage," 633.

10. Schwartz and Mare, "Trends in Educational Assortative Marriage," 640.

11. Philip Cohen reports that in 2011, 71 percent of college graduates married other college graduates, but his methodology is not identical to that in the Schwartz and Mare study. Philip Cohen, "College Graduates Marry Other College Graduates Most of the Time," *The Atlantic*, April 4, 2013, www.theatlantic.com/sexes/archive/2013/04/college-graduates-marry-other-college-graduates-most-of-the-time/274654.

12. Cohen observed that 60 percent of men with Ph.D's and 52 percent of those with professional degrees marry women with more education than a B.A. and that only 8 percent of men with professional degrees and 12 percent of those with Ph.D.s marry a woman without a college degree.

13. See, e.g., "Multiple Partner Fertility," Fragile Families Research Brief, No. 8, June 2008, www.aecf.org/upload/publicationfiles/multiple%20partner.pdf.

14. Richard Kahlenberg, "Class Act," *New Republic*, Aug. 8, 2012.

15. See Kay Hymowitz, Jason S. Carroll, W. Bradford Wilcox, and Kelleen Kay, "Knot Yet: The Benefits and Costs of Delayed Marriage in America," National Marriage Project Report, 2013, 8, fig. II, http://nationalmarriageproject.org/wp-content/uploads/2013/03/KnotYet-FinalForWeb.pdf. The median age of first marriage and first birth has continued to go up for college graduates. For those with less education, the median age of marriage has continued to go up, but the median age of first birth levels off after 1990 and now occurs at a younger age than the median age of marriage. Hymowitz et al., "Knot Yet," 8.

16. See Timothy Noah, *The Great Divergence: America's Growing Inequality Crisis and What We Can Do about It* (New York: Bloomsbury, 2012), 55–56 ("Among married couples in the United States, [Christine R.] Schwartz calculated, earnings inequality would, from 1967–2005, be 25 to 30 percent lower were it not for that period's greater correlation between spouses' incomes").

17. See Claudia Goldin and Robert A. Margo, "The Great Compression: The U.S. Wage Structure at Mid-Century," *Quarterly Journal of Economics* 107, no. 1 (1992): 1–34. For fond reminiscences, see Paul Krugman, "Introducing This Blog," Conscience of a Liberal blog, *New York Times*, Sept. 18, 2007, www.krugman.blogs.nytimes.com/2007/09/18/introducing-this-blog.

18. Willford I. King, *The Wealth and Income of the People of the United States* (New York: Macmillan, 1915), cited in Timothy Noah, "The United States of Inequality," *Slate*, Sept. 3, 2010, at www.slate.com/id/2266025/entry/2266026. Noah observes that a "more authoritative subsequent calculation puts the figure slightly higher, at about 18 percent."

19. "Income Growth for Bottom 90 Percent of Americans Averaged Just $59 over 4 Decades: Analysis," *Huffington Post*, March 25, 2013, www.huffingtonpost.com/2013/03/25/income-growth-americans_n_2949309.html.

20. Peter Robinson, "Top 1 percent Got 93 percent of Income Growth as Rich-Poor Gap Widened," Bloomberg News, Oct. 1, 2012, http://www.bloomberg.com/news/2012-10-02/top-1-got-93-of-income-growth-as-rich-poor-gap-widened.html.

21. Nicholas D. Kristof, "Our Banana Republic," *New York Times*, Nov. 6, 2010. http://www.nytimes.com/2010/11/07/opinion/07kristof.html.

22. Lawrence Mishel and Nicholas Finio, "Earnings of the Top 1.0 Percent Rebound Strongly in the Recovery," Economic Policy Institute Issue Brief no. 347 (Jan. 23, 2013), www.epi.org/publication/ib347-earnings-top-one-percent-rebound-strongly.

23. See Larry M. Bartels, *Unequal Democracy: The Political Economy of the New Gilded Age* (Princeton, NJ: Princeton University Press, 2008), 9. Bartels shows that during the period of the "Great Compression," which he identifies with the period 1947 to 1974, income grew at roughly the same rates for all sectors of American society, with the ninety-fifth percentile in fact growing somewhat less robustly than the other groups. In contrast, during the period of the "Great Divergence," which Bartels identifies with the years 1974–2005, the percentage increase in income growth increases with each increase in income. The twentieth percentile experiences a 10 percent growth; the fortieth percentile, a growth of 18.6 percent; the sixtieth percentile, a growth of 30.8 percent; the eightieth percentile, a growth of 42.9 percent; and the ninety-fifth percentile, a growth of 62.9 percent.

24. Lawrence Mishel and Natalie Sabadish, "CEO Pay and the Top 1 percent," Economic Policy Institute Issue Brief no. 331 (May 2, 2012), www.epi.org/publication/ib331-ceo-pay-top-1-percent; Lawrence Mishel, Jared Bernstein, and Sylvia Allegretto, *The State of Working America 2006/2007* (Ithaca, NY: Cornell University Press, 2007). See also Carola Frydman and Raven E. Saks, "Executive Compensation: A New View from a Long-Term Perspective, 1936–2005," FEDS Working Paper no. 2007–35 (July 6, 2007), http://federalreserve.gov/pubs/feds/2007/200735/200735abs.html (growth of CEO pay relative to worker pay increased from 30:1 in 1970 to 120:1 by 2000).

25. "In 2012, women held 14.3 percent of Executive Officer positions at *Fortune* 500 companies and 8.1 percent of Executive Officer top earner positions. In both 2011 and 2012, one-fifth of companies had 25 percent or more women Executive Officers, yet more than one-quarter had no women." Catalyst, "2012 Catalyst Census: Fortune 500 Women Executive Officers and Top Earners" (Dec. 11, 2012), www.catalyst.org/knowledge/2012-catalyst-census-fortune-500-women-executive-officers-and-top-earners. See Sheryl Sandberg, *Lean In: Women, Work, and the Will to Lead* (New York: Knopf, 2013).

26. Financial Crisis Inquiry Commission, "The Financial Crisis Inquiry Report," submitted pursuant to Public Law 111-21 (January 2011), 62, http://cybercemetery.unt.edu/archive/fcic/20110310173545/http://c0182732.cdn1.cloudfiles.rackspacecloud.com/fcic_final_report_full.pdf.

27. Financial Crisis Inquiry Commission, "Financial Crisis Inquiry Report," 62.

28. Frank Bass, "Shining Shoes Best Way Wall Street Women Outearn Men," Bloomberg, March 16, 2012, www.bloomberg.com/news/2012-03-16/shining-shoes-best-way-wall-street-women-outearn-men.html.

29. Alexander Eichler, "Gender Wage Gap Is Higher on Wall Street Than Anywhere Else," *Huffington Post*, March 19, 2012, www.huffingtonpost.com/2012/03/19/gender-wage-gap-wall-street_n_1362878.html.

30. Anthony T. Lo Sasso, Michael R. Richards, Chiu-Fang Chou, and Susan E. Gerber, "The $16,819 Pay Gap for Newly Trained Physicians: The Unexplained Trend of Men Earning More Than Women," *Health Affairs* 30, no. 2 (2011): 193–201.

31. Barbara M. Flom and Stephanie A. Scharf for the National Association of Women Lawyers (NAWL) and the NAWL Foundation, "Report of the Sixth Annual National Survey on Retention and Promotion of Women in Law Firms" (October 2011), http://nawl.timberlakepublishing.com/files/NAWL%202011%20Annual%20Survey%20Report%20FINAL%20Publication-ready%2011-9-11.pdf.

32. See FrancineD.BlauandLawrenceM.Kahn,"TheU.S.GenderPayGapinthe1990s:Slow-ing Convergence," Princeton University Industrial Relations Section Working Paper no. 508 (March 2006), 17, http://dataspace.princeton.edu/jspui/bitstream/88435/dsp01gb19f581g/1/508.pdf (finding that wage gains for married women in the 1970s and 1980s tended to be greatest for women married to middle- and high-wage men).

33. During the eighties, women's median weekly earnings increased by $128 for full-time college graduates in comparison with $120 increase for the men, and since the start-ing point for women was lower than for the men the percentage increase in wages was significantly higher for the women. During the relatively lean years in the early nine-ties, women college graduates continued to outpace the men, with median weekly earnings that increased $101 between 1990 and 1995 in comparison with only a $79 increase for the men. U.S. Bureau of Labor Statistics (BLS), "Highlights of Wom-en's Earnings in 2009," BLS Report no. 1025, June 2010, tbl. 17, www.bls.gov/cps/cpswom2009.pdf.

34. BLS, "Highlights of Women's Earnings in 2009," tbl. 17.

35. Catalyst, "Women's Earnings and Income" (Sept. 18, 2013), www.catalyst.org/knowledge/womens-earnings-and-income.

36. See, e.g., Marianne Bertrand, Claudia Goldin, and Lawrence F. Katz, "Dynamics of the Gender Gap for Young Professionals in the Financial and Corporate Sectors," unpub-lished paper, Sept. 30, 2008, http://fairmodel.econ.yale.edu/ec483/katz.pdf.

37. Blau and Kahn, "U.S. Gender Pay Gap in the 1990's."

38. U.S. Bureau of Labor Statistics and U.S. Census Bureau, Current Population Survey, Annual Social and Economic Supplement (2009), tbl. PINC-03, www.census.gov/hhes/www/cpstables/032009/perinc/new03_175.htm.

39. See, e.g., Hannah Rosin, *The End of Men and the Rise of Women* (New York: Penguin, 2012).

40. For financial aid purposes *dependent* is defined as an undergraduate who is twenty-four or younger and unmarried, does not have children, and is not a veteran or a ward of the court.

41. See Mary Beth Marklein, "College Gender Gap Widens: 57 percent Are Women," *USA Today*, Oct. 19, 2005, http://usatoday30.usatoday.com/news/education/2005-10-19-male-college-cover_x.htm (showing male representation on college campuses by race and income using data compiled by the National Center for Education Statistics). For updated statistics, which indicate that the gender gap in education has leveled off since 2004, and remains largely class-based, see Jacqueline E. King, "Gender Equity in Higher Education: 2010," American Council on Education Report, 2010, https://bookstore. acenet.edu/products/gender-equity-higher-education-2010-pdf (in 2007–2008, for blacks, it was 48 percent, down from 54 percent in 2004 but still up from 41 percent in 1995; for Hispanics, it was 48 percent, down from 51 percent in 2004; for Asians, it was 52 percent, down from 54 percent on 2004).

42. See King, "Gender Equity in Higher Education: 2010"; Marklein, "College Gender Gap Widens"; also see Thomas A. DiPrete and Claudia Buchman, *The Rise of Women: The Growing Gender Gap in Education and What It Means for American Schools* (Ithaca, NY: CUP Services, 2013).

43. Kelly Musick, Jennie E. Brand, and Dwight Davis, "Variation in the Relationship be-tween Education and Marriage: Marriage Market Mismatch?" *Journal of Marriage and Family* 74, no. 1 (2012): 53–69.

44. U.S. Bureau of Labor Statistics and U.S. Census Bureau, Current Population Survey, tbl. PINC-03.

45. U.S. Bureau of Labor Statistics and U.S. Census Bureau, Current Population Survey, tbl. PINC-03.

46. King, "Gender Equity in Higher Education, 2010," 11-12, tbls. 2 and 3.

47. Sam Roberts, "For Young Earners in Big City, a Gap in Women's Favor," *New York Times*, Aug. 3, 2007, www.nytimes.com/2007/08/03/nyregion/03women.html.

48. Roberts, "For Young Earners in Big City, a Gap in Women's Favor."

49. Philip N. Cohen, "The End of Men Is Not True: What Is Not and What Might Be on the Road toward Gender Equality," 93, B.U. L. Rev. 1157, 1160 (2013).

50. Banks, *Is Marriage for White People?* 3.

51. Kate Bolick, "All the Single Ladies," *The Atlantic*, Sept. 30, 2011, www.theatlantic.com/magazine/archive/2011/11/all-the-single-ladies/308654.

52. See Eric D. Gould and M. Daniele Paserman, "Waiting for Mr. Right: Rising Inequality and Declining Marriage Rates," *Journal of Urban Economics*, 53, no. 2 (2003): 257–281.

53. David M. Buss, Todd K. Shakelford, Lee A. Kirkpatrick, and Randy J. Larsen, "A Half Century of Mate Preferences: The Cultural Evolution of Values," *Journal of Marriage and Family* 63, no. 2 (2001): 491–503.

54. Christine R. Schwartz, "Earnings Inequality and the Changing Association between Spouses' Earnings," *American Journal of Sociology* 115, no. 5 (2010): 1524–1557.

55. Schwartz, "Earnings Inequality."

56. Michael Greenstone and Adam Looney, "The Marriage Gap: The Impact of Economic and Technological Change on Marriage Rates," Brookings blog, Feb. 3, 2012, www.brookings.edu/up-front/posts/2012/02/03-jobs-greenstone-looney.

57. Inequality in the United States taken from 2006 U.S. Census Data, http://wiki.econwiki.com/index.php/Inequality_in_the_US#cite_note-6.

58. U.S. Census Bureau, "Race: The Black Alone Population in the United States, 2011," tbl. 1, www.census.gov/population/race/data/ppl-ba11.html.

59. Jeffrey S. Passel, Wendy Wang, and Paul Taylor, "Marrying Out: One-in-Seven New U.S. Marriages Is Interracial or Interethnic," Pew Research Center Social & Demographic Trends Report, rev. June 15, 2010, ii, http://pewsocialtrends.org/files/2010/10/755-marrying-out.pdf.

60. William J. Wilson, *The Truly Disadvantaged: The Inner City, the Underclass, and Public Policy* (Chicago: University of Chicago Press, 1987), 83.

61. Sterling C. Lloyd, "Gender Gap in Graduation," *Education Week*, July 6, 2007, www.edweek.org/rc/articles/2007/07/05/sow0705.h26.html.

62. Banks, *Is Marriage for White People?* 38.

63. Erik Eckholm, "Plight Deepens for Black Men, Studies Warn," *New York Times*, March 20, 2006, www.nytimes.com/2006/03/20/national/20blackmen.html?pagewanted=all.

64. Kristen Harknett and Sara McLanahan, "Racial and Ethnic Differences in Marriage after the Birth of a Child," *American Sociological Review* 69, no. 6 (2004): 790, 799.

65. Adam Litpak, "1 in 100 U.S. Adults behind Bars, New Study Says," *New York Times*, Feb. 28, 2008, www.nytimes.com/2008/02/28/us/28cnd-prison.html; "One in 100: Behind Bars in America in 2008," Pew Center on the States Report, n.d., www.pewstates.org/uploadedFiles/PCS_Assets/2008/one%20in%20100.pdf.

66. Banks, *Is Marriage for White People?* 39.

67. Braman, *Doing Time on the Outside*, 91.

68. Braman, *Doing Time on the Outside*, 93. For further discussion of these issues see Daniel. T. Lichter, George Kephart, Diane K. McLaughlin, and David J. Laundry, "Race and the Retreat from Marriage: A Shortage of Marriageable Men?" *American Sociological Review* 57, no. 6 (1991): 781. The authors note that Wilson assumed both that all single women were in the marriage market and that they sought to marry only employed men. The authors add that empirical studies demonstrate that, compared with men, "women have stronger preferences for spouses with job stability, high earnings, and more education than their own" (784).

69. Sex ratios, adjusted to factor in men's employment rates, also explained more of the racial differences in marriage patterns than welfare availability or women's employment (which

had a positive effect on marriage rates). Lichter et al., "Race and the Retreat from Marriage," 796. Nonetheless, the studies varied significantly in how much of the racial differences the gender ratio analysis explained. For a summary of these studies, see Harknett and McLanahan, "Racial and Ethnic Differences in Marriage after the Birth of a Child."

70. Indeed, the supply of alternative partners had a significant effect on the likelihood of marriage even among couples cohabiting at the time of the child's birth and was a more powerful predictor of the likelihood of marriage than individual factors such as attitudes toward marriage or gender roles. Harknett and McLanahan, "Racial and Ethnic Differences in Marriage after the Birth of a Child," 807–808.

71. This was true along all four of the dimensions measured: (a) more supportive relationships, (b) less conflict, (c) greater paternal involvement, and (d) a lower likelihood that the father has additional children with another woman. Kristen Harknett, "Mate Availability and Unmarried Parent Relationships," *Demography* 45, no. 3 (2008): 555–571.

72. Kristen Harknett and Arielle Kuperberg, "Education, Labor Markets and the Retreat from Marriage," *Social Forces* 90, no. 1 (2011): 41–63; see also Liana C. Sayer, Paula England, Paul D. Allison, and Nicole Kangas, "She Left, He Left: How Employment and Satisfaction Affect Women's and Men's Decisions to Leave Marriages," *American Journal of Sociology* 116, no. 6 (2011): 1982–2018. This study found more generally that male unemployment increased divorce rates but that female employment had little effect unless the women were unhappy in the marriage.

73. Christopher Jencks pointed out, for example, that the decline in the proportion of African-American men who were married was almost as great among the employed as the unemployed. Christopher Jenks, *Rethinking Social Policy: Race, Poverty, and the Underclass* (New York: HarperCollins, 1992). Mare and Winship used individual employment data to predict the likelihood that a particular individual would marry and found that those data explained only 20 percent of the decline in marriage among young black men during the sixties and seventies. Robert D. Mare and Christopher Winship, "Socioeconomic Change and the Decline of Marriage for Blacks and Whites," in *The Urban Underclass*, ed. Christopher Jencks and Paul E. Peterson (Washington, DC: Brookings Institution, 1992).

74. Kathryn Edin and Maria Kefalas, *Promises I Can Keep: Why Poor Women Put Motherhood before Marriage* (Berkeley: University of California Press, 2005), 81.

75. Edin and Kefalas, *Promises I Can Keep*.

76. William J. Wilson, *When Work Disappears: The World of the New Urban Poor* (New York: Vintage, 1996), 99.

77. Wilson, *When Work Disappears*, 105.

78. Kathryn Edin and Joanna M. Reed, "Why Don't They Just Get Married? Barriers to Marriage among the Disadvantaged," *The Future of Children* 15, no. 2 (2005): 117, http://futureofchildren.org/futureofchildren/publications/docs/15_02_07.pdf, p. 123.

79. Laura Tach, Kathy Edin, and Sara McLanahan, "Multiple Partners and Multiple Partner Fertility in Fragile Families," Fragile Families Working Paper no. WP11-10-FF (Feb. 10, 2011), http://crcw.princeton.edu/workingpapers/WP11-10-FF.pdf (fragile families were defined as biological parents who were not married when their child was born); see Sharon H. Bzostek, Sara S. McLanahan, and Marcia J. Carlson, "Mothers' Repartnering after a Nonmarital Birth," *Social Forces* 90, no. 3 (2011): 817, 826, http://sf.oxfordjournals.org/content/90/3/817 ("At the time of the child's birth, slightly more than half of all unmarried mothers were living with the child's father, 30 percent were dating the child's father, and about a fifth were not romantically involved with the child's father. Five years later, 38 percent of mothers were living with the focal child's father (about 55 percent of those who were cohabiting at birth still lived together), and 31 percent had a new partner").

80. Harknett and McLanahan, "Racial and Ethnic Differences in Marriage after the Birth of a Child."

81. Harknett and McLanahan, "Racial and Ethnic Differences in Marriage after the Birth of a Child," 806.

82. Harknett and McLanahan, "Racial and Ethnic Differences in Marriage after the Birth of a Child," 794, 806.

83. Braman, *Doing Time on the Outside,* 95.

84. See Sara McLanahan, "Family Instability and Complexity after a Nonmarital Birth: Outcomes for Children in Fragile Families," in *Social Class and Changing Families in an Unequal America,* ed. Marcia J. Carlson and Paula England (Stanford, CA: Stanford University Press, 2011), 108, 119. McLanahan found that at the five-year follow-up point the Fragile Families study found that parents married at the birth of their child were approximately half as likely as cohabiting couples to experience any residential or dating change.

85. Edin and Kefalas, *Promises I Can Keep,* 194.

86. Ryan D. King, Michael Massoglia, and Ross MacMillan, "The Context of Marriage and Crime: Gender, the Propensity to Marry, and Offending in Early Adulthood," *Criminology* 45, no. 1 (2007): 33–65.

87. McLanahan and Percheski conclude that "all the studies show that male unemployment or underemployment has a large negative effect on union formation and stability." Sara McLanahan and Christine Percheski, "Family Structure and the Reproduction of Inequalities," *Annual Review of Sociology* 34 (Aug. 2008): 257, 262. See also Sayer et al., "She Left, He Left."

88. Jerry A. Jacobs and Kathleen Gerson, "Who Are the Overworked Americans?" *Review of Social Economy* 56, no. 4 (1998): 442, 457.

89. Charles Murray, *Coming Apart: The State of White America, 1960–2010* (New York: Random House, 2013), 176.

90. Murray, *Coming Apart,* 173.

91. Murray, *Coming Apart,* 175.

92. "Hispanic Unemployment Edges Up to 9.7 Percent," *Hispanic Business.com,* Feb. 4, 2013, www.hispanicbusiness.com/2013/2/4/hispanic_unemployment_edges_up_to_97. htm. Citing U.S. Bureau of Labor Statistics, the report found that in January 2013 the unemployment rate for men twenty years and older nationally was 6.5 percent for Asians, 7 percent for whites, 9.7 percent for Hispanics, and 13.8 percent for blacks.

93. Samreen Hooda, "Unemployment Rates Highest amongst Black and Latinos," *Huffington Post,* Sept. 10, 2012 (Last updated Nov. 8, 2012), www.huffingtonpost.com/2012/09/10/ unemployment-rates-highest-amongst-black-and-latinos_n_1871453.html, citing Bureau of Labor Statistics, "The Employment Situation—2013," news release, www.bls.gov/news. release/pdf/empsit.pdf.

94. Kalleberg, *Good Jobs, Bad Jobs,* 93.

95. Kalleberg, *Good Jobs, Bad Jobs,* 103–104.

96. Richard Wilkinson and Kate Pickett, *The Sprit Level: Why Greater Equality Makes Societies Stronger* (New York: Bloomsbury, 2011).

97. Kalleberg, *Good Jobs, Bad Jobs.*

98. Murray, *Coming Apart,* 193.

99. Murray, *Coming Apart,* 191.

100. Murray, *Coming Apart,* 157.

101. W. Bradford Wilcox and Elizabeth Marquardt, eds., "When Marriage Disappears: The New Middle America," *The State of Our Unions: Marriage in America,* 2010, 40, fig. 16, http://stateofourunions.org/2010/SOOU2010.pdf.

102. Murray, *Coming Apart,* 153.

103. W. Bradford Wilcox and Elizabeth Marquardt, eds., "When Marriage Disappears: The New Middle America," *The State of Our Unions: Marriage in America,* 2010, 30, fig. 9, http://stateofourunions.org/2010/SOOU2010.pdf.

104. Wilcox and Marquardt, "When Marriage Disappears," 32, fig. 11.

105. Wilcox and Marquardt, "When Marriage Disappears," 29, fig. 8, http://stateofourunions. org/2010/SOOU2010.pdf.

106. Wilcox and Marquardt, "When Marriage Disappears," 33, fig. 12.

107. Andrew J. Cherlin, *The Marriage-Go-Round: The State of Marriage and the Family in America Today* (New York: Vintage, 2009), 163.

108. Andrew J. Cherlin, "Between Poor and Prosperous: Do the Family Patterns of Moderately-Educated Americans Deserve a Closer Look?" in Carlson and England, *Social Class and Changing Families in an Unequal Society*, 68–84.

109. For the suggestion that an imbalance in gender ratios decreases marriage for the over-represented group but does not change the level of homogamy, see Bernardo Queiroz, "The Impacts of Sex Ratios on Marriage Markets in the United States," paper presented at Annual Meeting of the Population Association of America, Boston, April 2004.

110. We have not looked specifically at Asians and Latinos, in part, because the data do not capture differences over time as effectively. Most Asian figures on marriage, divorce, and non-marital births resemble the rates of whites. Latino immigrants differ significantly from African Americans with the same socioeconomic characteristics. Men outnumber women to a significant degree among immigrants, and Latino men are more likely to be employed than African-American men, especially among the foreign born. So the gender ratios are significantly different both in aggregate and in comparing employed men to the available women within a given social class. Nonetheless, these factors are all changing rapidly, as immigration rates drop, male employment falls, and the native born live in different communities with different attitudes from those of the foreign-born. Queiroz, "Impacts of Sex Ratios on Marriage Markets."

111. We can find no empirical work testing the impact of current income changes on the marriage rates of elite groups. The most intriguing work was published at the turn of the twenty-first century by Gould and Paserman, who compared marriage rates of those in their twenties in various American cities. They found that differences in male income inequality explained about 25 percent of the drop in marriage rates and that changes in female choice rather than male choice explain the results. Gould and Paserman, "Waiting for Mr. Right," 257 (2003); see also D. S. Loughran, "The Effect of Male Wage Inequality on Female Age at First Marriage," *Review of Economics and Statistics* 84, no. 2 (2002): 237–250 (linking increased inequality with higher average ages of marriage). Tristan P. Coughlin and Scott D. Drewianka also examined the relationship between marriage rates and inequality, finding a strong relationship between rising inequality in the seventies and eighties and declining marriage rates but not in the later years. Their study differed from Gould and Paserman's in that they looked at all ages, not just at people in their twenties. They did not, however, examine class-based differences in marriage rates. In addition, unlike Gould and Paserman, who used city-specific data, Coughlin and Drewianka used statewide data, which would not correlate as closely with specific marriage markets, and the study does not appear to have been published in a peer-reviewed journal. Coughlin and Drewianka, "Can Rising Inequality Explain Aggregate Trends in Marriage? Evidence from U.S. States, 1977–2005," *B.E. Journal of Economic Analysis & Policy* 11, no. 1 (2011): 1–33. The studies, however, are not necessarily inconsistent.

112. Pickett and Wilkinson, *The Sprit Level*, 133–134.

113. Indeed, sociologist Andrew Cherlin questions whether the middle really is a distinct group, though he indicates that high school graduates still tend to marry each other if they do marry and that the patterns for African Americans, Latinos, and whites are distinct from each other (whites marry and divorce more, Latinos have more stable relationships if they do marry, and African Americans marry less and have fewer cohabiting partnerships than whites) and from both college graduates and high school dropouts. Cherlin, "Between Poor and Prosperous."

114. "Rutgers Study: Protective Effect of Education on Marriage Differs between White and African-American Women, Rutgers," *Rutgers Today*, March 6, 2013, http://news.rutgers.edu/medrel/news-releases/2013/march-2013/rutgers-study-protec-20130304.

115. See Mary Beth Marklein, "College Gender Gap Widens: 57 percent Are Women," *USA Today*, Oct. 19, 2005, http://usatoday30.usatoday.com/news/education/2005-10-19-male-college-cover_x.htm (showing male representation on college campuses by race and income using data compiled by the National Center for Education Statistics).

116. Justin Lahart, "Number of the Week: Falling Wages for Young College Grads," *Real Time Economics* blog, *Wall Street Journal*, Oct. 8, 2011, http://blogs.wsj.com/economics/2011/10/08/number-of-the-week-falling-wages-for-young-college-grads.

117. Jefffrey J. Selingo, "The Diploma's Vanishing Value," *Wall Street Journal*, April 26, 2013, http://online.wsj.com/article_email/SB10001424127887324874204578440901216478088-lMyQjAxMTAzMDIwOTEyNDkyWj.html?mod=wsj_valettop_email; Jeffrey J. Selingo, *College (Un)Bound: The Future of Higher Education and What It Means for Students* (New York: Houghton Mifflin Harcourt, 2013).

Chapter 7

1. Jason DeParle, "For Poor, Leap to College Often Ends in a Hard Fall," *New York Times*, Dec. 22, 2013, www.nytimes.com/2012/12/23/education/poor-students-struggle-as-class-plays-a-greater-role-in-success.html?_r=0.

2. Sean F. Reardon, "The Widening Academic Achievement Gap between the Rich and the Poor: New Evidence and Possible Explanations," in *Whither Opportunity? Rising Inequality, Schools, and Children's Life Chances*, ed. Greg J. Duncan and Richard J. Murnane (New York: Sage, 2011), 91–116.

3. Sabrina Tavernise, "Education Gap Grows between Rich and Poor, Studies Say," *New York Times*, Feb. 9, 2012), www.nytimes.com/2012/02/10/education/education-gap-grows-between-rich-and-poor-studies-show.html?pagewanted=all.

4. Anne Fernald, Virginia A. Marchman, and Adriana Weisleder, "SES Differences in Language Processing Skill and Vocabulary Are Evident at 18 Months," *Developmental Science* 16, no. 2 (2013): 234–248.

5. Fernald et al., "SES Differences," 235.

6. Fernald et al., "SES Differences," 244.

7. Twin studies indicate that at higher SES levels, genetic variation accounts for a substantial portion of the difference in children's performance. For children raised in poverty, the genetic component drops to close to zero, but environmental factors explain 60 percent of the variation. Fernald et al., "SES Differences," 243.

8. Reardon, "Widening Academic Achievement Gap between the Rich and the Poor," 17.

9. Robert D. Putnam, Carl B. Frederick, and Kaisa Snellman, "Growing Class Gaps in Social Connectedness among American Youth, 1975–2009," unpublished paper, Kennedy School of Government, July 12, 2012, 10, www.hks.harvard.edu/saguaro/pdfs/SaguaroReport_DivergingSocialConnectedness.pdf.

10. Kim Parker and Wendy Wang, "Modern Parenthood: Roles of Moms and Dads Converge as They Balance Work and Family," Pew Research Center Report, March 14, 2013, 24, www.pewsocialtrends.org/files/2013/03/FINAL_modern_parenthood_03-2013.pdf.

11. See June Carbone, "Is Fertility the Unspoken Issue in the Debate between Liberal and Conservative Family Values?" 32 LAW & SOC. INQUIRY 809, 822 (2007) (reviewing Linda C. McClain, *The Place of Families: Fostering Capacity, Equality, and Responsibility* (Cambridge, MA: Harvard University Press, 2006).

12. Sara McLanahan, "Diverging Destinies: How Children Are Faring under the Second Demographic Transition," *Demography* 41, no. 4 (2004): 607, 608.

13. See Paula England, Elizabeth Aura McClintock, and Emily Fitzgibbons Shafer, "Birth Control Use and Early, Unintended Births: Evidence for a Class Gradient," in *Social Class and Changing Families in an Unequal America*, ed. Marcia Carlson and Paula England (Stanford, CA: Stanford University Press, 2011), 21–49.

14. Greg J. Duncan and Richard J. Murnane, "Introduction: The American Dream, Then and Now," in *Whither Opportunity? Rising Inequality, Schools, and Children's Life Chances*, ed. Greg J. Duncan and Richard J. Murnane (New York: Sage, 2011), 3, 9, www. russellsage.org/sites/all/files/Duncan_Murnane_Chap1.pdf.

15. Duncan and Murnane, *Whither Opportunity?* 13, and Elizabeth O. Ananat, Anna Gassman-Pines, and Christina M. Gibson-Davis, "The Effects of Local Employment Losses on Children's Educational Achievement," in Duncan and Murnane, *Whither Opportunity?* 299.

16. Duncan and Murnane, *Whither Opportunity?*, 13.

17. Robert Putnam, *Our Kids: The American Dream in Crisis* (Simon & Schuster, 2015) 225.

18. Annette Lareau, *Unequal Childhoods: Class, Race, and Family Life*, 2nd ed. (Berkeley: University of California Press, 2011).

19. Annette Lareau and Amanda Cox, "Social Class and the Transition to Adulthood: Differences in Parents' Interactions with Institutions," in Carlson and England, *Social Class and Changing Families*, 134.

20. National Center for Education Statistics, "Indicator 34: Immediate Transition to College," in NCES Report no. 2012-045, "The Condition of Education 2012," May 2012, 85, fig. 34-1.

21. See Martha J. Bailey and Susan M. Dynarski, "Gains and Gaps: Changing Inequality in U.S. College Entry and Completion," in Duncan and Murnane, *Whither Opportunity?*; Thomas A. DiPrete and Claudia Buchman, *The Rise of Women: The Growing Gender Gap in Education and What It Means for American Schools* (New York: Sage, 2013) (suggesting that part of the reason why boys do worse than girls is that their performance depends more on school and community reinforcement; both boys and girls do better in better schools, but the impact of better schools on boys is greater).

22. "Recent Deep State Higher Education Cuts May Harm Students in the Economy for Years to Come," March 19, 2013, www.cbpp.org\cms\?fa=view&&id=3927. Joan C. Williams, *Reshaping the Work-Family Debate: Why Men and Class Matter* (Cambridge, MA: Harvard University Press, 2010), 162.

23. William G. Bowen, Matthew M. Chingos, and Michael S. McPherson, *Crossing the Finish Line: Completing College at America's Public Universities* (Princeton, NJ: Princeton University Press, 2009), 6.

24. Bowen et al., *Crossing the Finish Line*, 8.

Chapter 8

1. W. Bradford Wilcox and Elizabeth Marquardt, eds., "When Marriage Disappears: The New Middle America," The State of Our Unions: Marriage in America, 2010 (2010), 38, http://stateofourunions.org/2010/SOOU2010.pdf; David Popenoe and Barbara Dafoe Whitehead, 'Who Wants to Marry a Soul Mate?' in "The State of Our Unions 2001," National Marriage Project Report, 2001, 6–16, www.stateofourunions.org/pdfs/SOOU2001.pdf; Paul Amato, Alan Booth, David R. Johnson, and Stacy J. Rogers, *Alone Together: How Marriage in America Is Changing* (Cambridge, MA: Harvard University Press, 2007), 71.

2. William Kristol, "Women's Liberation: The Relevance of Tocqueville," in *Interpreting Tocqueville's Democracy in America*, ed. Ken Masugi (Lanham, MD: Rowman & Littlefield, 1991), 480, 491.

3. Adrienne Rich, "Compulsory Heterosexuality and Lesbian Existence," *Signs* 5, no. 4 (1980): 631, 654.

4. Rich, "Compulsory Heterosexuality."

5. James Q. Wilson, *The Marriage Problem: How Our Culture Has Weakened Families* (New York: HarperCollins, 2002), 89–99.

6. Wilson, *The Marriage Problem*, 89.

7. One need only compare the Muslim Brotherhood with the Southern Baptist convention. See David D. Kirkpatrick and Mayy El Sheikh, "Muslim Brotherhood's Statement on Women Stirs Liberals' Fears," *New York Times*, March 14, 2013, www.nytimes.com/2013/03/15/world/middleeast/muslim-brotherhoods-words-on-women-stir-liberal-fears.html?emc=eta1&_r=0.

8. Leslie Bennetts, "JFK Intern Mimi Alford's Shocking Affair Tell-All," *Newsweek*, Feb. 13, 2012, www.thedailybeast.com/newsweek/2012/02/12/jfk-intern-mimi-alford-s-shocking-affair-tell-all.html.

9. Jacqueline Kennedy, *Historic Conversations on Life with John F. Kennedy* (New York: Hyperion, 2011), xxvi.

10. See Annual of the 2007 Southern Baptist Convention, June 12–13, San Antonio, Texas, www.sbcec.org/bor/2007/2007sbcannual.pdf.

11. Betsey Stevenson and Justin Wolfers, "Bargaining in the Shadow of the Law: Divorce Laws and Family Distress," *Quarterly Journal of Economics* 121, no. 1 (2006): 267.

12. Andrew J. Cherlin, "The Deinstitutionalization of American Marriage," *Journal of Marriage and Family* 66, no. 4 (2004): 848–861, citing F. M. Cancian, *Love in America: Gender and Self-Development* (Cambridge: Cambridge University Press, 1987) (characterizing the increased references to these qualities as a transition "from role to self.").

13. Amato et al., *Alone Together*.

14. Bureau of Labor Statistics, "Employment Characteristics of Families in 2005," news release, April 27, 2006, tbl. 4, www.bls.gov/news.release/archives/famee_04272006.pdf (approximately 66 percent of married mothers worked outside the home in 2004–2005); Eileen Patten and Kim Parker, "A Gender Reversal on Career Aspirations," Pew Research Center Social & Demographic Trends Report, April 19, 2012, www.pewsocialtrends.org/2012/04/19/a-gender-reversal-on-career-aspirations.

15. CNN Political Unit, "CNN Poll: Support for Working Women Almost Unanimous," Political Ticker blog, April 16, 2012, http://politicalticker.blogs.cnn.com/2012/04/16/poll-support-for-working-women-almost-unanimous.

16. Amato et al., *Alone Together*, 110.

17. Eileen Patten and Kim Parker, *A Gender Reversal On Career Aspirations*, April 19, 2012, http://www.pewsocialtrends.org/2012/04/19/a-gender-reversal-on-career-aspirations/.

18. Kim Parker and Wendy Wang, "Modern Parenthood: Roles of Moms and Dads Converge as They Balance Work and Family," Pew Research Center Report, March 14, 2013, 16, 58, http://www.pewsocialtrends.org/files/2013/03/FINAL_modern_parenthood_03-2013.pdf.

19. Sheryl Sandberg, *Lean In: Women, Work, and the Will to Lead* (New York: Knopf, 2013); Richard Fry and D'Vera Cohn, "Women, Men and the New Economics of Marriage," Pew Research Center Social & Demographic Trends Report, Jan. 19, 2010, 17, http://pewsocialtrends.org/files/2010/11/new-economics-of-marriage.pdf.

20. See Naomi Cahn and June Carbone, "Five Myths about Working Mothers," *Washington Post*, May 30, 2010, www.washingtonpost.com/wp-dyn/content/article/2010/05/28/AR2010052802268.html.

21. June Carbone and Naomi Cahn, "Casualty of the One Percent," *New York Times*, April 1, 2013, www.nytimes.com/roomfordebate/2013/03/31/why-has-salary-parity-still-not-happened/gender-equality-is-a-casualty-of-the-one-percent.

22. Sylvia DeMott and Kathy Lynch, "Defining Paternity Leave," Boston College Center for Work & Family Executive Brief (n.d.; last viewed May 18, 2013), www.bc.edu/content/dam/files/centers/cwf/research/publications/pdf/paternityleave_ebs.pdf.

23. Jeffery Leving and Kenneth Dachman, *Fathers' Rights: Hard-Hitting and Fair Advice for Every Father Involved in a Custody Dispute* (New York: Basic Books, 1997). But see

Suzanne M. Bianchi, John P. Robinson, and Melissa A. Milkie, *Changing Rhythms of American Family Life* (New York: Sage, 2007), 91 (putting the number at 82 percent).

24. Liana C. Sayer, Suzanne M. Bianchi, and John P. Robinson, "Are Parents Investing Less in Children? Trends in Mothers' and Fathers' Time with Children," *American Journal of Sociology* 110, no. 1 (2004): 1–43, http://csde.washington.edu/downloads/bianchi_ AJS_paper.pdf. See also Sara McLanahan, "Diverging Destinies: How Children Are Faring after the Second Demographic Transition," *Demography* 41, no. 4 (2004).

25. See Catherine Rampell, "In Most Rich Countries, Women Work More Than Men," Economix blog, *New York Times*, Dec. 19, 2012, http://economix.blogs.nytimes. com/2012/12/19/in-most-rich-countries-women-work-more-than-men.

26. Philip Cohen, "Exaggerating Gender Changes," FamilyInequality blog, Aug. 13, 2012, http://familyinequality.wordpress.com/2012/08/13/exaggerating-gender-changes.

27. Amato et al., *Alone Together*, 198–200.

28. Amato et al., *Alone Together*, 145.

29. Amato et al., *Alone Together*, 149–150.

30. Amato et al., *Alone Together*, 150.

31. Amato et al., *Alone Together*, 161.

32. Kathryn Edin and Timothy J. Nelson, *Doing the Best I Can: Fatherhood in the Inner City* (Berkeley: University of California Press, 2013), 78.

33. Robert L. Griswold, *Fatherhood in America: A History* (New York: Basic Books, 1993), 2.

34. See Mary Blair-Loy, *Competing Devotions: Career and Family among Women Executives* (Cambridge, MA: Harvard University Press, 2003), 83–84; http://www. pewsocialtrends.org/2010/11/18/the-decline-of-marriage-and-rise-of-new-families/ Pew Research Center Report, "The Decline of Marriage and the Rise of New Families," (November 18, 2010), iii, Pew Research Center Social & Demographic Trends Report, http://www.pewsocialtrends.org/2010/11/18/the-decline-of-marriage-and-rise-of- new-families/ ("When asked in the current Pew Research Center survey how important it is that a woman be able to support a family financially in order to be ready for marriage, only 33 percent say this is very important. When asked a parallel question about men, 67 percent say it is very important that a man be able to support a family").

35. See, e.g., Daniel Schneider, "Market Earnings and Household Work: New Tests of Gender Performance Theory," *Journal of Marriage and Family* 73, no. 4 (Aug. 2011): 845–860.

36. Suzanne Bianchi, "Changing Families, Changing Workplaces," *Future of Children* 21, no. 2 (2011): 26.

37. Andrew J. Cherlin, *The Marriage-Go-Round: The State of Marriage and the Family in America Today* (New York: Vintage, 2009), 163.

38. Kathleen Gerson, *The Unfinished Revolution: How a New Generation Is Reshaping Family, Work, and Gender in America* (New York: Oxford University Press, 2010), 164.

39. Jonathan Rauch, "The No Good, Very Bad Outlook for the Working-Class American Man," *National Journal*, Dec. 5, 2012, www.nationaljournal.com/next-economy/ the-no-good-very-bad-outlook-for-the-working-class-american-man-20121205.

40. Sarah Jane Glynn, "The New Breadwinners: 2010 Update; Rates of Women Supporting Their Families Economically Increased since 2007," Center for American Progress Issue Brief, April 16, 2012, www.americanprogress.org/issues/2012/04/epd_breadwinners. html.

41. Susan Gregory Thomas, "When the Wife Has a Fatter Paycheck: Female Breadwinners Can Make for Frustrated Husbands—Unless the Man Holds His Own with Income," *Wall Street Journal*, July 12, 2012, http://online.wsj.com/article_email/ SB10000872396390444873204577537161203859878-lMyQjAxMTAyMDIwMTAy- ODE3Wj.html?mod=wsj_valettop_email.

42. Hanna Rosin, *The End of Men and the Rise of Women* (New York: Penguin, 2012), 2 (describing a single mother as "queen of her castle").

43. Rosin, *The End of Men*, 3.
44. See, e.g., Schneider, "Market Earnings and Household Work," 845.
45. Rosin, *The End of Men*, 71. See also Marianne Bertrand, Jessica Pan, and Emir Kamenica, *Gender Identity and Relative Income Within Households* (2013), http://www.nber.org/papers/w19023.
46. Tony Dokoupil, "Lifestyle: Laid-Off Men Don't Do Dishes," *Newsweek*, Feb. 20, 2009, www.newsweek.com/2009/02/20/men-will-be-men.html.
47. CNN Political Unit, "CNN Poll: Support for Working Women Almost Unanimous."
48. Charles Murray, *Coming Apart: The State of White America, 1960–2010* (New York: Random House, 2013), 151.
49. Amato et al., *Alone Together*, 101.
50. Amato et al., *Alone Together*, 111.
51. Parker and Wang, "Modern Parenthood," 24.
52. See, e.g., Anne-Marie Slaughter, "Why Women Still Can't Have It All," *The Atlantic*, July/August 2012, www.theatlantic.com/magazine/archive/2012/07/why-women-still-cant-have-it-all/309020.
53. Lynda Laughlin, "Maternity Leave and Employment Patterns of First-Time Mothers, 1961–2008," U.S. Census Bureau Current Population Report no. P70-128, October 2011, 11, tbl. 7, www.census.gov/prod/2011pubs/p70-128.pdf.
54. Amato et al., *Alone Together*, 123–124.
55. Amato et al., *Alone Together*, 124.
56. Amato et al., *Alone Together*. See also Steven L. Nock and Margaret F. Brinig, "Weak Men and Disorderly Women: Divorce and the Division of Labor," in *The Law and Economics of Marriage and Divorce*, ed. Antony W. Dnes and Robert Rowthorn (Cambridge: Cambridge University Press, 2002), 171–190 (greater involvement in traditionally female housework by either partner is associated with higher chances of divorce or separation, though relationships are more stable if the husband acknowledges that the wife does more housework and he views the result as unfair).
57. Tony Dokoupil, "Men Will Be Men: When Guys Lose Jobs, the TV, Den and Gym Win. Women? Sex? Not So Much," *Newsweek*, March 2, 2009, 50.
58. Sarah Moore, Leon Grunberg, Richard Anderson-Connolly, and Edward S. Greenberg, "Physical and Mental Health Effects of Surviving Layoffs: A Longitudinal Examination," Institute of Behavioral Science Working Paper PEC2003–0003, November, 2003, www.colorado.edu/ibs/pubs/pec/pec2003-0003.pdf.
59. Tony Dokoupil, "Lifestyle: Laid-Off Men Don't Do Dishes"; see also Clifford L. Broman, V. Lee Hamilton, and William S. Hoffman, "The Impact of Unemployment on Families," *Michigan Family Review* 2, no. 2 (1996).
60. See Richard Wilkinson and Kate Pickett, *The Spirit Level: Why Greater Equality Makes Societies Stronger* (New York: Bloomsbury, 2009).
61. See Rosin, *The End of Men*, 2.

Chapter 9

1. Heather Havrilesky, "The Divorce Delusion," *New York Times Magazine*, July 6, 2011, www.nytimes.com/2011/07/10/magazine/the-divorce-delusion.html?pagewanted=1.
2. Havrilesky, "The Divorce Delusion."
3. Naomi Cahn and June Carbone, *Red Families v. Blue Families: Legal Polarization and the Creation of Culture* (New York: Oxford University Press, 2010).
4. Carl Schneider calls this "the channelling function in family law." Carl E. Schneider, *The Channelling Function in Family Law*, 20 Hofstra L. Rev. 495 (1992).
5. Robert H. Mnookin and Lewis Kornhauser, *Bargaining in the Shadow of the Law: The Case of Divorce*, 88 Yale L.J. 950 (1979).

6. See generally Jacobus tenBroek, *California's Dual System of Family Law: Its Origin, Development, and Present Status* (pts. I, II, & II), 16 STAN. L. REV. 257 (1964), 16 STAN. L. REV. 900 (1964), 17 STAN. L. REV. 614 (1965). These divisions between the family law of rich and poor, private and public, voluntary and involuntary family associations have been the subject of extensive subsequent commentary. See, e.g., Tonya L. Brito, *The Welfarization of Family Law*, 48 U. KAN. L. REV. 229, 238–250 (2000); Naomi R. Cahn, *Children's Interests in a Familial Context: Poverty, Foster Care, and Adoption*, 60 OHIO ST. L.J. 1189, 1211–1215 (1999); Deborah Harris, *Child Support for Welfare Families: Family Policy Trapped in Its Own Rhetoric*, 16 N.Y.U. REV. L. & SOC. CHANGE 619, 621–629 (1988); Leslie Joan Harris, *The Basis for Legal Parentage and the Clash between Custody and Child Support*, 42 IND. L. REV. 611, 612–614 (2009); Jill Elaine Hasday, *Parenthood Divided: A Legal History of the Bifurcated Law of Parental Relations*, 90 GEO. L.J. 299, 368–371 (2002); Daniel L. Hatcher, *Child Support Harming Children: Subordinating the Best Interests of Children to the Fiscal Interests of the State*, 42 WAKE FOREST L. REV. 1029, 1043–1044 (2007); Amy E. Hirsch, *Income Deeming in the AFDC Program: Using Dual Track Family Law to Make Poor Women Poorer*, 16 N.Y.U. REV. L & SOC. CHANGE 713, 715–716 (1988).

7. tenBroek, *California's Dual System of Family Law* (pt. II), 907.

8. Andrew J. Cherlin, *The Marriage Go-Round: The State of Marriage and Family in America Today* (New York: Vintage, 2009).

9. Hanna Rosin, *The End of Men and the Rise of Women* (New York: Penguin, 2012), 47.

10. See, e.g., James Q. Wilson, *The Marriage Problem: How Our Culture Has Weakened Families* (New York: HarperCollins, 2002), 89.

11. *Griswold v. Connecticut*, 381 U.S. 479 (1965); *Eisenstadt v. Baird*, 405 U.S. 438 (1972).

12. Naomi Cahn and June Carbone, *Red Families v. Blue Families: Legal Polarization and the Creation of Culture* (New York: Oxford University Press, 2010), 87.

13. *Carey v. Population Servs. Int'l*, 431 U.S. 678 (1977).

14. See, e.g., Elizabeth Warren and Amelia Warren Tyagi, *The Two-Income Trap: Why Middle-Class Parents Are Going Broke* (New York: Basic Books, 2003).

15. For a discussion of these changes see Deborah A. Widiss, *Changing the Marriage Equation*, 89 WASH. U. L. REV. 721 (2012).

16. Richard Fry and D'Vera Cohn, "Women, Men and the New Economics of Marriage," Pew Research Social & Demographic Trends Report, Jan. 19, 2010, 8, http://pewsocialtrends.org/files/2010/11/new-economics-of-marriage.pdf; Pew Research Center, "On Pay Gap, Millennial Women Near Parity – For Now," Dec. 11, 2013, http://www.pewsocialtrends.org/files/2013/12/gender-and-work_final.pdf.

17. For a discussion of bargaining over custody and support, see generally Paula England and Nancy Folbre, "Involving Dads: Parental Bargaining and Family Well-Being," in *Handbook of Father Involvement: Multidisciplinary Perspectives*, ed. Catherine S. Tamis-LeMonda and Natasha Cabrera (Mahwah, NJ: Erlbaum, 2002), 387.

18. Nelson Manfred Blake, *The Road to Reno* (New York: Macmillan, 1962).

19. Within marriage, husbands but not wives controlled expenditure of joint funds, and married women could not get credit without their husband's approval. See Leslie Joan Harris, June Carbone, and Lee E. Teitelbaum, *Family Law*, 4th ed. (New York: Aspen, 2009).

20. See June Carbone, *From Partners to Parents: The Second Revolution in Family Law* (New York: Columbia University Press, 2000), 99.

21. See, e.g., Andrew Hacker, *Mismatch: The Growing Gulf between Men and Women* (New York: Scribner, 2003) (finding in the mid-nineties that women initiated 60.7 percent of all divorces and 64 percent of those with children); Margaret F. Brinig and Douglas W. Allen, *"These Boots Are Made for Walking": Why Most Divorce Filers Are Women*, 2 AM. L. & ECON. REV. 126, 128 tbl. 1, 136–137 (2000) (stating that two-thirds of those filing for divorce are women).

22. Economists, influenced by the Coase theorem, argue that couples bargain around the legal changes. See, e.g., Betsey Stevenson and Justin Wolfers, "Marriage and Divorce: Changes and Their Driving Forces," *Journal of Economic Perspectives* 21, no. 2: 46 (summarizing literature); Justin Wolfers, "Did Unilateral Divorce Raise Divorce Rates? A Reconciliation and New Results," *American Economic Review* 96, no. 5 (2006): 1802–1820.

23. Stéphane Mechoulan, *Divorce Laws and the Structure of the American Family*, 35 J. LEGAL STUD. 143, 163–164 (2006) ("the impact of a no-fault regime for grounds regime is to decrease age at first marriage, although not statistically significantly, while the effect of no fault for property is to significantly delay marriage").

24. Betsey Stevenson and Justin Wolfers, "Bargaining in the Shadow of the Law: Divorce Laws and Family Distress," *Quarterly Journal of Economics* 121, no. 1 (2006): 267–288.

25. Betsey Stevenson, "The Impact of Divorce Laws on Investment in Marriage-Specific Capital," *Journal of Labor Economics* 25, no. 1 (2007): 75–94; Betsey Stevenson, "Divorce-Law Changes, Household Bargaining, and Married Women's Labor Supply Revisited," *mimeo*, University of Pennsylvania.

26. Cherlin, *Marriage Go-Round*, 88.

27. Leslie Harris, June Carbone, Lee Teitlelbaum, *Family Law*, 4th ed. (Aspen, 2009).

28. Harris et al., *Family Law*.

29. Harris et al., *Family Law*.

30. See, e.g., American Law Institute (ALI), *Principles of the Law of Family Dissolution: Analysis and Recommendations* § 4.09 (2002) (recognizing a presumption of equal division). See also Marsha Garrison, *How Do Judges Decide Divorce Cases? An Empirical Analysis of Discretionary Decision Making*, 74 N.C. L. REV. 401, 452–458 (1996) (finding that judges stay fairly close to a fifty-fifty division). Compare Marsha Garrison, *Good Intentions Gone Awry: The Impact of New York's Equitable Distribution Law on Divorce Outcomes*, 57 BROOK. L. REV. 621, 673–674, tbls. 18 and 20 (1991) (concluding that settled property divisions are much more variable than court-ordered ones).

31. Carolyn Frantz and Hanoch Dagan, *Properties of Marriage*, 104 COLUM. L. REV. 75, 77 (2004). See also Elizabeth S. Scott, *Rational Decisionmaking about Marriage and Divorce*, 76 VA. L. REV. 9, 12 (1990) (arguing that modern marriage, understood in terms of the rational pursuit of mutual self-interest, still involves commitment to the creation of an interdependent regime, not lightly dissolved simply because emotional satisfaction does not meet "soul mate" expectations).

32. See *Orr v. Orr*, 440 U.S. 268 (1979) (dismantling the gendered nature of support).

33. Harris et al., Family Law, 927, n10 (3d ed., 2005); June Carbone, *The Futility of Coherence: The ALI's Principles of the Law of Family Dissolution, Compensatory Spousal Payments*, 4 J.L. & FAM. STUD. 43 (2002): 43.

34. Katharine K. Baker, Homogenous Rules for Heterogeneous Families: The Standardization of Family Law When There Is No Standard Family, 2012 U. ILL. L. REV. 319, 340 (2012).

35. Nehami Baum, "'Separation Guilt' in Women Who Initiate Divorce," *Clinical Social Work Journal* 35, no. 1 (2006): 47, 48.

36. *Berger v. Berger*, 747 N.W.2d 336, 352–353 (Mich. App. 2008).

37. See, e.g., Nehami Baum, "'Separation Guilt' in Women Who Initiate Divorce," *Clinical Social Work Journal* 35, no. 1 (2006): 47, 48 (women initiate divorce at twice the rate of men). Older women who are not currently homemakers, however, incur the least sympathy in studies of juror attitudes. Ira Mark Ellman and Sanford L. Braver, *Lay Intuitions about Family Obligations: The Case of Alimony*, 13 THEORETICAL INQUIRIES L. 209 (2012).

38. See Judith G. McMullen, "ALIMONY: What Social Science and Popular Culture Tell Us about Women, Guilt and Spousal Support after Divorce" (2011), ExpressO, http://works.bepress.com/judith_mcmullen/1. More recently, some states have reaffirmed the availability of long-term spousal support for women who divorce after long marriages,

but the duration of such awards varies widely and depends on the payor spouse's income, the court's findings about the payee's capacity for workforce participation, and the length of the marriage. See Katharine K. Baker, *The Stories of Marriage*, 12 J.L. & FAM. STUD. 1, 49–50 (2010). The doctor who makes $400,000 per year can be expected to support a wife with four special needs children who last worked for $15 per hour in a medical clinic. *Martindale v. Martindale*, 2005 WL 94366 (Tenn. Ct. App. 2005).

39. See Katharine K. Baker, *The Stories of Marriage*, 12 J.L. & FAM. STUD. 1, 49–50 (2010).

40. Terry Martin Hekker, "Paradise Lost (Domestic Division)," *New York Times*, Jan. 1, 2006, www.nytimes.com/2006/01/01/fashion/sundaystyles/01LOVE.html?pagewanted=all.

41. See Theresa Glennon, *Still Partners? Examining the Consequences of Post-Dissolution Parenting*, 41 FAM. L.Q. 105, 105 (2007).

42. "Results of Local, Regional Ballot Questions," 2004 election, *Boston Globe*, www.boston. com/news/special/politics/2004_results/general_election/questions_all_by_town. htm.

43. Sanford L. Braver, Ira Mark Ellman, Ashley Votruba, and William V. Fabricius, *Lay Judgments about Child Custody after Divorce*, 17 PSYCHOL. PUB. POL'Y & L. 212 (2011); Ira Mark Ellman, Sanford L. Braver, and Robert J. MacCoun, *Abstract Principles and Concrete Cases in Intuitive Lawmaking*, 36 LAW & HUM. BEHAV. 96 (2012), (earlier version (Feb. 5, 2011) available at http://papers.ssrn.com/sol3/papers.cfm?abstract_id=1755707); Ira Mark Ellman, Sanford L. Braver, and Robert J. MacCoun, *Intuitive Lawmaking: The Example of Child Support*, 6 J. EMPIRICAL LEGAL STUD. 69 (2009).

44. See Judith G. McMullen, *Alimony: What Social Science and Popular Culture Tell Us about Women, Guilt, and Spousal Support after Divorce*, 19 DUKE J. GENDER L. & POL'Y 41 (2011) (discussing women's feeling of guilt about initiating divorce as factor in lack of alimony awards). See also Judith S. Wallerstein and Joan B. Kelly, *Surviving the Breakup: How Children and Parents Cope with Divorce* (New York: Basic Books, 1996), 23 (party initiating divorce likely to ask for less financial support).

45. June Carbone, *From Partners to Parents: The Second Revolution in Family Law* (New York: Columbia University Press, 2000), 180 n.12.

46. See, e.g., Margaret F. Brinig, *Does Parental Autonomy Require Equal Custody at Divorce?* 65 LA. L. REV. 1345, 1367–1368 (2005) (finding a decrease in child support after statutory changes in custody provisions took effect); Margaret F. Brinig, *Penalty Defaults in Family Law: The Case of Child Custody*, 33 FLA. ST. U. L. REV. 779, 806 (2006) (noting there was an increase in joint custody where couples separated after the statute took effect).

47. Martha Albertson Fineman, *The Illusion of Equality: The Rhetoric and Reality of Divorce Reform* (Chicago: University of Chicago Press, 1994), ch. 5; Martha Albertson Fineman, *The Neutered Mother, the Sexual Family, and Other Twentieth Century Tragedies* (New York: Routledge, 1995), 82–83. Much earlier, of course, Mnookin and Kornhauser also observed that any change to gender-neutral custody rules would weaken women's bargaining power at divorce. Mnookin and Kornhauser, *Bargaining in the Shadow of the Law*, 978.

48. Margaret F. Brinig and Douglas W. Allen, *"These Boots Are Made for Walking": Why Most Divorce Filers Are Women*, 2 AM. L. & ECON. REV. 126, 128 tbl. 1, 136–137 (2000) (stating that two-thirds of those filing for divorce are women and that custody laws affect willingness to file).

49. See, e.g., Wis. Stat § 767.41(2) (2011) (establishing that joint legal custody is presumed) and § 767.41(4) (noting that the court "shall set a placement schedule that allows the child to have regularly occurring meaningful periods of placement" and "maximizes the amount of time the child may spend with each parent"). See generally, Leslie Bennetts, *The Feminine Mistake: Are We Giving Up Too Much?* (New York: Hyperion, 2007).

50. Kay Hymowitz, Jason S. Carroll, W. Bradford Wilcox, and Kelleen Kaye, "Knot Yet: The Benefits and Costs of Delayed Marriage in America," National Marriage Project Report,

2013, http://nationalmarriageproject.org/wp-content/uploads/2013/03/KnotYet-Final-ForWeb.pdf. Better-educated men and less-educated women have the most to lose from inopportune marriages in the new system, and it should come as no surprise that these groups express the greatest skepticism about marriage to their current live-in partners.

51. See, e.g., Paul R. Amato, *Good Enough Marriages: Parental Discord, Divorce, and Children's Well-Being*, 9 VA. J. SOC. POL'Y & L. 71 (2002) (concluding that children benefit from divorce in high-conflict cases but not from the more common "good enough marriages").

52. William J. Wilson, *When Work Disappears: The World of the New Urban Poor* (New York: Vintage, 1996), 103–104.

53. Jason DeParle and Sabrina Tavernise, "For Women under 30, Most Births Occur Outside Marriage, *New York Times*, Feb. 17, 2012, www.nytimes.com/2012/02/18/us/for-women-under-30-most-births-occur-outside-marriage.html?pagewanted=all&_r=1&.

54. Mark Regnerus and Jeremy Uecker, *Premarital Sex in America: How Young Americans Meet, Mate, and Think about Marrying* (New York: Oxford University Press, 2011), 192.

55. Lauren Schutte, "Michael Jordan Set to Marry for the Second Time," *Hollywood Reporter*, Dec. 29, 2011, www.hollywoodreporter.com/news/michael-jordan-engaged-christmas-yvette-prieto-276669.

56. W. Bradford Wilcox and Elizabeth Marquardt, eds., "When Marriage Disappears: The New Middle America," *The State of Our Unions: Marriage in America* (2010), 40, fig. 16, http://stateofourunions.org/2010/SOOU2010.pdf (53 percent of the least educated and 43 percent of the moderately educated report that marriage has not worked out for people they know in comparison with 17 percent of the highly educated).

57. Kathryn Edin and Timothy J. Nelson, *Doing the Best I Can: Fatherhood in the Inner City* (Berkeley: University of California Press, 2013), 205.

58. Kathleen Gerson, *The Unfinished Revolution: Coming of Age in a New Era of Gender, Work, and Family* (New York: Oxford University Press, 2010), 11–12, 127–128.

59. Gerson, *Unfinished Revolution*, 127.

60. Gerson, *Unfinished Revolution*, 130.

61. Lenore Skomal, "Women Who Pay Alimony: It's More Frequent Than You Think," Divorce360, www.divorce360.com/divorce-articles/alimony/information/women-paying-alimony.aspx?artid=1065&page=2.

62. Katharine K. Baker, *Homogenous Rules for Heterogeneous Families: The Standardization of Family Law When There Is No Standard Family*, 2012 U. ILL. L. REV. 319 (2012).

63. Hanna Rosin, *The End of Men and the Rise of Women* (New York: Penguin, 2012), 3–4.

64. Hymowitz et al., "Knot Yet," 28; also, 26–29 ('The Great Crossover: The Why'), http://twentysomethingmarriage.org/the-great-crossover-the-why.

65. See, e.g., Alison Wolf, *The XX Factor: How the Rise of Working Women Has Created a Far Less Equal World* (London: Profile Books, 2013), 206, 207; Christine R. Schwartz, "Trends and Variation in Assortative Mating: Causes and Consequences," *Annual Review of Sociology* 39 (July 2013): 451, 460 (noting an increase in educational homogamy).

66. Molly Lanzarotta, "Kathryn Edin on Poverty in America," interview, April 21, 2008, http://www.hks.harvard.edu/news-events/publications/insight/social/kathryn-edin.

67. Edin and Nelson, *Doing the Best I Can*, 205.

68. Kathryn Edin and Maria Kefalas, *Promises I Can Keep: Why Poor Women Put Motherhood before Marriage* (Berkeley: University of California Press, 2005), 108.

69. Edin and Nelson, *Doing the Best I Can*, 17, 18, 208.

70. See Edin and Nelson, *Doing the Best I Can*, 209 ("fulfilling the aspiration to father consistently and well requires both commitment and strong emotional mettle—what we call psychological resources"). For a discussion of the role of uncertainty on the attitudes of African-American women, see generally Linda M. Burton and M. Belinda Tucker, *Romantic Unions in an Era of Uncertainty: A Post-Moynihan Perspective on African American Women and Marriage*, 621 ANNALS AM. ACAD. POL. & SOC. SCI. 132 (2009). Burton and Tucker observe, for example, that African-American women identified the following

risks from romantic involvement: "financial (many had finally obtained some degree of financial stability and were concerned that monetary entanglements with another would deplete their resources), physical (older men were more likely to become infirm, require care, and become dependent), and psychological (they preferred a life of independence, finally free from the demands of others—something they had been denied)" (135–136).

Chapter 10

1. Kristen Harknett and Sara McLanahan, "Racial and Ethnic Differences in Marriage after the Birth of a Child," *American Sociological Review* 69, no. 6 (2004); W. Bradford Wilcox and Elizabeth Marquardt, eds., "When Marriage Disappears: The New Middle America," *The State of Our Unions: Marriage in America,* 2010.

2. Linda M. Burton, Andrew Cherlin, Donna-Marie Winn, Angela Estacion, and Clara Holder-Taylor, "The Role of Trust in Low-Income Mothers' Intimate Unions," *Journal of Marriage and Family* 71, no. 5 (2009): 1107–1124, www.ncbi.nlm.nih.gov/pmc/articles/PMC2788951/pdf/nihms151618.pdf; Kathryn Edin and Maria Kefalas, *Promises I Can Keep: Why Poor Women Put Motherhood before Marriage* (Berkeley: University of California Press, 2005).

3. Burton et al., "Role of Trust in Low-Income Mothers' Intimate Unions," 1117.

4. Edin and Nelson, *Doing the Best I Can: Fatherhood in the Inner City* (Berkeley: University of California Press, 2013), 99.

5. George A. Akerlof, Janet L. Yellen, and Michael L. Katz, "An Analysis of Out-of-Wedlock Childbearing in the United States," *Quarterly Journal of Economics* 111, no. 2 (1996).

6. Edin and Nelson, *Doing the Best I Can.*

7. See Sara McLanahan and Audrey N. Beck, "Parental Relationships in Fragile Families," *The Future of Children* 20, no. 2 (2010): 17–37.

8. Elites, of course, differ about the acceptability of abortion, but for college students statistically, abortion remains important in reinforcing a continuing norm against single-parent births while the disappearance of such a norm for those who do not graduate from college also reinforces norms against abortion. See discussion in Chapter 13 below.

9. June Carbone and Naomi Cahn, *Marriage, Parents and Child Support,* 45 FAM. L. Q. 219 (2011).

10. *Renaud v. Renaud,* 168 Vt. 306, 721 A.2d 463 (1998).

11. *Id.* at 309, 466. See also Rita Berg, *Parental Alienation Analysis, Domestic Violence, and Gender Bias in Minnesota Courts,* 5 LAW & INEQ. 29 (2011) (concluding that charges that one parent is undermining the child's relationship with the other parent often involve cases of physical or psychological abuse of the "alienating" partner and disproportionately result in custody awards to the father).

12. For a discussion of the impact of these legal changes, particularly on cases involving abuse and neglect, see Leslie Joan Harris, June Carbone, and Lee E. Teitelbaum, *Family Law,* 4th ed. (New York: Aspen, 2010), 657–658.

13. For discussion of these movements and the objections to them, see Margaret F. Brinig, *Penalty Defaults in Family Law: The Case of Child Custody,* 33 FLA. ST. U. L. REV. 779, 781 (2006).

14. Sanford L. Braver, Ira M. Ellman, Ashley M. Votruba, and William V. Fabricius, *Lay Judgments about Child Custody after Divorce,* 17 PSYCHOL. PUB. POL'Y & L. 212 (2011). See also Linda Nielsen, "Shared Parenting after Divorce: A Review of Shared Residential Parenting Research," *Journal of Divorce & Remarriage* 52, no. 8 (2011): 586–609; and "Results of Local, Regional Ballot Questions," 2004 election, *Boston Globe,* www.boston.com/news/special/politics/2004_results/general_election/questions_all_by_town.htm (proposition in favor of shared parenting passed overwhelmingly).

15. Braver et al., *Lay Judgments,* 236.

16. Patricia Brown and Steven T. Cook, "Children's Placement Arrangements in Divorce and Paternity Cases in Wisconsin," Institute for Research on Poverty Report, September 2011 (rev. November 2012), www.irp.wisc.edu/research/childsup/cspolicy/pdfs/2009-11/Task4A_CS_09-11_Final_revi2012.pdf.

17. Brown and Cook, "Children's Placement Arrangements," 19.

18. Brown and Cook, "Children's Placement Arrangements," 11.

19. Brown and Cook, "Children's Placement Arrangements," 17.

20. Harris et al., *Family Law*, 161, 166–167.

21. Harris et al., *Family Law*.

22. Harris et al., *Family Law*.

23. Harris et al., *Family Law*, 168.

24. A Wisconsin study indicates, however, that in child-support cases brought against fathers who have signed a VAP, custody by the mother remains the norm, accounting for 80 percent of the orders in 2006–2007. This constitutes a fall, however, from the 91 percent of sole custody orders ten years earlier. Brown and Cook, "Children's Placement Arrangements," 12.

25. For a systematic critique of the "privatization of dependency," see Martha Albertson Fineman, *The Neutered Mother, the Sexual Family, and Other Twentieth Century Tragedies* (New York: Routledge, 1995).

26. Jill Hasday observes, for example, that "From the start, this program [ADC] was grounded in a suspicion of fathers who had failed to support their families, on the assumption that there was almost no acceptable reason for that state of affairs." Jill Hasday, *Parenthood Divided: A Legal History of the Bifurcated Law of Parental Relations*, 90 GEO. L.J. 299, 357 (2002).

27. For a discussions of how paternity law is driven by welfare principles see Leslie Joan Harris, *The Basis for Legal Parentage and the Clash between Custody and Child Support*, 42 IND. L. REV. 611 (2009); Jane C. Murphy, *Legal Images of Fatherhood: Welfare Reform, Child Support Enforcement and Fatherless Children*, 81 NOTRE DAME L. REV. 325, 346 (2005); Tonya Brito, *The Welfarization of Family Law*, 48 KAN. L. REV. 229, 256–260 (2000).

28. Personal Responsibility and Work Opportunity Reconciliation Act of 1996, Pub. L. No. 104–193, 110 Stat. 2105 (1997). Section 103(a)(1) sets out goals for employment according to household status, provides that adults may receive cash assistance continuously for at most two years, and prohibits states from providing cash assistance to families in which adults have received assistance for five years. These provisions are codified at 42 U.S.C. §§ 607, 602(a)(1)(A)(ii), 608(a)(7)(A) (Supp. II 1996).

29. Personal Responsibility and Work Opportunity Reconciliation Act of 1996, 104 Pub. L. No. 193, 110 Stat. 2105, § 101 (codified at 42 U.S.C. § 601 (2007)); see also Gwendolyn Mink, *Welfare's End* (Ithaca, NY: Cornell University Press, 1998), 43 (emphasizing the legislative history of marriage, marital parenting, and paternal involvement); Tonya L. Brito, *From Madonna to Proletariat: Constructing a New Ideology of Motherhood in Welfare Discourse*, 44 VILL. L.Rev. 415 (1999).

30. Sara S. McLanahan and Irwin Garfinkel, "The Fragile Families and Child Well-Being Study: Questions, Design and a Few Preliminary Results," Institute for Research on Poverty Discussion Paper no. 1208–00, 41, http://irp.wisc.edu/publications/dps/pdfs/dp120800.pdf.

31. Marcia J. Carlson, Sara S. McLanahan, and Jeanne Brooks-Gunn, "Coparenting and Nonresident Fathers' Involvement with Young Children after a Nonmarital Birth," *Demography* 45, no. 2 (2008): 461–488.

32. See Nancy E. Dowd, *Redefining Fatherhood* (New York: NYU Press, 2000), 3; Katharine K. Baker, *Bargaining or Biology? The History and Future of Paternity Law and Parental Status*, 14 CORNELL J.L. & PUB. POL'Y 1 (2004); Leslie M. Harris, *Questioning Child Support Enforcement Policy for Poor Families*, 45 FAM. L.Q. 157 (2011).

33. Maureen R. Waller, "Viewing Low-Income Fathers' Ties to Families through a Cultural Lens: Insights for Research and Policy," *Annals of the American Academy of Political and Social Science* 629 (2010): 102–124, 109.

34. Edin and Nelson, *Doing the Best I Can*, 214.

35. Baker, *Bargaining or Biology?* 37. Men are also more likely to establish paternity if they have a close relationship with the mother. See Ronald Mincy, Irwin Garfinkel, and Lenna Nepomnyaschy, "In-Hospital Paternity Establishment and Father Involvement in Fragile Families," *Journal of Marriage and Family* 67 (2005): 611, 615. A smaller Wisconsin study found that almost half of the unmarried parents in the state filed VAPs within a few months of birth for children born in 2005. The parents were more likely to use VAPs if they were older or college educated and less likely to do so if the mother was receiving public support. Patricia R. Brown and Steven T. Cook, "A Decade of Voluntary Paternity Acknowledgment in Wisconsin: 1997–2007," Institute for Research on Poverty Report, May 2008, www.irp.wisc.edu/research/childsup/pubtopics/paternity_estab.htm.

36. Leslie Harris, *Questioning Child Support Enforcement Policy for Poor Families*, 45 FAM. L.Q. 157 (2011).

37. Lenna Nepomnyaschy and Irwin Garfinkel, "Child Support Enforcement and Fathers' Contributions to Their Nonmarital Children," Center for Research on Child Well-Being Working Paper no. 2006-09-FF, April 2007, crcw.princeton.edu.workingpapers/WP06-09-FF.pdf. See also Timothy S. Grall, "Custodial Mothers and Fathers and Their Child Support: 2007," Current Population Reports no. P60–237, November 2009; see Laurie Kohn, *Engaging Men as Fathers: The Courts, The Law, and Father-Absence in Low-Income Families*, 35 CARDOZO L. Rev. 511, 535 (2013) (noting that the federal system of assignment "renders all of these negotiations and arrangements untenable since the right to the support belongs to the government. Decisions by the custodial parent to accept informal payments could amount to welfare fraud").

38. Harris, *Questioning Child Support Enforcement Policy for Poor Families*, 165.

39. Harris, *Questioning Child Support Enforcement Policy for Poor Families*, 158.

40. See In re Marriage of Deborah & Michael Jackson, 136 Cal. App. 4th 980, 990, 994 (Cal. Ct. App. 2d Dist. 2006) (reversing order terminating mother's parental rights).

41. In re Marriage of Deborah & Michael Jackson.

42. See, e.g., Esther Wattenberg, "Paternity Actions and Young Fathers," in *Young Unwed Fathers: Changing Roles and Emerging Policies*, ed. Robert I. Lerman and Theodora J. Ooms (Philadelphia: Temple University Press, 1993), 213, 226.

43. Timothy S. Grall, "Custodial Mothers and Fathers and Their Child Support: 2009," Current Population Reports no. P60–240, December 2011, www.census.gov/prod/2011pubs/p60-240.pdf.

44. "Bristol Palin: Levi Johnston's a Deadbeat Dad," Tmz.com, April 7, 2012, www.tmz.com/2012/04/07/bristol-palin-levi-johnston-child-support.

45. Michael Y. Park, "Levi Johnston to Sue for Joint Custody of Son Tripp," People.com, Sept. 11, 2009, www.people.com/people/article/0,,20318502,00.html.

46. "Bristol Palin: Levi Johnston's a Deadbeat Dad."

47. *Stanley v. Illinois*, 405 U.S. 645 (1972).

48. *Stanley v. Illinois*, 405 U.S. at 646–647, 651 (recognizing deference to an unmarried father's private interest "in the children he has sired and raised").

49. For a discussion of these cases see June Carbone, *From Partners to Parents: The Second Revolution in Family Law* (New York: Columbia University Press, 2000), 166–170.

50. *Quilloin v. Walcott*, 434 U.S. 246 (1978).

51. *Caban v. Mohammed*, 441 U.S. 380 (1979).

52. *Lehr v. Robertson*, 463 U.S. 248 (1983).

53. Carbone, *From Partners to Parents: The Second Revolution in Family Law*, 169; Janet L. Dolgin, *Just a Gene: Judicial Assumptions about Parenthood*, 40 UCLA L. REV. 637, 671 (1993) ("A biological father does protect his paternity by developing a social relationship

with his child, but this step demands the creation of a family, a step itself depending upon an appropriate relationship between the man and his child's mother").

54. *Michael H. v. Gerald D.,* 491 U.S. 110, 114 (1989).

55. *Id.* at 113–114. The dissent contended that "the evidence is undisputed that Michael, Victoria, and Carole did live together as a family; that is, they shared the same household, Victoria called Michael 'Daddy,' Michael contributed to Victoria's support, and he is eager to continue his relationship with her." *Id.* at 143–144 (Brennan, J., dissenting).

56. *Id.*

57. Justice Byron White made the strongest case for the identification of fatherhood with biology but still limited constitutional recognition to men who stepped forward to seize the parental role. *See id.* at 157–160 (White, J., dissenting).

58. *See id.* at 142 (Brennan, J., dissenting) (framing the issue of the case as whether Michael and Victoria had a protected family unit relationship).

59. *Compare id.* at 124, *with id.* at 157 (White, J., dissenting). Justice Scalia explained:

> Justice Brennan insists that in determining whether a liberty interest exists we must look at Michael's relationship with Victoria in isolation, without reference to the circumstance that Victoria's mother was married to someone else when the child was conceived, and that that woman and her husband wish to raise the child as their own. We cannot imagine what compels this strange procedure of looking at the act which is assertedly the subject of a liberty interest in isolation from its effect upon other people—rather like inquiring whether there is a liberty interest in firing a gun where the case at hand happens to involve its discharge into another person's body. The logic of Justice Brennan's position leads to the conclusion that if Michael had begotten Victoria by rape, that fact would in no way affect his possession of a liberty interest in his relationship with her.

Id. at 124 n4 (majority opinion) (footnote omitted). The analysis is particularly pointed in this case as a factual matter because by the time the case reached the Supreme Court five years had passed, Gerald and Carole had remained together, had moved from California to New York, and had two additional children within the marriage. See June Carbone and Naomi Chan, *Which Ties Bind? Redefining the Parent-Child Relationship in an Age of Genetic Certainty,* 11 Wm. & Mary Bill Rts. J. 1011, 1045 (2003).

60. *Michael H.,* 491 U.S. at 133–144 (Brennan, J., dissenting).

61. *Id.* at 123 n3 (majority opinion).

62. Approximately two-thirds of the states similarly allow the non-marital father to challenge the marital presumption through either statute or case law. Uniform Parentage Act of 2002 § 607 cmt.

63. *In re* J.W.T., No. D-1742, 1993 Tex. LEXIS 101, at *31–32 (Tex. June 30, 1993), *withdrawn, In re* J.W.T., 872 S.W.2d 189, 197–198 (Tex. 1994).

64. *Id.* at 198.

65. *J.N.R. v. O'Reilly,* 264 S.W.3d 587, 596–597 (Ky. 2008) (Cunningham, J., concurring).

66. See, e.g., *J.A.S. v. Bushelman,* 342 S.W.3d 850, 853 (Ky. 2011) (explicitly overruling *J.N.R.*).

67. See *Draper v. Heacock,* No. 2010-CA-000,112-ME, slip op. at 3, n1 (Ky. Ct. App. Jan. 21, 2011), opinions.kycourts.net/coa/2010-CA-000112.pdf.

68. See, e.g., *Courtney v. M. Roggy,* 302 S.W.3d 141, 149 (Mo. Ct. App. 2009) ("[A] man *alleging himself to be a father* . . . may bring an action *at any time* for the purpose of declaring the *existence or nonexistence* of the father and child relationship"; emphasis added) (quoting Mo. Ann. Stat. § 210.826 (West 2010)); *Fisher v. Tucker,* 697 S.E.2d 548, 550 (S.C. 2010) (holding that South Carolina's statutory presumption of paternity within marriage can be rebutted by blood tests); *Watermeier v. Moss,* No. W2009-00789-COA-R3-JV, 2009 WL 3486426, at *2 (Tenn. Ct. App. Oct. 29, 2009) (holding that a Tennessee statute required that for the marital presumption to preclude paternity for the biological father the married couple needed to have lived together at the time of conception

and remained together through the filing of the petition, and the husband and mother needed to sign an affidavit attesting to biological paternity).

69. David D. Meyer, *Parenthood in a Time of Transition: Tensions between Legal, Biological, and Social Conceptions of Parenthood*, 54 AM. J. COMP. L. 125, 138–139 (2006).

70. *J.N.R. v. O'Reilly*, 264 S.W.3d 587 (Ky. 2008); *J.A.S. v. Bushelman*, 342 S.W.3d 850, 853 (Ky. 2011).

71. See, e.g., In re Jesusa V., 85 P.3d 2, 13, 15 (Cal. 2004).

72. See June Carbone, "From Partners to Parents Revisited: How Will Ideas of Partnership Influence the Emerging Definition of California Parenthood?" *Whittier Journal of Child and Family Advocacy* 7, no. 1 (2007): 3, 5.

73. See Carbone, "From Partners to Parents Revisited"; *In re Jesusa V.*

74. See, e.g., In re Jesusa V.

75. *Gabriel P. v. Suedi D.*, 46 Cal. Rptr. 3d 437, 439 (Cal. Ct. App. 2006).

76. Over a series of cases, the courts have concluded that a person who welcomes the child into his household and holds out the child as his own is presumed the parent, and the fact that this person has no biological connection to the child does not rebut the presumption. See Carbone, "From Partners to Parents Revisited."

77. See, e.g., *H.S. v. Superior Court*, 108 Cal. Rptr. 3d 723, 726 (Cal. Ct. App. 2010) (recognizing that the statute does "allow the mother and her husband to prevent the biological father from ever establishing parental rights over a child"). In *Gabriel P.*, 46 Cal. Rptr. 3d at 439, the court noted that the mother, Suedi, allowed Anthony, the nonbiological father, to live with her, accompany her to the hospital, and voluntarily declare paternity.

78. See *Brian C. v. Ginger K.*, 92 Cal. Rptr. 2d 294, 297, 310–311 (Cal. Ct. App. 2000) (upholding the right of the biological father—who had lived with the mother and child and established a parental relationship with the child—to rebut the marital presumption).

79. *Black v. Librers*, 28 Cal. Rptr. 3d 188 (Cal. Ct. App. 2005).

Chapter 11

1. For African Americans, the patterns and timing have often been different. World War II provided the greatest expansion in access to relatively high paying manufacturing jobs and African-American income doubled in that period. By the sixties, the class-based divergence in family patterns that would later characterize whites was already well under way. See June Carbone, *From Partners to Parents: The Second Revolution in Family Law* (New York: Columbia University Press, 2000), 77–78.

2. See discussion in Chapter 8 describing the relatively small gap in achievement and in parent time spend on children between blue collar and white collar families in the sixties.

3. Fixing employment may in itself take care of the class division in the family. As Princeton sociologist Sara McLanahan pointed out in 2004, before the Great Recession, "[W]e need policies that increase the returns to work and make it possible for men and women in the bottom strata to achieve the living standard" they associate with stable families. Sara McLanahan, "Diverging Destinies: How Children are Faring under the Second Demographic Transition," *Demography* 41, no. 4 (2004): 607, 622.

4. Professors Claudia Goldin and Lawrence Katz also observe that the expansion of secondary education took off first in the wealthier and more equal parts of the country. They conclude that equality begets greater equality. See Claudia Goldin and Lawrence Katz, "Why the United States Led in Education: Lessons from Secondary School Expansion, 1910 to 1940." In D. Eltis, F. Lewis, K. Sokoloff, *Human Capital and Institutions* (Cambridge: Cambridge University Press, 2009), available at http://scholar.harvard.edu/files/lkatz/files/why_the_united_states_led_in_education_lessons_from_secondary_school_expansion_1910_to_1940_1.pdf.

5. Naomi Cahn and June Carbone, *Red Families v. Blue Families: Legal Polarization and the Creation of Culture* (New York: Oxford University Press, 2010).
6. E.g., William Easterly, "The Middle Class Consensus and Economic Development," World Bank Policy Research Working Paper no. 2346, May 2000, http://ssrn.com/abstract=630,718.
7. Dagmar Hertova, Luis F. Lopez-Calva, and Eduardo Ortiz-Juarez, "Bigger . . . But Stronger? The Middle Class in Chile and Mexico in the Last Decade," Research for Public Policy, Inclusive Development, ID-02-2010, www.revistahumanum.org/revista/wp-content/uploads/2012/02/02_10_rplac_id.pdf.
8. Adam Looney and Michael Greenstone, "A Record Decline in Government Jobs: Implications for the Economy and America's Workforce," Hamilton Project Paper, Aug. 2012, www.hamiltonproject.org/papers/a_record_decline_in_government_jobs_implications_for_todays_economy_an.
9. Sajinda O'Connell, "How Did the Peacock Get His Tail?" *The Independent* (London), Sept. 9, 2002, http://news.nationalgeographic.com/news/2002/09/0909_peacock_2.html.
10. "Goods production supplied about three-fifths of economic output in 1950 and about half of its jobs. By 2010, growth in the service sector has accounted for two-thirds of output and seven out of every 10 jobs." Jim Tankersley, "Shift to a Service-Driven Economy Delays Job Recovery," *Washington Post*, May 3, 2013, www.washingtonpost.com/business/economy/shift-to-services-delays-job-recovery/2013/05/03/a78ec0f0-b3f3-11e2-9a98-4be1688d7d84_story.html?wprss=rss_business.
11. See, e.g., Jim Tankersley, "Growth Isn't Enough to Help Middle Class," *Washington Post*, Feb. 13, 2013, http://articles.washingtonpost.com/2013-02-13/business/37070931_1_job-creation-growth-drives-recoveries.
12. Ro Khanna, "Five Myths about Manufacturing Jobs," *Washington Post*, Feb. 15, 2013, http://articles.washingtonpost.com/2013-02-15/opinions/37111109_1_gary-pisano-job-growth-service-sector.
13. "Rewarding Work: The Case for Subsidizing Worker Pay; Interview with Edmund Phelps," *Challenge* 40, no. 4 (1997): 15–26, www.challengemagazine.com/Challenge%20interview%20pdfs/phelps.pdf. See also Edmund S. Phelps, *Rewarding Work: How to Restore Participation and Self-Support to Free Enterprise* (Cambridge, MA: Harvard University Press, 1997).
14. Indeed, an intense debate exists on the sources of inequality, with most scholars in agreement that single-minded examinations of the role of technology or globalization do not explain the changes in any satisfying way. See, e.g., Margaret Jacobson and Filippo Occhino, "Labor's Declining Share of Income and Rising Inequality," Commentary, Federal Reserve Bank of Cleveland, Sept. 25, 2012, www.clevelandfed.org/research/commentary/2012/2012-13.cfm (attributing greater inequality to a variety of factors, including technology, globalization, and labor market structure and organization); Jared Bernstein, "An Inequality Debate Heats Up," *Huffington Post*, Jan. 18, 2013, www.huffingtonpost.com/jared-bernstein/income-inequality_b_2502007.html.
15. "Elephant Seal," *National Geographic*, n.d., http://animals.nationalgeographic.com/animals/mammals/elephant-seal (last visited Oct. 18, 2013).
16. "Elephant Seal Reproduction," Marine Science blog, n.d., www.marinebio.net/marinescience/05nekton/esrepro.htm (last visited Oct. 20, 2013).
17. Journalist Chris Hayes concludes that greater inequality and the competition that produces it increase the social distance from the top to the bottom, making it more likely that the top group will neither know nor care about the plight of others. He describes it as a pervasive issue, equally affecting the failure to prosecute the misconduct underlying the financial crisis and Penn State's reluctance to inquire into Jerry Sandusky's abuse of young boys. "Twilight of the Elites: Chris Hayes on How the Powerful Rig the System, from Penn State to Wall St.," *Democracy Now!* July 17, 2012, www.democracynow.org/2012/7/17/twilight_of_the_elites_chris_hayes.

18. See Laurent Belsie, "The Causes of Rising Income Inequality," *NBER Digest*, December 2008, www.nber.org/digest/dec08/w13982.html. See also "Symposia: The Top 1 Percent," *Journal of Economic Perspectives* 27, no. 3 (2013): 3, www.aeaweb.org/articles. php?doi=10.1257/jep.27.3 (summarizing the arguments on both sides).

19. Lawrence Mishel and Natalie Sabadish, "CEO Pay and the Top 1 percent: How Executive Compensation and Financial-Sector Pay Have Fueled Income Inequality," Economic Policy Institute Report, May 2, 2012, www.epi.org/publication/ib331-ceo-pay-top-1-percent.

20. Emmanuel Saez, "Striking It Richer: The Evolution of Top Incomes in the United States," unpublished paper, Sept. 3, 2013, http://elsa.berkeley.edu/~saez/saez-UStopincomes-2012.pdf.

21. Belsie, "Causes of Rising Income Inequality," para.8.

22. Lynne L. Dallas, *Short-Termism, the Financial Crisis, and Corporate Governance*, 37 J. Corp. L. 265, 316 (2012).

23. Mary Schapiro, *Testimony Concerning the State of the Financial Crisis*, testimony before the Financial Crisis Inquiry Commission, Jan. 14, 2010, http://www.sec.gov/news/testimony/2010/ts011410mls.htm.

24. Kent Greenfield, *Reclaiming Corporate Law in a New Gilded Age*, 2 Harv. L & Pol'y Rev. 1, 12 (2008).

25. Sreedhari D. Desai, Donald Palmer, Jennifer George, and Arthur Brief, "When Executives Rake in Millions: The Callous Treatment of Lower Level Employees," ResearchGate. net, July 25, 2011, www.researchgate.net/publication/228181990_When_Executives_Rake_in_Millions_The_Callous_Treatment_of_Lower_Level_Employees. See also Jeffrey T. Brookman, Saeyoung Chang, and Craig G. Rennie, "CEO Equity Portfolio Incentives and Layoff Decisions," *Journal of Financial Research* 30, no. 2 (2007): 259–281 (finding that CEOs with at least one year of tenure who possess greater incentives from portfolios of restricted stock and stock option grants are more likely to announce layoffs and that these layoffs create shareholder value).

26. "Is it Time to Reform Executive Compensation and Stock Option Grants?" Brookings Institution panel discussion, Sept. 27, 2012, transcript at www.brookings.edu/~/media/events/2012/9/27%20executive%20compensation/20120927_executive_compensation.pdf.

27. For a comparison of this phenomenon in the United States and Germany, which has retained a greater number of high-paid, higher skill, mid-level jobs than has the United States, see Virginia Doellgast, *Disintegrating Democracy at Work: Labor Unions and the Future of Good Jobs in the Service Economy* (Ithaca, NY: Cornell University Press, 2012). See also Mort Zuckerman, "A Jobless Recovery Is a Phony Recovery," *Wall Street Journal*, July 15, 2013, http://online.wsj.com/article/SB10001424127887323740804578601472 261953366.html (noting the decline in overall workforce participation and move toward part-time employment with fewer benefits).

28. Eileen Appelbaum, "Reducing Inequality and Insecurity: Rethinking Labor and Employment Policy for the 21st Century," Center for Economic and Policy Research Working Paper, November 2012, www.cepr.net/documents/publications/inequality-insecurity-2012-11.pdf.

29. Executive tenure has declined as executive pay has increased. See Joanne S. Lublin, "The Serial CEO," *Wall Street Journal*, Sept. 19, 2005, http://online.wsj.com/news/articles/SB112709114986644489; Steven N. Kaplan and Bernadette A. Minton, "How Has CEO Turnover Changed?" unpublished paper, August 2008, faculty.chicagobooth.edu/steven.kaplan/research/km.pdf ("There is some evidence that the increases in turnover and turnover-performance sensitivity are related to increases in block shareholder ownership, board independence, and Sarbanes-Oxley").

30. Paul Davidson, "Study Says Shortage of Skilled Workers Not That Severe," *USA Today*, Oct. 15, 2012, http://www.usatoday.com/story/money/business/2012/10/14/jobs-skills-gap-study/1630359.

31. Adam Davidson, "Skills Don't Pay the Bills," *New York Times*, Nov. 20, 2012, www.nytimes.com/2012/11/25/magazine/skills-dont-pay-the-bills.html?pagewanted=all.

32. Andrew Hacker and Paul Pierson, *Winner-Take-All Politics: How Washington Made the Rich Richer—And Turned its Back on the Middle Class* (Simon & Shuster 2010), 166-67 Lee Epstein, William M. Landes, and Richard A. Posner, *How Business Fares in the Supreme Court*, 97 Minn. L. Rev. 1431 (2013) (documenting the conservative orientation of the Supreme Court and showing that the Chamber of Commerce wins 70 percent of the cases with which it is associated).

33. See Belsie, "Causes of Rising Income Inequality."

34. Belsie, "Causes of Rising Income Inequality."

35. Belsie, "Causes of Rising Income Inequality." Labor force participation has continued to decline, with Mort Zuckerman, chairman and editor-in-chief of *U.S. News & World Report*, observing in a July 15, 2013, *Wall Street Journal* op-ed that "The measure of those adults who can work and have jobs, known as the civilian workforce-participation rate, is currently 63.5 percent—a *drop* of 2.2 percent since the recession ended." Zuckerman, "Jobless Recovery Is a Phony Recovery."

36. Brett McDonnell, "Two Goals for Executive Compensation Reform," Minnesota Legal Studies Research Paper no. 07-34, 2007, http://ssrn.com/abstract=1008356.

37. See, e.g., Roberta Romano and Sanjai Bhagat, *Reforming Executive Compensation: Focusing and Committing to the Long-Term*, 26 Yale J. on Reg. 359 (2009), http://digitalcommons.law.yale.edu/cgi/viewcontent.cgi?article=2969&context=fss_papers. For a discussion of clawbacks see Miriam A. Cherry and Jarrod Wong, *Clawbacks: Prospective Contract Measures in an Era of Excessive Executive Compensation and Ponzi Schemes*, 94 Minn. L. Rev. 368, 370 (2009) (detailing an exhaustive treatment of clawbacks). They define "clawback" as "a theory for recovering benefits that have been conferred under a claim of right, but that are nonetheless recoverable because unfairness would otherwise result" (371–372).

38. The Brookings Institution, "Is It Time to Reform Corporate Compensation and Stock Option Grants," Washington, D.C., Sept. 27, 2012, 37, http://www.brookings.edu/~/media/events/2012/9/27%20executive%20compensation/20120927_executive_compensation.pdf. The debate between shareholder primacy and stakeholder theory is a long and complex one. Ironically, one of the claims to emerge from the Great Depression was the need to restrain overreaching executives in order to protect shareholder interests. While we believe that considering the structure of the labor market is important for its impact on employment and that modern executive compensation should be questioned from the context of both shareholder primacy and stakeholder arguments, we leave the full debate to others. See generally, Edward S. Adams and John H. Matheson, *A Statutory Model for Corporate Constituency Concerns*, 49 Emory L.J. 1085 (2000); Stephen M. Bainbridge, *Interpreting Nonshareholder Constituency Statutes*, 19 Pepp. L. Rev. 971 (1992); William J. Carney, *Does Defining Constituencies Matter?* 59 U. Cin. L. Rev. 385 (1990); Timothy L. Fort, The *Corporation as Mediating Institution: An Efficacious Synthesis of Stakeholder Theory and Corporate Constituency Statutes*, 73 Notre Dame L. Rev. 173 (1997); James J. Hanks Jr., *Playing with Fire: Nonshareholder Constituency Statutes in the 1990s*, 21 Stetson L. Rev. 97 (1991); Jonathan R. Macey, *Fiduciary Duties as Residual Claim: Obligations to Nonshareholder Constituencies from a Theory of the Firm Perspective*, 84 Cornell L. Rev. 1266 (1999); Lawrence E. Mitchell, *A Theoretical and Practical Framework for Enforcing Corporate Constituency Statutes*, 70 Tex. L. Rev. 579 (1992); Brett H. McDonnell, *Corporate Constituency Statutes and Employee Governance*, 30 Wm. Mitchell L. Rev. 1227 (2004); Eric W. Orts, *Beyond Shareholders: Interpreting Corporate Constituency Statutes*, 61 Geo. Wash. L. Rev. 14 (1992); Jonathan D. Springer, *Corporate Constituency Statutes: Hollow Hopes and False Fears*, Ann. Surv. Am. L. 85 (1999); Steven M. H. Wallman, *The Proper Interpretation of Corporate Constituency Statutes and Formulation of Director Duties*, 21 Stetson L. Rev. 163 (1991); Committee on Corporate Law, *Other Constituencies Statutes: Potential for Confusion*, 45 Bus. Law 2253 (1990).

39. McDonnell, "Two Goals for Executive Compensation Reform."

40. Roland Bénabou and Jean Tirole, "Intrinsic and Extrinsic Motivation," *Review of Economic Studies* 70 (2003): 489–520, www.princeton.edu/~rbenabou/papers/RES2003.pdf.

41. Claudio Feser, "The Limits of Monetary Incentives," Chief Executive.net, Feb. 3, 2012, http://chiefexecutive.net/the-limits-of-monetary-incentives.

42. Appelbaum, "Reducing Inequality and Insecurity," 3 ("Even skilled workers are discarded rather than offered opportunities to develop their skills in industries in which technology advances quickly. Jobs long thought to be protected from the vagaries of market forces are now subject to new forms of insecurity and downward pressure on compensation").

43. Betsey Stevenson and Justin Wolfers, "The U.S. Economic Policy Debate Is a Sham," *Bloomberg Politics*, July 23, 2012, www.bloomberg.com/news/2012-07-23/the-u-s-economic-policy-debate-is-a-sham.html.

44. Josh Bivens and Heidi Shierholz, "Three Years into Recovery, Just How Much Has State and Local Austerity Hurt Job Growth?" Economic Policy Institute blog, July 6, 2012, www.epi.org/blog/years-recovery-state-local-austerity-hurt.

45. Paul Krugman, *End This Depression Now!* (New York: W. W. Norton, 2012), 46.

46. Arne L. Kalleberg, *Good Jobs, Bad Jobs: The Rise of Polarized and Precarious Employment Systems in the United States, 1970s to 2000s* (New York: Sage, 2011), 248, n. 5. For a review of the decline in the minimum wage and the lack of enforcement see Sarah Leberstein and Anastasia Christman, *Occupy Our Occupations: Why "We Are the 99 percent" Resonates with Working People and What We Can Do to Fix the American Workplace*, 39 FORDHAM URB. L.J. 1073 (2012). For a summary of economic thinking about the minimum wage see Betsey Stevenson, "Five Myths about the Minimum Wage," *Washington Post*, April 5, 2013, http://articles.washingtonpost.com/2013-04-05/opinions/38300337_1_minimum-wage-fair-labor-standards-act-workers.

47. Stevenson, "Five Myths about the Minimum Wage," para. 10 ("Paying workers more often leads them to feel better about their work and reduces stress, both of which increase productivity. And when workers produce more, employers' labor costs fall").

48. E.g., Edmund S. Phelps, "The Economy Needs a Bit of Ingenuity," *New York Times*, Aug. 6, 2010, www.nytimes.com/2010/08/07/opinion/07phelps.html?_r=0.

49. Dan Slater, "At Law Firms, Reconsidering the Model for Associates' Pay," *New York Times*, March 31, 2010, www.nytimes.com/2010/04/01/business/01LEGAL.html?pagewanted=all. Edmund Phelps also argues that underlying the erosion in jobs for the unskilled has been an increase in the cost of training relative to the wages paid. Phelps, "Rewarding Work."

50. See, e.g., Tyler Cowen, *Average Is Over: Powering America beyond the Age of the Great Stagnation* (New York: Penguin, 2013) (arguing that the new economy will inevitably produce a smaller number of high-wage jobs and the unemployment of a larger number of low-skill workers).

51. Phelps, "Rewarding Work."

52. "The Case for an Integrated Model of Growth, Employment and Social Protection," World Economic Forum Report no. 200112, 2012, www3.weforum.org/docs/WEF_GAC_CaseIntegratedModelGrowthEmploymentSocialProtection_Report_2012.pdf.

53. Michael Greenstone and Adam Looney, "A Record Decline in Government Jobs: Implications for the Economy and America's Workforce," Brookings on Job Numbers blog, Aug. 3, 2012, www.brookings.edu/blogs/jobs/posts/2012/08/03-jobs-greenstone-looney.

54. Kalleberg, *Good Jobs, Bad Jobs*.

55. Martha Alberston Fineman, *The Vulnerable Subject and the Responsive State*, 60 EMORY L.J. 251 (2010).

56. Jacob Hacker, *The Great Risk Shift: The New Economic Insecurity and the Decline of the American Dream* (New York: Oxford University Press, 2008), 165, 178 (describing increased economic insecurity and less reliable pension, healthcare, and other benefits).

57. See, e.g., Sara Sternberg Greene, *The Broken Safety Net: A Study of Earned Income Tax Credit Recipients and a Proposal for Repair*, 88 N.Y.U. L. Rev. 515 (2013).

58. See Fineman, *Vulnerable Subject and the Responsive State*, 269 ("Significantly, the counterpoint to vulnerability is not invulnerability, for that is impossible to achieve, but rather the resilience that comes from having some means with which to address and confront misfortune").

59. Tammy Erickson, "The Rise of the New Contract Worker," *Harvard Business Review*, blog, Sept. 7, 2012, http://blogs.hbr.org/erickson/2012/09/the_rise_of_the_new_contract_worker.html.

60. Mark Thoma, "Flexicurity," Economist's View blog, March 21, 2006, http://economistsview.typepad.com/economistsview/2006/03/flexicurity.html.

61. See, e.g., Hacker, *Great Risk Shift*, 182–192.

62. See, e.g., "Health Insurance Market Reforms: Portability," Kaiser Family Foundation Fact Sheet no. 8421, March 2013, http://kaiserfamilyfoundation.files.wordpress.com/2013/03/8421.pdf.

63. Greene, supra, at 108.

64. See, e.g., Kristen Harknett and Arielle Kuperberg, "Education, Labor Markets, and the Retreat from Marriage: Understanding Differences in Marriage by Education," *Social Forces* 90, no. 1 (2011): 41–63. They also note that there is less correlation for more highly educated women. This may be due to entrenched gender ideologies that still celebrate male breadwinners.

Chapter 12

1. Jason DeParle, "Two Classes, Divided by 'I Do,'" *New York Times*, July 14, 2012, www.nytimes.com/2012/07/15/us/two-classes-in-america-divided-by-i-do.html?ref=jasondeparle.

2. See, e.g., James J. Heckman, "The Economics of Inequality: The Value of Early Childhood Education," *American Educator* (spring 2011), www.aft.org/pdfs/americaneducator/spring2011/Heckman.pdf (showing that intact families provide more cognitive stimulation for young children than do single mothers or blended families).

3. See chapter 7.

4. Lee Fang, "Missouri Lawmaker on Child Hunger: 'Hunger Can Be a Positive Motivator,'" Think Progress.org, June 21, 2009, http://thinkprogress.org/politics/2009/06/21/46862/cynthia-davis-hunger/?mobile=nc.

5. June Carbone and Naomi Cahn, "The Conservative War on Single Mothers Like Jessica Schairer," *Huffington Post*, July 19, 2012, www.huffingtonpost.com/june-carbone/the-conservative-war-on-s_b_1685865.html.

6. See chapter 7 on the increasing class-based differences in parental time spent with children and children's feeling of isolation from their communities.

7. John F. Irwin, "Invest Wisely in Early Childhood," letter to the editor, *Baltimore Sun*, March 15, 2013, www.baltimoresun.com/news/opinion/readersrespond/bs-ed-child-health-letter-20130314,0,6670846.story. See also D. J. Barker, "The Developmental Origins of Adult Disease," *Journal of the American College of Nutrition* 23, no. 6 (supp. 2004), 588S–595S.

8. C. T. Beck, "The Effects of Postpartum Depression on Child Development: A Meta-Analysis," *Archives of Psychiatric Nursing* 12, no. 1 (1998): 12–20 (discussing effects of postpartum depression on children's long-term cognitive and emotional development).

9. John Cairney, Michael Boyle, David R. Offord, and Yvonne Racine, "Stress, Social Support and Depression in Single and Married Mothers," *Social Psychiatry and Psychiatric Epidemiology* 38, no. 8 (2003): 442–449.

10. *Medicaid's Role for Women across the Lifespan: Current Issues and the Impact of the Afford-able Care Act*, Kaiser Family Foundation Women's Issue Brief, Dec. 3, 2012, 3–4, http:// kff.org/womens-health-policy/issue-brief/medicaids-role-for-women-across-the-lifespan.

11. Kristen Kirkland and Susan Mitchell Herzfeld, "Final Report: Evaluating the Effective-ness of Home Visiting Services in Promoting Children's Adjustment in School," New York State Office of Children and Family Services Report, May 31, 2012, www.pews-tates.org/uploadedFiles/PCS_Assets/2013/School_Readiness_report.pdf.

12. "Why Business Should Support Early Childhood Education," Institute for a Competi-tive Workforce Report, 2010, www.smartbeginnings.org/Portals/5/PDFs/Research/ ICW_EarlyChildhoodReport_2010.pdf; Deborah Lowe Vandell, Jay Belsky, Margaret Burchinal, Laurence Steinberg, and Nathan Vandergrift, "Do Effects of Early Child Care Extend to Age 15 Years? Results for the NICHD Study of Early Child Care and Youth Development," *Child Development* 81, no. 3 (2010): 737–756. As the Institute for a Com-petitive Workforce notes, "[T]he research is clear. Early learning opportunities for chil-dren from birth to age five have great impact on a child's development and build a strong foundation for learning and success later in life" ("Why Business Should Support Early Childhood Education," 24).

13. See research discussed in Madeleine M. Kunin, *The New Feminist Agenda* (White River Junction, VT: Chelsea Green, 2012), 110–111.

14. See Donna Cooper and Kristina Costa, "Increasing the Effectiveness and Efficiency of Existing Public Investments in Early Childhood Education: Recommendations to Boost Program Outcomes and Efficiency," Center for American Progress Report, June 2012, 2, www.americanprogress.org/issues/2012/06/pdf/earlychildhood.pdf.

15. James J. Heckman and Dimitriy V. Masterov, "The Productivity Argument for Investing in Young Children," *Review of Agricultural Economics* 29, no. 3 (2007): 446, 449, http:// jenni.uchicago.edu/papers/Heckman_Masterov_RAE_2007_v29_n3.pdf; Arthur J. Reynolds, Judy A. Temple, Suh-Ruu Ou, Irma A. Arteaga, and Barry A. B. White, "School-Based Early Childhood Education and Age-28 Well-Being: Effects by Timing, Dosage, and Subgroups," *Science* 333, no. 6040 July 15, 2011. ("[W]e found that the most consistent and enduring effects were for preschool participation, which started at ages 3 or 4. Its impact was broad, including education, SES, health behavior, and crime outcomes").

16. James J. Heckman, "The American Family in Black and White: A Post-Racial Strategy for Improving Skills to Promote Equality," Institute for the Study of Labor (IZA) Discus-sion Paper no. 5495, February 2011, www.iza.org/en/webcontent/publications/papers/ viewAbstract?dp_id=5495.

17. Heckman, "American Family in Black and White," 22.

18. See also Lynn A. Karoly, M. Rebecca Kilburn, and Jill S. Cannon, "Early Childhood In-terventions: Proven Results, Future Promise," RAND Labor and Population Report, 2005, www.rand.org/content/dam/rand/pubs/monographs/2005/RAND_MG341. pdf.

19. Karoly et al., "Early Childhood Interventions," 130; see also "A Science-Based Frame-work for Early Childhood Policy," Center on the Developing Child Report, August 2007, http://developingchild.harvard.edu/index.php/resources/reports_and_working_ papers/policy_framework.

20. "A Science-Based Framework."

21. Travis Waldron, "How Investing in Pre-School Education Could Boost the Economy and Combat Income Inequality," Think Progress, Feb. 7, 2013, http://thinkprogress. org/economy/2013/02/07/1555401/universal-pre-k-plan.

22. Vincent Zafonte, "Why Universal Preschool Would Cost Taxpayers and Not Ben-efit Students," Heritage Foundation, Feb. 22, 2013, www.myheritage.org/news/ why-universal-preschool-would-cost-taxpayers-and-not-benefit-students.

23. See Lindsey Layton, "Preschool Can Pay Big Dividends," *Washington Post*, March 13, 2013, www.washingtonpost.com/postlive/policymakers-business-leaders-say-preschool-can-pay-big-dividends/2013/03/12/63108bc2-8a93-11e2-8d72-dc76641cb8d4_story.html.

24. "Science-Based Framework," 19.

25. "Science-Based Framework," 19.

26. See, e.g., "The Costs and Benefits of Universal Preschool in California," RAND Labor and Population Research Brief no. 9118-PF, 2005, www.rand.org/content/dam/rand/pubs/research_briefs/2005/RAND_RB9118.pdf.

27. See Susan Dynarski, Joshua Hyman, and Diane Whitmore Schanzenbach, "Experimental Evidence on the Effect of Childhood Investments on Postsecondary Attainment and Degree Completion," unpublished paper, Oct. 16, 2011, www.classsizematters.org/wp-content/uploads/2012/10/dynarski-120,426.pdf.

28. See Caroline M. Hoxby and Christopher Avery, "The Missing 'One-Offs': The Hidden Supply of High-Achieving, Low Income Students," National Bureau of Economic Research Working Paper no. 18586, December 2012, http://papers.nber.org/tmp/73802-w18586.pdf; David Leonhardt, "Better Colleges Failing to Lure Talented Poor," *New York Times*, March 16, 2012, www.nytimes.com/2013/03/17/education/scholarly-poor-often-overlook-better-colleges.html.

29. See Hoxby and Avery, "Missing 'One-Offs,'" 25–26.

30. See Stephen Vaisey, *What People Want: Rethinking Poverty, Culture, and Educational Attainment*, 629 ANNALS AM. ACAD. POL. & SOC. SCI. 75 (2010).

31. Vaisey, *What People Want*.

32. See Michelle Kelso, Naomi Cahn, and Barbara Miller, "Gender Equality in Employment: Policies and Practices in Switzerland and the United States," George Washington University Report, 2012, 40–42, www.gwu.edu/~igis/assets/docs/report-gender-equality-switzerland-2012.pdf.

33. See, e.g., Leonhardt, "Better Colleges Failing to Lure Talented Poor."

34. David Leonhardt, "A Nudge to Poorer Students to Aim High on Colleges," *New York Times*, Sept. 25, 2013, www.nytimes.com/2013/09/26/education/for-low-income-students-considering-college-a-nudge-to-aim-high.html; Leonhardt, "Better Colleges Failing to Lure Talented Poor."

35. Chapter 11; see generally Jacob Hacker, *The Great Risk Shift: The New Economic Insecurity and the Decline of the American Dream* (New York: Oxford University Press, 2008).

36. Jason Koebler, "Report: Community College Attendance Up, but Graduation Rates Remain Low," *U.S. News & World Report*, April 21, 2012, www.usnews.com/education/best-colleges/articles/2012/04/21/report-community-college-attendance-up-but-graduation-rates-remain-low; American Association of Community Colleges, 21st-Century Commission on the Future of Community Colleges, "Reclaiming the American Dream: Community Colleges and the Nation's Future," 2012, 8, 14, www.aacc.nche.edu/AboutCC/21stcenturyreport/21stCenturyReport.pdf.

37. American Association of Community Colleges, "Reclaiming the American Dream," 8, 14.

38. Sylvia Ann Hewlett and Carolyn Buck Luce, "Off-Ramps and On-Ramps: Keeping Talented Women on the Road to Success," *Big Picture*, March 2005, 48, 46, www.uwlax.edu/faculty/giddings/ECO336/week_3/Off_ramps_and_on_ramps.pdf.

39. Sheryl Sandberg, *Lean In: Women, Work, and the Will to Lead* (New York: Knopf, 2013).

40. Liz Watson and Jennifer E. Swanberg, "Flexible Workplace Solutions for Low-Wage Hourly Workers: A Framework for a National Conversation," Georgetown University Law Center, Workplace Flexibility 2010, May 2011, 5, http://workplaceflexibility2010.org/images/uploads/whatsnew/Flexible%20Workplace%20Solutions%20for%20Low-Wage%20Hourly%20Workers.pdf.

41. Karen Kornbluh, "The Parent Trap," *The Atlantic*, January/February 2003, www.theatlantic.com/issues/2003/01/kornbluh.htm.

42. Lynn Feinberg, Susan C. Reinhard, Ari Houser, and Rita Choula, "Valuing the Invaluable: 2011 Update, The Growing Contributions and Costs of Family Caregiving," AARP Public Policy Institute Report, 2011, http://assets.aarp.org/rgcenter/ppi/ltc/i51-caregiving.pdf.

43. Joan C. Williams and Heather Boushey, "The Three Faces of Work-Family Conflict: The Poor, the Professionals, and the Missing Middle," Center for American Progress Report, January 2010, www.worklifelaw.org/pubs/ThreeFacesofWork-FamilyConflict.pdf.

44. On paid leave see Sarah Jane Glynn, "Working Parents' Lack of Access to Paid Leave and Workplace Flexibility," Center for American Progress, Nov. 20, 2012, www.americanprogress.org/wp-content/uploads/2012/11/GlynnWorkingParents-1.pdf.

45. Eileen Appelbaum and Ruth Milkman, "Leaves That Pay: Employer and Worker Experiences with Paid Family Leave in California," Center for Economic Policy Research Report, January 15, 2011 http://www.cepr.net/documents/publications/paid-family-leave-1-2011.pdf.

46. California Unemployment Insurance Code § 2626; N.J. Dept. of Labor & Workforce Dev., "Family Leave Insurance," http://lwd.state.nj.us/labor/fli/fliindex.html (last visited Jan. 14, 2014).

47. Linda Houser and Thomas P. Vartanian, "Pay Matters: The Positive Economic Impacts of Paid Family Leave for Families, Businesses and the Public," Center for Women and Work Report, January 2012, 2, smlr.rutgers.edu/paymatters-cwwreport-january2012; Heather Boushey and Sarah Jane Glynn, "The Effects of Paid Family and Medical Leave on Employment Stability and Economic Security," Center for American Progress, Report, April 2012, 15, www.americanprogress.org/wp-content/uploads/issues/2012/04/pdf/BousheyEmploymentLeave1.pdf.

48. Majority Staff of the Joint Economic Committee, 111th Cong., "Invest in Women, Invest in America: A Comprehensive Review of Women in the U.S. Economy," Dec. 16, 2010, 12.

49. Sarah Beth Estes, Mary C. Noonan, and David J. Maume, "Is Work-Family Policy Use Related to the Gendered Division of Housework?" *Journal of Family and Economic Issues* 28, no. 4 (2007): 527, 538; Ellen Ernst Kossek and Brian Distelberg, "Work and Family Employment Policy for a Transformed Labor Force: Current Trends and Themes," in *Work-Life Policies*, ed. Ann C. Crouter and Alan Booth (Washington, DC: Urban Institute Press, 2009), 29.

50. "The Case for a National Family and Medical Leave Insurance Program (The FAMILY Act)," National Partnership for Women and Families Fact Sheet, August 2013, 2–3, www.nationalpartnership.org/site/DocServer/FAMILY_Act_Fact_Sheet.pdf?docID=11821; Appelbaum and Milkman, "Leaves That Pay."

51. See Joan Williams, Mary Blair-Loy, and Jennifer Berdahl, "The Flexibility Stigma: Work Devotion vs. Family Devotion," *Rotman Magazine*, Winter 2013, http://worklifelaw.org/wp-content/uploads/2012/12/TheFlexibilityStigma.pdf.

52. Ann O'Leary, Matt Chayt, and Eve Weissman, "Social Security Cares: Why American Is Ready for Paid Family and Medical Leave," Center for American Progress Report, Sept. 27, 2012, www.americanprogress.org/issues/labor/report/2012/09/27/39331/social-security-cares.

53. National Partnership for Women and Families, "The Case for a National Family and Medical Leave Insurance Program."

54. See Kristin Smith and Andrew Schaefer, "Who Cares for the Sick Kids? Parents' Access to Paid Time to Care for a Sick Child," Carsey Institute Issue Brief no. 51, Spring 2012, 2, tbl. 1, www.carseyinstitute.unh.edu/publications/IB-Smith-Paid-Sick-Leave-2012.pdf.

55. See, e.g., "Flexible Work Arrangements: A Definition and Examples," Georgetown University Law Center, Workplace Flexibility 2010, n.d., http://workplaceflexibility2010.org/images/uploads/general_information/fwa_definitionsexamples.pdf (last visited Oct. 19, 2010).

56. See Watson and Swanberg, "Flexible Workplace Solutions for Low-Wage Hourly Workers," 25–31.

57. Jennifer E. Swanberg, Jacquelyn B. James, and Mac Werner, "What Is Workplace Flexibility for Hourly Retail Workers?" Citi Sales Study Issue Brief no. 2, n.d., www.uky.edu/Centers/iwin/citisales/_pdfs/IB2-HourlyWorkers.pdf (last visited Oct. 19, 2013).

58. See "2012 Working Mother 100 Best Companies," Working Mother.com, n.d., www.workingmother.com/best-companies/2012-working-mother-100-best-companies; Kelso, Cahn, and Miller, "Gender Equality in Employment," 40–42.

Chapter 13

1. Naomi Cahn and June Carbone, *Red Families v. Blue Families: Legal Polarization and the Creation of Culture* (New York: Oxford University Press, 2010), 175.

2. See Linda Hirschman and Jane Larson, *Hard Bargains: The Politics of Sex* (New York: Oxford University Press, 1998).

3. From 2001 to 2006, the unintended pregnancy rate declined for teens and increased for women in their twenties. See Lawrence B. Finer and Mia R. Zolna, "Unintended Pregnancy in the United States: Incidence and Disparities, 2006," *Contraception* 84, no. 5 (2011): 478–485, tbl. 1.

4. Gladys Martinez, Casey E. Copen, and Joyce C. Abma, "Teenagers in the United States: Sexual Activity, Contraceptive Use, and Childbearing, 2006–2010 National Survey of Family Growth," *Vital and Health Statistics* 23, no. 31 (2011): 6, fig. 1, www.cdc.gov/nchs/data/series/sr_23/sr23_031.pdf.

5. Martinez et al., "Teenagers in the United States," 14, tbl. 1.

6. Mark Regnerus and Jeremy Uecker, *Premarital Sex in America: How Young Americans Meet, Mate, and Think about Marrying* (New York: Oxford University Press, 2011), 6.

7. Mark D. Regnerus, *Forbidden Fruit: Sex & Religion in the Lives of American Teenagers* (New York: Oxford University Press, 2007), 122.

8. John S. Santelli, Laura Duberstein Lindberg, Lawrence B. Finer, and Susheela Singh, "Explaining Recent Declines in Adolescent Pregnancy in the United States: The Contribution of Abstinence and Improved Contraceptive Use," *American Journal of Public Health* 97, no. 1 (2007): 150–156.

9. Martinez et al., "Teenagers in the United States."

10. In the years 2006–2010, first sex was described as "unwanted" by 11 percent of young women between the ages of eighteen and twenty-four who had had sex before age twenty, compared with 13 percent in 2002. For young men in the same age group, the share reporting first sex as unwanted decreased from 10 to 5 percent. "Facts on American Teens' Sexual and Reproductive Health," Guttmacher Institute In Brief: Fact Sheet, June 2013, www.guttmacher.org/pubs/FB-ATSRH.html. See also Lawrence B. Finer and Jesse M. Philbin, "Sexual Initiation, Contraceptive Use, and Pregnancy among Young Adolescents," *Pediatrics* 131 (2013): 886, http://pediatrics.aappublications.org/content/early/2013/03/27/peds.2012-3495. They also observe that, for the youngest groups, sex is much less likely to be consensual (888).

11. Democratic administrations have joined Republican ones in promoting abstinence; they rely, however, on "abstinence plus" efforts that include information about contraception. On their effectiveness see Laura Duberstein Lindberg and Isaac Maddow-Zimet, "Consequences of Sex Education on Teen and Young Adult Sexual Behaviors and Outcomes," *Journal of Adolescent Health* 51, no. 4 (2012): 332–338.

12. See Mark Regnerus and Jeremy Uecker, *Premarital Sex in America: How Young Americans Meet, Mate, and Think about Marrying* (New York: Oxford University Press, 2011).

13. Frank Newport, "Americans, Including Catholics, Say Birth Control Is Morally OK," Gallup poll, May 22, 2012, www.gallup.com/poll/154799/Americans-Including-Catholics-Say-Birth-Control-Morally.aspx.

14. Regnerus and Uecker, *Premarital Sex in America*, 92–93.

15. Regnerus and Uecker, *Premarital Sex in America*, 62–65 (describing persistence of the double standard in sexual relationships) and 162 (men reporting casual relationships reported the lowest rates of depression while female depression increased with the number of sexual partners). See also Michael Pollard and Kathleen Mullan Harris, "Cohabitation and Marriage Intensity: Consolidation, Intimacy, and Commitment," RAND Labor & Population Working Paper, June 2013, 14, www.rand.org/content/dam/rand/pubs/working_papers/WR1000/WR1001/RAND_WR1001.pdf (cohabitating males express lower levels of commitment to their existing relationships than do cohabiting females).

16. Regnerus and Uecker, *Premarital Sex in America*, 60.

17. Regnerus and Uecker, *Premarital Sex in America*, 61. See also Naomi Wolf, "The Porn Myth," *New York Magazine*, http://nymag.com/nymetro/news/trends/n_9437 (suggesting that women have to compete not only with each other but also with pornography).

18. Hanna Rosin, *The End of Men and the Rise of Women* (New York: Penguin, 2012), 23.

19. Regnerus and Uecker, *Premarital Sex in America*, 225, tbl. 7.4.

20. Regnerus and Uecker, *Premarital Sex in America*, 225, tbl. 7.4.

21. Evelyn M. Perry and Elizabeth A. Armstrong, "Evangelicals on Campus," Social Science Resource Council, Feb. 6, 2007, http://religion.ssrc.org/reforum/Perry_Armstrong.pdf.

22. Journalist Hanna Rosin writes that

> What makes this remarkable development [women's progress] possible is not just the pill or legal abortion but the whole new landscape of sexual freedom—the ability to delay marriage and have temporary relationships that don't derail education or career. To put it crudely, feminist progress right now largely depends on the existence of the hookup culture.... For college girls these days, an overly serious suitor fills the same role an accidental pregnancy did in the 19th century: a danger to be avoided at all costs, lest it get in the way of a promising future.

Rosin, "Boys on the Side," *The Atlantic*, September 2012, www.theatlantic.com/magazine/archive/2012/09/boys-on-the-side/309062/2; Guttmacher Instit., "Disparities in Unintended Pregnancy Grow, Even as National Rate Stagnates," Aug. 24, 2011, www.guttmacher.org\media\nr\2011\08\24\ (on unintended pregnancy rates); Regnerus and Uecker, *Premarital Sex in America*, 213, tbl 7.1, (on virginity among religious conservatives).

23. June Carbone and Naomi Cahn, *Embryo Fundamentalism*, 18 Wm. & Mary Bill Rts. J. 1015 (2010).

24. Carbone and Cahn, *Embryo Fundamentalism*.

25. Dan Cassino, "Changing the Subject: Abortion and Symbolic Masculinities among Young Evangelicals," *Journal of Men, Masculinities, and Spirituality* 1, no. 3 (2007), 201–214, http://www.jmmsweb.org/issues/volume1/number3/pp201-214.

26. David Schecter, "What Drives the Voting on Abortion Policy? Investigating Partisanship and Religion in the State Legislative Arena," *Women & Politics* 23, no. 4 (2001): 61–84.

27. Amy Deschner and Susan A. Cohen, "Contraceptive Use Is Key to Reducing Abortion Worldwide," *Guttmacher Report on Public Policy* 6, no. 4 (2003): 7, 10, www.guttmacher.org/pubs/tgr/06/4/gr060407.html; John Santelli, Theo Sandfort, and Mark Orr, "Transnational Comparisons of Adolescent Contraceptive Use: What Can We Learn from These Comparisons?" *Archives of Pediatrics & Adolescent Medicine* 162, no. 1 (2008): 92–94; Jeffrey F. Peipert, Tessa Madden, Jennifer E. Allsworth, and Gina M. Secura, "Preventing Unintended Pregnancies by Providing No-Cost Contraception," *Obstetrics & Gynecology Online*, Oct. 4, 2012, http://news.wustl.edu/news/Pages/24334.aspx (press release); http://www.ncbi.nlm.nih.gov/pubmed/23037916.

28. Rob Stein, "Premarital Abstinence Pledges Ineffective, Study Finds," *Washington Post*, Dec. 29, 2008, www.washingtonpost.com/wp-dyn/content/article/2008/12/28/AR2008122801588.html?hpid=topnews.

29. Ross Douthat, "Red Family, Blue Family," *New York Times*, May 9, 2010, www.nytimes.com/2010/05/10/opinion/10douthat.html.

30. See Lawrence B. Finer and Mia R. Zolna, "Unintended Pregnancy in the United States: Incidence and Disparities, 2006," *Contraception* 84, no. 5 (2011): 478–485; Rachel Benson Gold, "Rekindling Efforts to Prevent Unplanned Pregnancy: A Matter of 'Equity and Common Sense,'" *Guttmacher Policy Review* 9, no. 3 (2006), 2, www.guttmacher.org/pubs/gpr/09/3/gpr090302.html (showing abortion rates by income); Averil Y. Clarke, *Inequalities of Love: College-Educated Black Women and the Barriers to Romance and Family* (Durham, NC: Duke University Press, 2011), 246 (reporting that white women college graduates are most likely to terminate their unplanned pregnancies).

31. Melissa S. Kearney and Phillip B. Levine, "Why Is the Teen Birth Rate in the United States So High and Why Does It Matter?" 26 *Journal of Economic Perspectives* 26, no. 2 (2012): 141–163, www.nber.org/papers/w17965.pdf.

32. Thomas, "2008 Republican Party Platform Formally Addresses Education," Open Education.net, Sept. 2, 2008, www.openeducation.net/2008/09/02/2008-republican-party-platform-formally-addresses-education (last visited Oct. 20, 2013).

33. Edin and Kefalas, *Promises I Can Keep*, 43-44.

34. See, e.g., Linda McClain, *The Place of Families: Fostering Capacity, Equality and Responsibility* (Cambridge, MA: Harvard University Press, 2006).

35. McClain, *The Place of Families*; Maxine Eichner, *The Supportive State: Families, Governments and America's Political Ideals* (New York: Oxford University Press, 2010).

36. See Stephanie Mencimer, "The GOP's Dead-End Marriage Program," *Mother Jones*, June 25, 2012, www.motherjones.com/politics/2012/06/gops-dead-end-marriage-program; Madeleine Schwartz, "One Marriage under God," *Salon*, Feb. 2, 2013, www.salon.com/2013/02/02/one_marriage_under_god (book review noting that one of the authors makes clear that the history of marriage promotion shows a prejudice toward the poor).

37. See, e.g., Eichner, *Supportive State*.

38. Wendy Wang and Paul Taylor, "For Millennials, Parenthood Trumps Marriage," Pew Research Center Social & Demographic Trends Report, March 9, 2011, http://www.pewsocialtrends.org/2011/03/09/for-millennials-parenthood-trumps-marriage/2.

39. Melanie Hicken, "Average Cost to Raise a Child: $241,080," CNNMoney, Aug. 14, 2013, http://money.cnn.com/2013/08/14/pf/cost-children.

40. Lydia Saad, "In U.S., Half of Women Prefer a Job outside the Home," Gallup poll, Sept. 7, 2012, www.gallup.com/poll/157313/half-women-prefer-job-outside-home.aspx.

41. Charles Murray, *Losing Ground: American Social Policy, 1950–1980* (New York: Basic Books, 1984).

42. Alex Seitz-Wald, "Romney Flashback: Poor Mothers Should Be Required to Work outside the Home or Lose Welfare," Soda Head blog, April 15, 2012, www.sodahead.com/united-states/romney-flashback-poor-mothers-should-be-required-to-work-outside-the-home-or-lose-welfare/question-2589443.

43. Kristen Harknett and Arielle Kuperberg, "Education, Labor Markets and the Retreat from Marriage," *Social Forces* 90, no. 1 (2011): 41–63; Kathryn Edin and Timothy J. Nelson, *Doing the Best I Can: Fatherhood in the Inner City* (Berkeley: University of California Press, 2013).

44. Wang and Taylor, "For Millennials, Parenthood Trumps Marriage."

45. Cahn and Carbone, *Red Families v. Blue Families*, 162–163.

46. Linda M. Burton, Andrew Cherlin, Donna-Marie Winn, Angela Estacion, and Clara Holder Taylor, "The Role of Trust in Low-Income Mothers' Intimate Unions," *Journal of Marriage and Family* 71, no. 5 (2009): 1107–1124, www.ncbi.nlm.nih.gov/pmc/articles/PMC2788951/pdf/nihms151618.pdf.

47. Burton et al., "Role of Trust in Low-Income Mothers' Intimate Unions."

48. Marianne Bertrand, Jessica Pan, and Emir Kamenica, "Gender Identity and Relative Income within Households," National Bureau of Economic Research Working Paper no. 19023, May 2013, www.nber.org/papers/w19023.

49. See Cahn and Carbone, *Red Families v. Blue Families,* 175.
50. Janis Graham, "Other Reasons to Take the Pill," WebMD, n.d., www.webmd.com/sex/birth-control/features/other-reasons-to-take-the-pill (last visited Oct. 20, 2013).

Chapter 14

1. For discussion of the relationship between autonomy and vulnerability, see Martha Fineman, *The Vulnerable Subject: Anchoring Equality in the Human Condition,* 20 Yale J.L.& Feminism 1 (2008).
2. For a discussion of these cases see June Carbone, *From Partners to Parents: The Second Revolution in Family Law* (New York: Columbia University Press, 2000), 166–170.
3. In Chapters 7 and 9, we cited studies showing that both male and female married college graduates spend more time with children than they did in earlier decades and that while all parents spend, on average, more time with their children, the increases for unmarried and/or less educated men have been significantly less than the increases for more elite men.
4. Joy A. Schneer and Frieda Reitman, "Managerial Life Without a Wife: Family Structure and Managerial Career Success," *Journal of Business Ethics* (2002): 25–38.
5. See, e.g., Alison Wolf, *The XX Factor: How the Rise of Working Women Has Created a Far Less Equal World* (London: Profile Books, 2013).
6. "Decades after O'Connor, Role of Women Judges Still Growing," *Third Branch News,* March 29, 2013, news.uscourts.gov/decades-after-oconnor-role-women-judges-still-growing.
7. Katharine K. Baker, *Homogenous Rules for Heterogeneous Families: The Standardization of Family Law When There is No Standard Family,* Ill. L. Rev. 319 (2012).
8. We also showed, in *Red Families v. Blue Families,* Chapter 9, how ideological division led appellate courts in Alabama to withdraw from passing judgment on parents in custody battles, deferring instead to the trial court decisions even when the reasons for the trial courts decisions were opaque (no written opinions and a limited written record) or unfair. For a comparison of state willingness to issue written opinions see Stephen J. Choi, Mitu Gulati, and Eric A. Posner, *Judicial Evaluations and Information Forcing: Ranking State High Courts and Their Judges,* 58 Duke L.J. 1313 (2009), http://scholarship.law.duke.edu/cgi/viewcontent.cgi?article=1403&context=dlj.
9. Richard Fry and D'Vera Cohn, "Women, Men and the New Economics of Marriage," Pew Research Center Social & Demographic Trends Report, Jan. 19, 2010, 16, http://pewsocialtrends.org/files/2010/11/new-economics-of-marriage.pdf.
10. The position of college-graduate men is not parallel with that of college-graduate women. College-graduate men are more likely than college-graduate women to marry a fellow college graduate, and these men tend to marry women who earn less than they do to a greater degree than do men with less education. Fry and Cohn, "Women, Men and the New Economics of Marriage." See also Philip Cohen, "College Graduates Marry Other College Graduates Most of the Time," *The Atlantic,* April 4, 2013, www.theatlantic.com/sexes/archive/2013/04/college-graduates-marry-other-college-graduates-most-of-the-time/274654. This is true in part because there are more college women than men overall.
11. See discussion in chapter 9, supra.
12. Jack Mirkinson, "All-Male Fox Panel Freaks Out about Female Breadwinners," *Huffington Post,* www.huffingtonpost.com/2013/05/30/fox-female-breadwinners_n_3358926.html?utm_hp_ref=email_share.
13. See, e.g., Hanna Rosin, *The End of Men and the Rise of Women* (New York: Penguin, 2012).
14. See Nancy E. Dowd, *The Man Question: Male Subordination and Privilege* (New York: NYU Press, 2010), 13–73, 105–123; Nancy E. Dowd, *Asking the Man Question: Masculinities Analysis and Feminist Theory,* 33 Harv. J.L. & Gender 415, 430 (2010); Nancy E. Dowd, *Masculinities and Feminist Legal Theory,* 23 Wis. J.L. Gender & Soc'y 201, 248 (2008).

15. See, e.g., Daniel Schneider, "Market Earnings and Household Work: New Tests of Gender Performance Theory," *Journal of Marriage and Family* 73, no. 4 (2011): 845–860.

16. Marianne Bertrand, Jessica Pan, and Emir Kamenica, "Gender Identity and Relative Income within Households," National Bureau of Economic Research Working Paper no. 19023, May 2013, http://www.nber.org/papers/w19023.

17. Indeed, the persistence of gendered expectations of behavior and roles is stronger among the working class, even though working class men may be less able to realize stereotypical definitions of male success. See Richard A. Lippa, *Gender, Nature and Nurture* (Mahwah, NJ: Erlbaum, 2005), 183 (poor and working-class children tend to have more rigid gender stereotypes); Joan C. Williams, *Reshaping the Work-Family Debate: Why Men and Class Matter* (Cambridge, MA: Harvard University Press, 2010), 59.

18. Indeed, a rigorous, three-year federally funded marriage-promotion program, Building Strong Families, found that it had "had no effect on couples' relationship quality or the likelihood that they remained romantically involved or got married." Robert G. Wood, Quinn Moore, Andrew Clarkwest, Alexandra Killewald, and Shannon Monahan, "The Long-Term Effects of Building Strong Families: A Relationship Skills Education Program for Unmarried Parents, Executive Summary," OPRE Report no. 2012-28B, November 2012, vi, www.mathematica-mpr.com/publications/PDFs/family_support/BSF_36month_impact_ES.pdf.

19. The median net worth is under $80,000 (half of all households are above; half are below). Equal division will generally mean dividing debt. Kathleen Pender, "Household Incomes, Net Worth Rising," SFGate, March 11, 2013, www.sfgate.com/business/networth/article/Household-incomes-net-worth-rising-4346405.php.

20. The American Law Institute (ALI) has established a rebuttable presumption that a couple has created a "domestic partnership" if they have cohabited for the requisite number of years. Domestic partnership status essentially means the application of principles of property division and alimony adapted from divorce law. ALI, *Principles of the Law of Family Dissolution: Analysis and Recommendations* §§ 6.01–.06 (2002).

21. Leslie Joan Harris, June Carbone and Lee E. Teitelbaum, *Family Law* 4th ed. (New York: Aspen, 2010), chapter 4.

22. Jonathan Zimmerman, "Alimony Myth Persists in New Jersey's Divorce-Reform Drive," Philly.com, June 5, 2012, http://articles.philly.com/2012-06-05/news/32056763_1_alimony-divorce-reform-women.

23. Philip Cohen, "End-of-Men-Richer-Sex Equality Check," FamilyInequality.com, Sept. 10, 2012, http://familyinequality.wordpress.com/2012/09/10/end-of-men-richer-sex-reality-check-40-years-of-pants-edition.

24. Sarah Jane Glynn, "The New Breadwinners: 2010 Update; Rates of Women Supporting Their Families Economically Increased since 2007," Center for American Progress Issue Brief, April 16, 2012, 3, fig. 2, www.americanprogress.org/issues/labor/report/2012/04/16/11377/the-new-breadwinners-2010-update. While 40 percent of white wives earned as much or more than their husbands, this was true for more than half of black wives.

25. See, e.g., *Courtney v. M. Roggy*, 302 S.W.3d 141, 146 (Mo. Ct. App. 2009).

26. June Carbone and Naomi Cahn, *Which Ties Bind? Redefining the Parent-Child Relationship in an Age of Genetic Certainty*, 11 WM. & MARY BILL RTS. J. 1011 (2003).

27. In the case of the use of a sperm donor, for example, the intended parents should be free to waive DNA testing, and the presence or absence of such testing should not affect recognition of the parental status of the intended parents. Even in the case where the intended parents believe they are the two biological progenitors, waiver would mean that neither parent could contest his own or the other partner's parental status. A man who later discovered that he was not the biological father would therefore still be liable for support, and the mother could not interfere with his effort to obtain shared custody because of the lack of biological ties. He would still be a legal parent.

28. See Baker, *Homogenous Rules for Heterogeneous Families: The Standardization of Family Law When There is No Standard Family.*

29. *In re* J.W.T., No. D-1742, 1993 Tex. LEXIS 101, at *31–32 (Tex. June 30, 1993), *withdrawn, In re* J.W.T., 872 S.W.2d 189, 197–198 (Tex. 1994).

30. *Pearson v Pearson*, 182 P.3d 353 (Utah 2008) (protecting husband's ongoing relationship with the child).

31. For a discussion of the legal developments, see Nancy Polikoff, "Where Can a Child Have Three Parents?", Beyond (Straight and Gay) Marriage, July 14, 2012, http://beyondstraightandgaymarriage.blogspot.com/2012/07/where-can-child-have-three-parents.html; Nancy Polikoff, "Three parents (or more) okay in California—by adoption or otherwise," Beyond (Straight and Gay) Marriage, Aug. 5, 2013, http://beyondstraightandgaymarriage.blogspot.com/2013/10/three-parents-or-more-okay-in.html.

32. Fathers' income has a consistently robust and positive impact on relationship quality. See, e.g., Marcia Carlson, Sara S. McLanahan, and Jeanne Brooks-Gunn, *Co-parenting and Nonresident Fathers' Involvement with Young Children after a Nonmarital Birth, Demography* 45, no. 2 (2008): 461–488.

33. See June Carbone, "From Partners to Parents Revisited: How Will Ideas of Partnership Influence the Emerging Definition of California Parenthood?" *Whittier Journal of Child and Family Advocacy* 7, no. 1 (2007):3, 5.

34. Louisiana recognizes a theory of dual paternity; see June Carbone, *The Legal Definition of Parenthood: Uncertainty at the Core of Family Identity*, 65 LA. L. REV. 1295 (2005); Rachel L. Kovach, Comment, *Sorry Daddy—Your Time Is Up: Rebutting the Presumption of Paternity in Louisiana*, 56 LOY. L.REV. 651 (2010).

35. See Carbone, "From Partners to Parents Revisited."

36. Korvach, *Sorry Daddy—Your Time Is Up.*

37. See American Law Institute (ALI), Principles of the Law of Family Dissolution § 2.03 (2002). Indeed, many states already recognize a second non-biological, non-marital parent, using the doctrine of de facto parenthood.

38. A statute adopted in 2013 in California allows the award of custody to three parents only in accordance with a showing that the child would otherwise suffer detriment.

39. Fry and Cohn, "Women, Men and the New Economics of Marriage."

40. David M. Buss, Todd K. Shakelford, Lee A. Kirkpatrick, and Randy J. Larsen, "A Half Century of Mate Preferences: The Cultural Evolution of Values," *Journal of Marriage and Family* 63, no. 2 (2001): 491–503.

41. As Kathryn Edin told Hanna Rosin, "'I think something feminists have missed . . . is how much power women have' when they're not bound by marriage. The women, she explained, 'make every important decision'—whether to have a baby, how to raise it, where to live." Rosin, *End of Men*, 92.

42. John T. Jost, "The End of the End of Ideology," *American Psychologist* 61, no.7 (2006): 651, 654 (emphasis in original). Jost found "a clear tendency for conservatives to score higher on measures of dogmatism, intolerance of ambiguity, needs for order, structure, and closure and to be lower in openness to experience and integrative complexity than moderates and liberals. Several studies demonstrate that in a variety of perceptual and aesthetic domains, conservatism is associated with preferences for relatively simple, unambiguous, and familiar stimuli, whether they are paintings, poems, or songs" (662). See also Dan M. Kahan, Donald Braham, Paul Slovic, John Gastil, and Geoffrey L. Cohen, "The Second National Risk and Culture Study: Making Sense of—and Making Progress in—The American Culture War of Fact," Yale Law School Public Law Working Paper no. 154, Sept. 26, 2007.

43. Jost, "The End of the End of Ideology."

44. Larry M. Bartels, *Unequal Democracy: The Political Economy of the New Gilded Age* (Princeton, NJ: Princeton University Press, 2008), 160.

INDEX

Note: Page numbers in *italics* refer to graphs or tables.